Fodor's Fifth Edition

Norway

The complete guide, thoroughly up-to-date

Packed with details that will make your trip

The must-see sights, off and on the beaten path

What to see, what to skip

Mix-and-match vacation itineraries

City strolls, countryside adventures

Smart lodging and dining options

Essential local do's and taboos

Transportation tips, distances and directions

Key contacts, savvy travel tips

When to go, what to pack

Clear, accurate, easy-to-use maps

Books to read, videos to watch

Excerpted from *Fodor's Scandinavia*

Fodor's Norway

EDITORS: Andrew Collins, Tania Inowlocki

Editorial Contributors: Daniel Cash, Roderick Craig, Lauren Myers
Editorial Production: Brian Vitunic
Maps: David Lindroth, *cartographer;* Rebecca Baer, Bob Blake, *map editors*
Design: Fabrizio La Rocca, *creative director;* Guido Caroti, *art director;* Jolie Novak, *photo editor*
Cover Design: Pentagram
Production/Manufacturing: Mike Costa
Cover Photograph: E. Nagele/FPG International

Copyright

Fifth Edition

ISBN 0–679–00402–5

ISSN 1073–6603

Special Sales

Fodor's Travel Publications are available at special discounts for bulk purchases for sales promotions or premiums. Special editions, including personalized covers, excerpts of existing guides, and corporate imprints, can be created in large quantities for special needs. For more information, contact your local bookseller or write to Special Markets, Fodor's Travel Publications, 201 East 50th Street, New York, NY 10022. Inquiries from Canada should be directed to your local Canadian bookseller or sent to Random House of Canada, Ltd., Marketing Department, 2775 Matheson Boulevard East, Mississauga, Ontario L4W 4P7. Inquiries from the United Kingdom should be sent to Fodor's Travel Publications, 20 Vauxhall Bridge Road, London, England SW1V 2SA.

PRINTED IN THE UNITED STATES OF AMERICA

10 9 8 7 6 5 4 3 2 1

Important Tip

Although all prices, opening times, and other details in this book are based on information supplied to us at press time, changes occur all the time in the travel world, and Fodor's cannot accept responsibility for facts that become outdated or for inadvertent errors or omissions. So **always confirm information when it matters,** especially if you're making a detour to visit a specific place.

CONTENTS

Maps

ON THE ROAD WITH FODOR'S

THE TRIPS YOU TAKE this year and next are going to be significant trips, if only because they'll be your first in the new millennium. Acutely aware of that fact, we've pulled out all stops in preparing *Fodor's Norway.* To guide you in putting together your Norwegian experience, we've created multiday itineraries and neighborhood walks. And to direct you to the places that are truly worth your time and money in these important years, we've rallied the team of endearingly picky know-it-alls we're pleased to call our writers. Having seen all corners of Norway, they're real experts. If you knew them, you'd poll them for tips yourself.

Trained in graphic design and documentary film production, **Daniel Cash** spent some two years in the Norwegian capital, Oslo, working as an editor on an international shipping publication. An Australian national and a keen cricket fan, Dan co-updated *Norway* before returning to live and work in Melbourne. Co-updater **Roderick Craig** (aka Roddy) is a journalist and editor living in Oslo. A British na-

tional, Roddy has worked for Times Mirror International Publishers, Dorling Kindersley, and the Quarto group. In Oslo, Roddy has worked on the desk of an English-language shipping newspaper, *TradeWinds,* as well as freelancing for various clients, including the Norwegian Trade Council. He enjoys the Norwegian way of life, as well as Oslo's manageable size and spectacular setting, but is keen for more foreigners to take up residence here.

Don't Forget to Write

We love feedback—positive and negative—and follow up on all suggestions. So contact the Norway editor at editors@fodors.com or c/o Fodor's, 201 East 50th Street, New York, New York 10022. Have a wonderful trip!

Karen Cure

Karen Cure
Editorial Director

Norway

ATLANTIC OCEAN

Norwegian Sea

TO SVALBARD

North Cape

Vardø
Vadsø
Hammerfest
Kirkenes
Alta
Karasjok
Tromsø
Kautokeino

FINLAND

Harstad
Svolvær
Narvik
VESTERÅLEN
LOFOTEN
Vestfjorden
Bodø   Fauske
Polarsirkelsenteret

Arctic Circle

Mo i Rana
Sandnessjøen   Mosjøen
Brønnøysund
E6

Rørvik
Namsos
Steinkjer

SWEDEN

Trondheim   Meråker
Støren
Kristiansund   Røros
Molde   70   Oppdal
Ålesund   Åndalsnes   Tynset
Geiranger   Dombås   Østerdalen
Nordfjord   Lom   Otta   Koppang
Florø   Jostedalsbreen   Rena
Sognefjord   Lillehammer
Voss   Geilo   Gol   Lake   Hamar
Bergen   Hønefoss   Mjøsa   Eidsvoll
Hardangerfjord   Drammen   ★ Oslo
Haugesund   Kongsberg   Fredrikstad
Dalen   Larvik   Oslofjord
Stavanger   Valle   Porsgrunn   Halden
Sandnes   Evje   Arendal
Mandal   Grimstad   Skagerrak   Kattegat
Kristiansand

Gulf of Bothnia

Baltic Sea

N

0   200 miles
0   300 km

Scandinavia

KEY
----- Ferry

0 — 200 miles
0 — 300 km

Barents Sea

RUSSIA

Vardø
Vadsø
Kirkenes
Uljsjok
Ivalo
Inari
Karasjok
Kautokeino
Enontekiö
Muonio
Kittilä
Sodankylä
Kemijärvi
Rovaniemi
Kemi
Tornio
Tornea

North Cape
TO SVALBARD
Hammerfest
Alta
Kilpisjärvi

Torniojoki
Torneälv

Kiruna
Jokkmokk
Arjeplog
Arvidsjaur
Piteå
Skellefteå
Umeå

Tromsø
Harstad
Narvik
Vesttfjorden
VESTERÅLEN
LOFOTEN
Bodø
Fauske
Mo i Rana

Arctic Circle

Tärnaby
Sorsele
Storuman
Lycksele
Åsele
Strömsund
Ångermanälven

SVERIGE
(SWEDEN)

Sandnessjøen
Mosjøen
Brønnøysund
Rørvik
Namsos
Steinkjer
Meråker
Trondheim
Kristiansund

Norwegian Sea

ATLANTIC OCEAN

TO ICELAND

Suomussalmi
Kuusamo
Posio
Pudasjärvi
Puolanka
Kuhmo
Kajaani
Otanmäki
Otanmäki
Nurmes
Pielinen
Iisalmi
SUOMI
(FINLAND)
Oulu
Radhe
Pulkkila
Kalajoki
Nivala
Haapajärvi
Kärsämäki
Kokkola
Gulf of Bothnia

Kalix
Luleå

Arctic Circle

Raufarhöfn
Húsavík
Bakkaflói
Þórshöfn
Vopnafjörður
Vopnafjörður
Héraðsflói
Egilsstaðir
Neskaupstaður
Breiðdalsvík
Djúpivogur
Höfn
Hornafjörður
Hornafjarðarós
Faguhólsmyri
Kirkjubæjarklaustur

Skjálfandi
Dalvík
Akureyri
Vatnajökull
Vík
Westmann Islands

Siglufjörður
Ísafjörður
Húnaflói
Vestfirðir
Búðardalur
Reykholt
Langjökull
Hofsjökull
Mýrdalsjökull
Hella
Hveragerði

Þingeyri
Stykkishólmur
Búðir
Breiðafjörður
Breiðafjörður
Faxaflói
Reykjavík
Hafnarfjörður

ISLAND
(ICELAND)

World Time Zones

Numbers below vertical bands relate each zone to Greenwich Mean Time (0 hrs.).
Local times frequently differ from these general indications,
as indicated by light-face numbers on map.

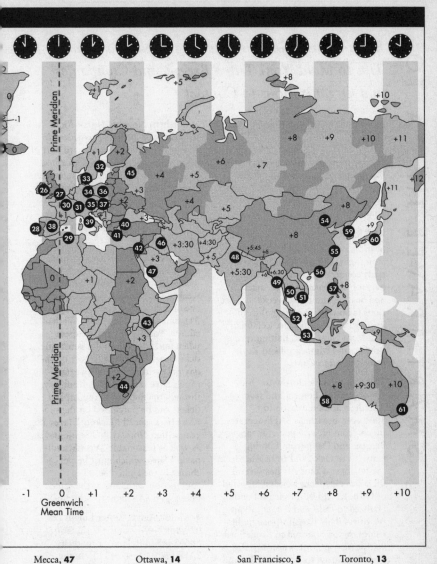

-1   0   +1   +2   +3   +4   +5   +6   +7   +8   +9   +10
Greenwich
Mean Time

SMART TRAVEL TIPS A TO Z

Basic Information on Traveling in Norway, Savvy Tips to Make Your Trip a Breeze, and Companies and Organizations to Contact

AIR TRAVEL

BOOKING YOUR FLIGHT

When you book **look for nonstop flights** and **remember that "direct" flights stop at least once.** Try to avoid connecting flights, which require a change of plane.

CARRIERS

Scandinavian Airlines has daily non-stop flights to Oslo from Newark; daily connections to Oslo via Copen-hagen from Chicago, Los Angeles, and Seattle; and twice-weekly connec-tions (also via Copenhagen) from Toronto and Anchorage. Icelandair flies from New York, Baltimore, Boston, and Minneapolis to Reyk-javík and on to Oslo.

SAS flies from Heathrow to Oslo, Stavanger, and Bergen, and from Aberdeen and Newcastle to Stavanger. Braathens SAFE operates flights from Newcastle to Stavanger, Bergen, and Oslo, from London Gatwick to Oslo, and from Aberdeen to Stavanger. Color Air has several flights weekly from London Stansted to Oslo. KLM UK flies from London Stansted to Oslo and Bergen. Ryan Air offers daily bargain-price flights from London Stansted to Sandefjord. British Airways offers nonstop flights from Heathrow to Bergen, Oslo, and Stavanger. Aer Lingus and Icelandair also have flights between Great Britain or Ireland and major Scandi-navian cities.

Within Norway, SAS serves most major cities, including Svalbard. Braathens SAFE is the major domestic airline, serving cities throughout the country and along the coast as far north as Tromsø and Svalbard. It also has international routes from Oslo to Billund, Denmark; Malmö, Sweden; and Newcastle, England. Widerøe serves smaller airports (with smaller planes), mostly along the coast, and in northern Norway. Norsk Air, a subsidiary of Widerøe, provides similar services in the southern part of the country. Coast Air and Norlink, an SAS subsidiary, are commuter systems linking both smaller and larger airports. All flights within Scandinavia are no-smoking, as are all airports in Norway, except in designated areas.

A number of special fares are avail-able within Norway year-round, including air passes, family tickets, weekend excursions, youth (up to the age of 25), student (up to the age of 31), and senior (older than 67) dis-counts. Youth fares are cheapest when purchased from the automatic ticket machines at the airport on the day of departure. All Norwegian routes have reduced rates from July through the middle of August, and tickets can be purchased on the spot. SAS offers special **"Jackpot"** fares all year within Norway and Scandinavia, as well as reasonable **"Visit Scandi-navia"** fares, which must be pur-chased in the United States in conjunction with, and at the same time as, an SAS flight to Scandinavia.

➤ MAJOR AIRLINES: Aer Lingus (☎ 020/8899–4747 in the U.K., ☎ 01/886–8888 in Ireland). **Braathens SAFE** (☎ 020/7473–1155 in the U.K., ☎ 67/58–60–00 in Norway). **British Airways** (☎ 0345/222–111 in the U.K.). **Coast Air** (☎ 55/99–82–17 in Norway). **Color Air** (☎ 012/7968–0500 in the U.K.). **Finnair** (☎ 800/950–5000). **Icelandair** (☎ 800/223–5500 in the U.S., ☎ 020/7388–5599 in the U.K.). **KLM UK** (☎ 087/0507–4074 in the U.K.). **Norlink** (☎ 77/67–57–80 in Norway). **Norsk Air** (☎ 33/48–26–00 in Norway). **Ryan Air** (☎ 015/4156–9569). **Scandinavian Airlines (SAS)** (☎ 800/221–2350 in the U.S., 810/03–300 in Norway). **Widerøe** (☎ 810/01–200 in Norway).

CHECK-IN & BOARDING

Assuming that not everyone with a ticket will show up, airlines routinely overbook planes. When that happens, airlines ask for volunteers to give up their seats. In return these volunteers usually get a certificate for a free flight and are rebooked on the next flight out. If there are not enough volunteers, the airline must choose who will be denied boarding. The first to get bumped are passengers who checked in late and those flying on discounted tickets, so **get to the gate and check in as early as possible,** especially during peak periods.

Always **bring a government-issued photo I.D. to the airport.** You may be asked to show it before you are allowed to check in.

CUTTING COSTS

Braathens SAFE sells a **Visit Norway** pass, which includes the Scandinavian BonusPass. It is available at **Passage Tours of Scandinavia** (☏ 800/548–5960) and **Borton Overseas** (☏ 800/843–0602). **Widerøe** offers the Explore **Norway** ticket, which provides unlimited travel over 2 weeks.

The least expensive airfares to Norway must usually be purchased in advance and are nonrefundable. It's smart to **call a number of airlines, and when you are quoted a good price, book it on the spot**—the same fare may not be available the next day. Always **check different routings** and look into using different airports. Travel agents, especially low-fare specialists (☞ Discounts & Deals, *below*), are helpful.

Consolidators are another good source. They buy tickets for scheduled international flights at reduced rates from the airlines, then sell them at prices that beat the best fare available directly from the airlines, usually without restrictions. Sometimes you can even get your money back if you need to return the ticket. Carefully read the fine print detailing penalties for changes and cancellations, and **confirm your consolidator reservation with the airline.**

When you **fly as a courier** you trade your checked-luggage space for a ticket deeply subsidized by a courier service. There are restrictions on when you can book and how long you can stay.

➤ CONSOLIDATORS: **Cheap Tickets** (☏ 800/377–1000). **Up & Away Travel** (☏ 212/889–2345). **Discount Airline Ticket Service** (☏ 800/576–1600). **Unitravel** (☏ 800/325–2222). **World Travel Network** (☏ 800/409–6753).

ENJOYING THE FLIGHT

For more legroom **request an emergency-aisle seat.** Don't sit in the row in front of the emergency aisle or in front of a bulkhead, where seats may not recline. If you have dietary concerns, **ask for special meals when booking.** These can be vegetarian, low-cholesterol, or kosher, for example. On long flights, try to maintain a normal routine, to help fight jet lag. At night **get some sleep.** By day **eat light meals, drink water** (not alcohol), and **move around the cabin** to stretch your legs.

FLYING TIMES

Flying time from New York to Oslo, 7½ hours. A nonstop flight from London to Oslo is about 1¾ hours and about 1½ hours to Stavanger.

HOW TO COMPLAIN

If your baggage goes astray or your flight goes awry, complain right away. Most carriers require that you **file a claim immediately.**

➤ AIRLINE COMPLAINTS: U.S. Department of Transportation **Aviation Consumer Protection Division** (✉ C-75, Room 4107, Washington, DC 20590, ☏ 202/366–2220). **Federal Aviation Administration Consumer Hotline** (☏ 800/322–7873).

AIRPORTS

The major gateway to Norway is Gardermoen Airport, which is about 53 km (33 mi) northeast of Oslo and opened in 1998. Other international airports are in Bergen, Kristiansand, Sandefjord, Stavanger, and Trondheim.

➤ AIRPORT INFORMATION: **Gardermoen Airport** (☏ 011–47–6481–0000).

BIKE TRAVEL

BIKES IN FLIGHT

Most airlines accommodate bikes as luggage, provided they are dismantled and boxed. For bike boxes, often free at bike shops, you'll pay about $5 (at least $100 for bike bags) from airlines. International travelers can sometimes substitute a bike for a piece of checked luggage at no charge; otherwise, the cost is about $100. Domestic and Canadian airlines charge $25–$50.

BOAT & FERRY TRAVEL

Taking a ferry isn't only fun, it's often necessary in Scandinavia. Many companies arrange package trips, some offering a rental car and hotel accommodations as part of the deal.

Ferry crossings often last overnight. The trip between Copenhagen and Oslo, for example, takes approximately 16 hours, most lines leaving at about 5 PM and arriving about 9 the next morning. The direct cruise between Stockholm and Helsinki takes 12 hours, usually leaving at about 6 PM and arriving the next morning at 9. The shortest ferry route runs between Helsingør, Denmark, and Helsingborg, Sweden; it takes only 25 minutes.

Ferries and passenger ships remain important means of transportation within Norway. Along west-coast fjords, car ferries are a way of life. More specialized boat service includes hydrofoil-catamaran trips between Stavanger, Haugesund, and Bergen. There are also fjord cruises out of these cities and others in the north. Color Line is a major carrier in Norwegian waters.

Norway's most renowned boat trip is *Hurtigruten,* or the *Coastal Steamer,* which departs from Bergen and stops at 36 ports in six days, ending with Kirkenes, near the Russian border, before turning back. Tickets can be purchased for the entire journey or for individual legs. Tickets are available through Bergen Line travel agents or directly from the companies that run the service: FFR, OVDS, Hurtigruten Coastal Express Bookings, and TFDS.

➤ FERRIES: **Color Line** (✉ Box 1422, Vika 0115, Oslo, ☎ 810/00–811, FAX 22/83–07–76). **Bergen Line travel agents** (✉ 405 Park Ave., New York,

NY 10022, ☎ 800/323–7436). **FFR** (✉ 9615 Hammerfest, ☎ 78/40–70–90). **OVDS** (✉ 8501 Narvik, ☎ 76/96–76–96). **Hurtigruten Coastal Express Bookings** (☎ 810/30–000). **TFDS** (✉ 9000 Tromsø, ☎ 77/64–82–00).

FROM THE UNITED KINGDOM

Two ferry lines serve Norway from the United Kingdom. Fjord Line has three departures a week among Bergen, Stavanger, and Newcastle during the summer (mid-May–end of Sept.) and two during the rest of the year. Crossings take about 22 hours. Monday and Wednesday sailings stop first in Stavanger and arrive in Bergen six hours later. The Saturday service stops first in Bergen. P&O Scottish Ferries operates a twice-weekly summer service (mid-May–early Sept.) from Aberdeen to Bergen via Lerwick. There is a Monday service from Aberdeen to Lerwick with an onward connection to Bergen with Smyril Lines (contact P&O Scottish Ferries).

➤ BOAT & FERRY INFORMATION: **Fjord Line** (✉ Norway House, Royal Quays, North Shields [near Newcastle], NE29 6EG, ☎ 091/296–1313). **Color Line** (✉ Box 30, DK–985O Hirsthals, Denmark, ☎ 45/99–56–20–00, FAX 45/99–56–20–20; Hjortneskaia, Box 1422 Vika, N–0115 Oslo, Norway, ☎ 47/22–94–44–00, FAX 47/22–83–04–30; c/o Bergen Line, Inc., 405 5th Ave., New York, NY 10022, ☎ 800/323–7436, FAX 212/983–1275; Tyne Commission Quay, North Shields NE29 6EA, Newcastle, England, ☎ 091/296–1313, FAX 091/296–1540). **P&O Scottish Ferries** (✉ Box 5, Jamieson's Quay, Aberdeen AB11 5NP, ☎ 012/2457–2615). **ScandLines** (✉ Box 1, DK–300O Helsingør, Denmark, ☎ 45/33–15–15–15, FAX 45/33–15–10–20; Knutpunkten 44, S–252 78 Helsingborg, Sweden, ☎ 46/42–18–61–00, FAX 46/42–18–74–10).

FERRIES FROM ENGLAND

The chief operator between England and many points within Scandinavia is DFDS/Scandinavian Seaways, with ships connecting Harwich and Newcastle to Göteborg and Amsterdam.

➤ MAJOR OPERATOR: **DFDS/Scandinavian Seaways** (✉ Sankt Annae Plads 30, DK–1295 Copenhagen, Denmark, ☎ 45/33–42–30–00, FAX 45/33–42–33–41; DFDS Travel Centre, 15 Hanover St., London W1R 9HG, ☎ 020/7409–6060, FAX 020/7409–6035; DFDS Seaways USA Inc., 6555 NW 9th Ave., Suite 207, Fort Lauderdale, FL 33309, ☎ 800/533–3755, FAX 305/491–7958; Box 8895, Scandiahamnen, S–402 72 Göteborg, Sweden, ☎ 46/31–650–610).

PLYING SCANDINAVIAN WATERS

Connections from Denmark to Norway and Sweden are available through DFDS and the Stena Line. Fjord Line sails along the magnificent west coast of Norway. Connections to the Faroe Islands from Norway and Denmark are available through the Smyril Line. Silja Line and Viking Line offer a variety of cruises to Finland, with departures from Stockholm to Mariehamn in the Åland archipelago, Turku (Åbo) and Helsinki (Helsingfors), and a crossing from Umeå to Vaasa.

➤ MAJOR OPERATORS: **DFDS Seaways** (☞ *above*). **Stena Line** (✉ Trafikhamnen, DK–9900 Frederikshavn, Denmark, ☎ 45/96–20–02–00, FAX 45/96–20–02–80; Jernbanetorget 2, N–0154 Oslo 1, Norway, ☎ 47/23–17–90–00, FAX 47/23–17–90–60; Scandinavia AB, S–405 19 Göteborg, Sweden, ☎ 46/31–704–0000, FAX 46/31–241–038). **Fjord Line** (✉ Skoltegrunnskaien, Box 7250, N–5020 Bergen, Norway, ☎ 47/55–54–88–00, FAX 47/55–54–86–01). **Smyril Line** (☞ DFDS Seaways, *above*; or J. Brocksgøta 37, Box 370, FO-110 Tórshavn, Faroe Islands, ☎ 298/31–59–00, FAX 298/31–57–07; Slottsgate 1, Box 4135 Dreggen, N–5023 Bergen, Norway, ☎ 47 /55–32–09–70, FAX 47/55–96–02–72). **Silja Line** (✉ Kungsgatan 2, S–111 43 Stockholm, Sweden, ☎ 46/8–666–3512, FAX 46/8–611–9162; c/o Scandinavian Seaways, Parkeston Quay Scand. House, Harwich, Essex, England CO12 4QG, ☎ 44/255–240–240, FAX 44/255–244–382).

CAR FERRIES

Travel by car in Scandinavia often necessitates travel by ferry. Some well-known vehicle and passenger ferries run between Dragør, Denmark (just south of Copenhagen), and Limhamn, Sweden (just south of Malmö); between Helsingør, Denmark, and Helsingborg, Sweden; and between Copenhagen and Göteborg, Sweden. On the Dragør/Limhamn ferry (ScandLines), taking a car one-way costs SKr 395 (about $60 or £39). The Helsingør/Helsingborg ferry (ScandLines also) takes only 25 minutes; taking a car along one-way costs SKr 330 (about $50 or £33). Fares for round-trip are cheaper, and on weekends the Öresund Runt pass (for crossing between Dragoør and Limhamn one way and Helsingborg and Helsingoør the other way) costs only SKr 495 (about $75 or £49).

➤ MAJOR OPERATORS: **Stena Line** (Sweden, ☎ 46–31/775–00–00). **ScandLines** (☞ *above*).

BUS TRAVEL

Bus tours can be effective for smaller regions within Norway, Sweden, Finland, and Denmark, but all have excellent train systems, which offer much greater coverage in less time than buses. Detailed information on bus routes is available through local tourist offices.

Every end station of the railroad is supported by a number of bus routes, some of which are operated by NSB, others by local companies. Long-distance buses usually take longer than the railroad, and fares are only slightly lower. Virtually every settlement on the mainland is served by bus, and for anyone with a desire to get off the beaten track, a pay-as-you-go open-ended bus trip is the best way to see Norway.

Most long-distance buses leave from Bussterminalen, close to Oslo Central Station. Nor-Way Bussekspress has more than 40 different bus services, covering 10,000 km (6,200 mi) and 500 destinations, and can arrange any journey. It offers the Nor-Way Bus-Pass, which provides one or two weeks of unlimited travel. One of its participating services, Feriebussen, offers package tours with English-speaking guides.

➤ Bus Information: **Bussterminalen** (⊠ Galleriet Oslo, Schweigaardsgt., 10). **Nor-Way Bussekspress** (⊠ Bussterminalen, ☎ 814/44–444, FAX 22/00–24–49). **Feriebussen** (⊠ Østerdal Billag A/S, 2560 Alvdal, ☎ 62/48–74–00).

BUSINESS HOURS

BANKS

Banks are open weekdays 8:30–3:30. In summer, banks open at 8:15 and close at 3, with a Thursday closing at 5.

POST OFFICES

Most post offices are open weekdays 8 to 5, Saturday 9 to 1. In small towns, post offices are often closed on Saturdays.

SHOPS

Most shops are open 9 or 10 to 5 weekdays, Thursday until 7, Saturday 9 to 2, and are closed Sunday. In some areas, especially in larger cities, stores stay open later on weekdays. Large shopping centers, for example, are usually open until 8 weekdays and 6 on Saturdays. Supermarkets are open until 8 or 10 weekdays and until 6 on Saturdays. During the summer, most shops close weekdays at 4 and at 1 on Saturday.

CAMERAS & PHOTOGRAPHY

➤ Photo Help: **Kodak Information Center** (☎ 800/242–2424). *Kodak Guide to Shooting Great Travel Pictures,* available in bookstores or from Fodor's Travel Publications (☎ 800/533–6478; $16.50 plus $4 shipping).

EQUIPMENT PRECAUTIONS

Always **keep your film and tape out of the sun.** Carry an extra supply of batteries, and **be prepared to turn on your camera or camcorder** to prove to security personnel that the device is real. Always **ask for hand inspection of film,** which becomes clouded after successive exposures to airport X-ray machines, and **keep videotapes away from metal detectors.**

CAR RENTAL

Rates in Oslo begin at $111 a day and $284 a week. This does not include tax on car rentals, which is 23% in Norway.

➤ Major Agencies: **Alamo** (☎ 800/522–9696; 020/8759–6200 in the U.K.). **Avis** (☎ 800/331–1084; 800/879–2847 in Canada; 02/9353–9000 in Australia; 09/525–1982 in New Zealand). **Budget** (☎ 800/527–0700; 0144/227–6266 in the U.K.). **Dollar** (☎ 800/800–6000; 020/8897–0811 in the U.K., where it is known as Eurodollar; 02/9223–1444 in Australia). **Hertz** (☎ 800/654–3001; 800/263–0600 in Canada; 0990/90–60–90 in the U.K.; 02/9669–2444 in Australia; 03/358–6777 in New Zealand). **National InterRent** (☎ 800/227–3876; 0345/222525 in the U.K., where it is known as Europcar InterRent).

CUTTING COSTS

To get the best deal **book through a travel agent who will shop around.** Do **look into wholesalers,** companies that do not own fleets but rent in bulk from those that do and often offer better rates than traditional car-rental operations. Payment must be made before you leave home.

➤ Wholesalers: **Auto Europe** (☎ 207/842–2000 or 800/223–5555, FAX 800–235–6321). **Europe by Car** (☎ 212/581–3040 or 800/223–1516, FAX 212/246–1458). **DER Travel Services** (⊠ 9501 W. Devon Ave., Rosemont, IL 60018, ☎ 800/782–2424, FAX 800/282–7474 for information; 800/860–9944 for brochures). **Kemwel Holiday Autos** (☎ 914/825–3000 or 800/678–0678, FAX 914/381–8847).

INSURANCE

When driving a rented car you are generally responsible for any damage to or loss of the vehicle. Before you rent see what coverage your personal auto-insurance policy and credit cards already provide.

Collision policies that car-rental companies sell for European rentals usually do not include stolen-vehicle coverage. Before you buy it, check your existing policies—you may already be covered.

REQUIREMENTS & RESTRICTIONS

Ask about age requirements: Several countries require drivers to be over 20 years old, but some car-rental companies require that drivers be at least 25. In Scandinavia your own driver's license is acceptable for a limited time; check with the country's tourist board before you go. An International Driver's Permit is a good idea; it's available from the American or Canadian automobile association, or, in the United Kingdom, from the Automobile Association or Royal Automobile Club.

SURCHARGES

Before you pick up a car in one city and leave it in another **ask about drop-off charges or one-way service fees,** which can be substantial. Note, too, that some rental agencies charge extra if you return the car before the time specified in your contract. To avoid a hefty refueling fee **fill the tank just before you turn in the car,** but be aware that gas stations near the rental outlet may overcharge.

CAR TRAVEL

Excellent, well-marked roads make driving a great way to explore Scandinavia—but beware that gasoline costs more than $1 per liter of lead-free gas, roughly four times the typical U.S. price. Ferry costs can be steep, and reservations are vital. Tolls on some major roads add to the expense, as do the high fees for city parking; tickets for illegal parking are painfully costly.

Also be aware that there are relatively low legal blood-alcohol limits and tough penalties for driving while intoxicated in Scandinavia. Penalties include suspension of the driver's license and fines or imprisonment and are enforced by random police roadblocks in urban areas on weekends. In addition, an accident involving a driver with an illegal blood-alcohol level usually voids all insurance agreements, so the driver becomes responsible for his own medical bills and damage to the cars.

All vehicles registered abroad are required to carry international liability insurance and an international accident report form, which can be obtained from automobile clubs. Collision insurance is recommended. One important rule when driving in

Norway: yield to the vehicle approaching from the right.

In a few remote areas, especially in northern Norway, road conditions can be unpredictable, and careful planning is required for safety's sake. It is wise to **use a four-wheel-drive vehicle** and to **travel with at least one other car** in these areas.

Keep your headlights on at all times; this is required by law in most of Scandinavia. Also by Scandinavian law, everyone, including infants, must **wear seat belts.**

AUTO CLUBS

➤ IN AUSTRALIA: **Australian Automobile Association** (☎ 02/6247–7311).

➤ IN CANADA: **Canadian Automobile Association** (CAA, ☎ 613/247–0117).

➤ IN NEW ZEALAND: **New Zealand Automobile Association** (☎ 09/377–4660).

➤ IN THE U.K.: **Automobile Association** (AA, ☎ 0990/500–600). **Royal Automobile Club** (RAC, ☎ 0990/722–722 for membership; 0345/121–345 for insurance).

➤ IN THE U.S.: **American Automobile Association** (☎ 800/564–6222).

EMERGENCY ASSISTANCE

Norsk Automobil Forbund (✉ NAF, ☎ 810/00–606 or 810/00–505 for 24-hour service) patrols main roads and has emergency telephones on mountain roads.

GASOLINE

Gas stations are plentiful, and *blyfri bensin* (unleaded gasoline) and diesel fuel are sold everywhere from self-service pumps. Those marked *kort* are 24-hour pumps, which take oil-company credit cards or bank cards, either of which is inserted directly into the pump. Gas costs approximately NKr 8–8.50 per liter.

ROAD CONDITIONS

Four-lane highways are the exception and are found only around major cities. Outside of main routes, roads tend to be narrow and twisting, with only token guardrails, and during the summer roads are always crowded. Along the west coast, waits for ferries and passage through tunnels can be significant. Don't expect to cover more than 240 km (150 mi) in a day, especially in fjord country.

Norwegian roads are well marked with directional, distance, and informational signs. Some roads, particularly those over mountains, can close for all or part of the winter. If you drive outside major roads in winter, make sure the car is equipped with studded tires. Roads are not salted but are left with a hard-packed layer of snow on top of the asphalt. If you're renting, choose a small car with front-wheel drive. Also bring an ice scraper, snow brush, small shovel, and heavy clothes for emergencies. Although the weather along the coast is sunny, a few hours inland, temperatures may be 15°F colder, and snowfall is the rule rather than the exception.

RULES OF THE ROAD

Driving is on the right. The maximum speed limit is 90 kph (55 mph) on major motorways. On other highways, the limit is 80 kph (50 mph). The speed limit in cities and towns is 50 kph (30 mph), and 30 kph (18 mph) in residential areas.

Dimmed headlights are mandatory at all times, as is the use of seat belts and children's seats (when appropriate) in both front and rear seats. All cars must carry red reflecting warning triangles to be placed a safe distance from a disabled vehicle. Norway has strict drinking-and-driving laws, and there are routine roadside checks. The legal limit is a blood-alcohol percentage of 0.05%, which corresponds to a glass of wine or a bottle of low-alcohol beer. If you are stopped, you may be required to take a breath test. If it is positive, you must submit to a blood test. No exceptions are made for foreigners, who can lose their licenses on the spot.

Speeding is also punished severely. Most roads are monitored by radar and cameras in gray metal boxes. Signs warning of *Automatisk Trafikkontroll* (Automatic Traffic Monitoring) are posted periodically along appropriate roads. Radar

controls are frequent. Make sure you have an up-to-date map before you venture out, because some highway numbers have changed in the past few years, particularly routes beginning with "E."

CHILDREN IN NORWAY

In Norway children are to be seen *and* heard and are genuinely welcome in most public places. If you are renting a car don't forget to **arrange for a car seat** when you reserve.

DISCOUNTS

Children are entitled to discount tickets (often as much as 50% off) on buses, trains, and ferries throughout Scandinavia, as well as reductions on special City Cards. Children under 12 pay half-price and children under 2 pay 10% on SAS and Linjeflyg round-trips. The only restriction on this discount is that the family travel together and return to the originating city in Scandinavia at least two days later. With the Scanrail Pass (☞ Discount Passes *in* Train Travel, *below*)—good for rail journeys throughout Scandinavia—children under 4 (on lap) travel free; those 4–11 pay half-fare and those 12–25 can get a Scanrail Youth Pass, providing a 25% discount off of the adult fare.

FLYING

If your children are two or older **ask about children's airfares.** As a general rule, infants under two not occupying a seat fly at greatly reduced fares or even for free. When booking **confirm carry-on allowances** if you're traveling with infants. In general, for babies charged 10% of the adult fare, you are allowed one carry-on bag and a collapsible stroller; if the flight is full the stroller may have to be checked or you may be limited to less.

Experts agree that it's a good idea to use safety seats aloft for children weighing less than 40 pounds. Airlines set their own policies: U.S. carriers usually require that the child be ticketed, even if he or she is young enough to ride free, since the seats must be strapped into regular seats. Do **check your airline's policy about using safety seats during takeoff and landing.** And since safety seats are not allowed just everywhere in the plane, get your seat assignments early.

When reserving, **request children's meals or a freestanding bassinet** if you need them. But note that bulkhead seats, where you must sit to use the bassinet, may lack an overhead bin or storage space on the floor.

LODGING

Most hotels in Norway allow children under a certain age to stay in their parents' room at no extra charge, but others charge for them as extra adults; be sure to **find out the cutoff age for children's discounts.**

SIGHTS & ATTRACTIONS

Places that are especially good for children are indicated by a rubber duckie icon in the margin.

CONSUMER PROTECTION

Whenever shopping or buying travel services in Norway, **pay with a major credit card** so you can cancel payment or get reimbursed if there's a problem. If you're doing business with a particular company for the first time, **contact your local Better Business Bureau and the attorney general's offices** in your state and the company's home state, as well. Have any complaints been filed? Finally, if you're buying a package or tour, always **consider travel insurance** that includes default coverage (☞ Insurance, *below*).

➤ LOCAL BBBs: **Council of Better Business Bureaus** (✉ 4200 Wilson Blvd., Suite 800, Arlington, VA 22203, ☎ 703/276–0100, ☎ 703/525–8277).

CUSTOMS & DUTIES

Residents of non-European countries who are over 18 may import duty-free into Norway 200 cigarettes or 500 grams of tobacco goods, and souvenirs and gifts to the value of NKr 1,200. Residents of European countries who are over 18 may import 200 cigarettes or 250 grams of tobacco or cigars, a small amount of perfume, and other goods to the value of NKr 1,200. Anyone over 20 may bring in 1 liter of wine and 1 liter of liquor or 2 liters of wine or beer.

When shopping, **keep receipts** for all purchases. Upon reentering the country, **be ready to show customs officials what you've bought.** If you feel a duty is incorrect or object to the way your clearance was handled, note the inspector's badge number and ask to see a supervisor. If the problem isn't resolved, write to the appropriate authorities, beginning with the port director at your point of entry.

IN NORWAY

Limits on what you can bring in duty-free vary from country to country. **Check with individual country tourist boards for limits on alcohol, cigarettes, and other items.** Also be careful to check before bringing food of any kind into Iceland.

IN AUSTRALIA

Australia residents who are 18 or older may bring home $A400 worth of souvenirs and gifts (including jewelry), 250 cigarettes or 250 grams of tobacco, and 1,125 ml of alcohol (including wine, beer, and spirits). Residents under 18 may bring back $A200 worth of goods. Prohibited items include meat products. Seeds, plants, and fruits need to be declared upon arrival.

➤ INFORMATION: **Australian Customs Service** (Regional Director, ✉ Box 8, Sydney, NSW 2001, ☎ 02/9213–2000, ☎ 02/9213–4000).

IN CANADA

Canadian residents who have been out of Canada for at least 7 days may bring home C$500 worth of goods duty-free. If you've been away less than 7 days but more than 48 hours, the duty-free allowance drops to C$200; if your trip lasts 24–48 hours, the allowance is C$50. You may not pool allowances with family members. Goods claimed under the C$500 exemption may follow you by mail; those claimed under the lesser exemptions must accompany you. Alcohol and tobacco products may be included in the 7-day and 48-hour exemptions but not in the 24-hour exemption. If you meet the age requirements of the province or territory through which you reenter Canada, you may bring in, duty-free, 1.14 liters (40 imperial ounces) of wine or liquor *or* 24 12-ounce cans or bottles of beer or ale. If you are 16 or older you may bring in, duty-free, 200 cigarettes and 50 cigars. Check ahead of time with Revenue Canada or the Department of Agriculture for policies regarding meat products, seeds, plants, and fruits.

You may send an unlimited number of gifts worth up to C$60 each duty-free to Canada. Label the package UNSOLICITED GIFT—VALUE UNDER $60. Alcohol and tobacco are excluded.

➤ INFORMATION: **Revenue Canada** (✉ 2265 St. Laurent Blvd. S, Ottawa, Ontario K1G 4K3, ☎ 613/993–0534; 800/461–9999 in Canada).

IN NEW ZEALAND

Homeward-bound residents 17 or older may bring back $700 worth of souvenirs and gifts. Your duty-free allowance also includes 4.5 liters of wine or beer; one 1,125-ml bottle of spirits; and either 200 cigarettes, 250 grams of tobacco, 50 cigars, or a combination of the three up to 250 grams. Prohibited items include meat products, seeds, plants, and fruits.

➤ INFORMATION: **New Zealand Customs** (Custom House, ✉ 50 Anzac Ave., Box 29, Auckland, New Zealand, ☎ 09/359–6655, FAX 09/359–6732).

IN THE U.K.

If you are a U.K. resident and your journey was wholly within the European Union (EU), you won't have to pass through customs when you return to the United Kingdom. If you plan to bring back large quantities of alcohol or tobacco, check EU limits beforehand. From countries outside the EU, including Norway, you may import, duty-free, 200 cigarettes or 50 cigars; 1 liter of spirits or 2 liters of fortified or sparkling wine or liqueurs; 2 liters of still table wine; 60 milliliters of perfume; 250 milliliters of toilet water; plus £136 worth of other goods, including gifts and souvenirs.

➤ INFORMATION: **HM Customs and Excise** (✉ Dorset House, Stamford St., Bromley Kent BR1 1XX, ☎ 020/7202–4227).

IN THE U.S.

U.S. residents who have been out of the country for at least 48 hours (and who have not used the $400 allowance or any part of it in the past 30 days) may bring home $400 worth of foreign goods duty-free. U.S. residents 21 and older may bring back 1 liter of alcohol duty-free. In addition, regardless of your age, you are allowed 200 cigarettes and 100 non-Cuban cigars. Antiques, which the U.S. Customs Service defines as objects more than 100 years old, enter duty-free, as do original works of art done entirely by hand, including paintings, drawings, and sculptures.

You may also send packages home duty-free: up to $200 worth of goods for personal use, with a limit of one parcel per addressee per day (and no alcohol or tobacco products or perfume worth more than $5); label the package PERSONAL USE and attach a list of its contents and their retail value. Do not label the package UNSOLICITED GIFT or your duty-free exemption will drop to $100. Mailed items do not affect your duty-free allowance on your return.

➤ INFORMATION: **U.S. Customs Service** (inquiries, ✉ 1300 Pennsylvania Ave. NW, Washington, DC 20229, ☎ 202/927–6724; complaints, ✉ Office of Regulations and Rulings, 1300 Pennsylvania Ave. NW, Washington, DC 20229; registration of equipment, ✉ Registration Information, 1300 Pennsylvania Ave. NW, Washington, DC 20229, ☎ 202/927–0540).

DINING

Norway's major cities offer a full range of dining choices, from traditional to international restaurants. Restaurants in smaller towns stick to traditional local fare. Local dishes can be very good, especially in the seafood and game categories, but bear in mind that northern climes beget exceptionally hearty, and heavy, meals. Sausage appears in a thousand forms, likewise potatoes. Some particular northern tastes can seem very different, such as the fondness for pickled and fermented fish—to be sampled carefully at first—and a universal obsession with sweet pastries, ice cream, and chocolate. Other novelties for the visitor might be the use of fruit in main dishes and soups, or sour milk on breakfast cereal, or preserved fish paste as a spread for crackers, or the prevalence of tasty, whole-grain crisp breads and hearty rye breads. The Swedish *smörgåsbord* and its Scandinavian cousins are often the traveling diner's best bet, providing you find an authentic sampling. They include fresh fish and vegetables alongside meat and starches, and are also among the lower-priced menu choices.

Restaurant meals are a big-ticket item throughout Norway, but there are ways to keep the cost of eating down. Take full advantage of the large, buffet breakfast usually included in the cost of a hotel room. At lunch, look for the "menu" that offers a set two- or three-course meal for a set price, or limit yourself to a hearty appetizer. Some restaurants now include a trip to the salad bar in the dinner price. At dinner, pay careful attention to the price of wine and drinks, since the high tax on alcohol raises these costs considerably. For more information on affordable eating, *see* Money Matters, *below.*

Properties indicated by an ✕🍴 are lodging establishments whose restaurant warrants a special trip.

RESERVATIONS & DRESS

Reservations are always a good idea: we mention them only when they're essential or are not accepted. Book as far ahead as you can, and reconfirm as soon as you arrive. We mention dress only when men are required to wear a jacket or a jacket and tie.

DISABILITIES & ACCESSIBILITY

Facilities for travelers with disabilities in Norway are generally good, and most of the major tourist offices offer special booklets and brochures on travel and accommodations.

LODGING

Best Western offers properties with wheelchair-accessible rooms in Oslo. If wheelchair-accessible rooms are not available, ground-floor rooms are provided.

When discussing accessibility with an operator or reservations agent **ask hard questions.** Are there any stairs, inside *or* out? Are there grab bars next to the toilet *and* in the shower/tub? How wide is the doorway to the room? To the bathroom? For the most extensive facilities meeting the latest legal specifications **opt for newer accommodations.**

➤ WHEELCHAIR-FRIENDLY CHAIN: **Best Western** (☎ 800/528–1234).

TRANSPORTATION

➤ COMPLAINTS: **Disability Rights Section** (✉ U.S. Department of Justice, Civil Rights Division, Box 66738, Washington, DC 20035-6738, ☎ 202/514–0301; 800/514–0301; 202/514–0301 TTY; 800/514–0301 TTY, 🖷 202 /307–1198) for general complaints. **Aviation Consumer Protection Division** (☞ Air Travel, *above*) for airline-related problems. **Civil Rights Office** (✉ U.S. Department of Transportation, Departmental Office of Civil Rights, S-30, 400 7th St. SW, Room 10215, Washington, DC 20590, ☎ 202/366–4648, 🖷 202/366–9371) for problems with surface transportation.

TRAVEL AGENCIES

In the United States, although the Americans with Disabilities Act requires that travel firms serve the needs of all travelers, some agencies specialize in working with people with disabilities.

➤ TRAVELERS WITH MOBILITY PROBLEMS: **Access Adventures** (✉ 206 Chestnut Ridge Rd., Rochester, NY 14624, ☎ 716/889–9096), run by a former physical-rehabilitation counselor. **Accessible Journeys** (✉ 35 W. Sellers Ave., Ridley Park, PA 19078, ☎ 610/521–0339 or 800/846–4537, 🖷 610/521–6959). **CareVacations** (✉ 5-5110 50th Ave., Leduc, Alberta T9E 6V4, ☎ 780/986–6404 or 877/478–7827, 🖷 780/986–8332) has group tours and is especially helpful with cruise vacations. **Flying Wheels Travel** (✉ 143 W. Bridge St., Box 382, Owatonna, MN 55060, ☎ 507/451–5005 or 800/535–6790, 🖷 507/451–1685). **Hinsdale Travel Service** (✉ 201 E. Ogden Ave., Suite 100,

Hinsdale, IL 60521, ☎ 630/325–
1335, FAX 630/325–1342).

DISCOUNTS & DEALS

Be a smart shopper and **compare all
your options** before making decisions.
A plane ticket bought with a promotional coupon from travel clubs,
coupon books, and direct-mail offers
may not be cheaper than the least
expensive fare from a discount ticket
agency. And always keep in mind that
what you get is just as important as
what you save.

DISCOUNT RESERVATIONS

To save money **look into discount-
reservations services** with toll-free
numbers, which use their buying
power to get a better price on hotels,
airline tickets, even car rentals. When
booking a room, always **call the
hotel's local toll-free number** (if one is
available) rather than the central
reservations number—you'll often get
a better price. Always ask about
special packages or corporate rates.

When shopping for the best deal on
hotels and car rentals **look for guaranteed exchange rates,** which protect
you against a falling dollar. With your
rate locked in, you won't pay more,
even if the price goes up in the local
currency.

➤ AIRLINE TICKETS: ☎ **800/FLY–4–
LESS.**

➤ HOTEL ROOMS: **International
Marketing & Travel Concepts** (☎
800/790–4682). **Steigenberger Reservation Service** (☎ 800/223–5652).
Travel Interlink (☎ 800/888–5898).

PACKAGE DEALS

Don't confuse packages and guided
tours. When you buy a package, you
travel on your own, just as though
you had planned the trip yourself.
Fly/drive packages, which combine
airfare and car rental, are often a
good deal. If you **buy a rail/drive
pass** you may save on train tickets
and car rentals. All Eurail- and Europass holders get a discount on
Eurostar fares through the Channel
Tunnel. Also check rates for Scanrail
Passes (☞ Discount Passes *in* Train
Travel, *below*).

ELECTRICITY

To use your U.S.-purchased electric-
powered equipment **bring a converter
and adapter.** The electrical current in
Norway is 220 volts, 50 cycles alternating current (AC); wall outlets take
Continental-type plugs, with two
round prongs.

If your appliances are dual-voltage
you'll need only an adapter. Don't use
110-volt outlets, marked FOR SHAVERS
ONLY, for high-wattage appliances
such as blow-dryers. Most laptops
operate equally well on 110 and 220
volts and so require only an adapter.

EMBASSIES

The United States, Canada, and the
United Kingdom have embassies in
Oslo.

➤ EMBASSIES IN OSLO: **U.S.** (✉ Drammensvn. 18, 0255 Oslo, ☎ 22/44–
85–50). **Canada** (✉ Oscars Gt. 20,
0352 Oslo, ☎ 22/46–69–55). **U.K.**
(✉ Thomas Heftyes Gt. 8, 0244
Oslo, ☎ 22/55–24–00).

EMERGENCIES

Ambulance, fire, and police assistance
is available 24 hours in Norway.

➤ EMERGENCIES: **Police** ☎ **122. Fire**
☎ **110. Ambulance** ☎ **113.**

GAY & LESBIAN TRAVEL

➤ GAY- AND LESBIAN-FRIENDLY TRAVEL
AGENCIES: **Different Roads Travel** (✉
8383 Wilshire Blvd., Suite 902, Bev-
erly Hills, CA 90211, ☎ 323/651–
5557 or 800/429–8747, FAX 323/651–
3678). **Kennedy Travel** (✉ 314 Jeri-
cho Turnpike, Floral Park, NY
11001, ☎ 516/352–4888 or 800/
237–7433, FAX 516/354–8849). **Now
Voyager** (✉ 4406 18th St., San Fran-
cisco, CA 94114, ☎ 415/626–1169
or 800/255–6951, FAX 415/626–8626).
Skylink Travel and Tour (✉ 1006
Mendocino Ave., Santa Rosa, CA
95401, ☎ 707/546–9888 or 800/
225–5759, FAX 707/546–9891), serving lesbian travelers.

INSURANCE

The most useful travel insurance plan
is a comprehensive policy that includes coverage for trip cancellation
and interruption, default, trip delay,

and medical expenses (with a waiver for preexisting conditions).

Without insurance you will lose all or most of your money if you cancel your trip, regardless of the reason. Default insurance covers you if your tour operator, airline, or cruise line goes out of business. Trip-delay covers expenses that arise because of bad weather or mechanical delays. Study the fine print when comparing policies.

If you're traveling internationally, a key component of travel insurance is coverage for medical bills incurred if you get sick on the road. Such expenses are not generally covered by Medicare or private policies. U.K. residents can buy a travel-insurance policy valid for most vacations taken during the year in which it's purchased (but check pre-existing-condition coverage). Always **buy travel policies directly from the insurance company**; if you buy it from a cruise line, airline, or tour operator that goes out of business you probably will not be covered for the agency or operator's default, a major risk. Before you make any purchase **review your existing health and home-owner's policies** to find what they cover away from home.

➤ TRAVEL INSURERS: In the U.S. **Access America** (✉ 6600 W. Broad St., Richmond, VA 23230, ☎ 804/285–3300 or 800/284–8300), **Travel Guard International** (✉ 1145 Clark St., Stevens Point, WI 54481, ☎ 715/345–0505 or 800/826–1300). In Canada **Voyager Insurance** (✉ 44 Peel Center Dr., Brampton, Ontario L6T 4M8, ☎ 905/791–8700; 800/668–4342 in Canada).

➤ INSURANCE INFORMATION: In the U.K. the **Association of British Insurers** (✉ 51–55 Gresham St., London EC2V 7HQ, ☎ 020/7600–3333, FAX 020/7696–8999). In Australia the **Insurance Council of Australia** (☎ 03/9614–1077, FAX 03/9614–7924).

LANGUAGE

Despite the fact that four of the five Scandinavian tongues are in the Germanic family of languages, it is a myth that someone who speaks German can understand Danish, Icelandic,

Swedish, and Norwegian. Fortunately, English is widely spoken in Scandinavia. German is the most common third language. English becomes rarer outside major cities, and it's a good idea to **take along a dictionary or phrase book.** Even here, however, anyone under the age of 50 is likely to have studied English in school.

Danish, Norwegian, and Swedish are similar, and fluent Norwegian and Swedish speakers can generally understand each other. While Finns must study Swedish (the second national language) in school, they much prefer to speak English with their Scandinavian counterparts.

Norwegian has three additional vowels: æ, ø, and å. Æ is pronounced as a short "a." The ø, sometimes printed as *oe*, is the same as *ö* in German and Swedish, pronounced very much like a short "u." The *å* is a contraction of the archaic "aa" and sounds like long "o." These three letters appear at the end of alphabetical listings.

There are two officially sanctioned Norwegian languages, Bokmål and Nynorsk. Bokmål is used by 84% of the population and is the main written form of Norwegian, the language of books, as the first half of its name indicates. Nynorsk, which translates as "new Norwegian," is actually a compilation of older dialect forms from rural Norway. Every Norwegian also receives at least seven years of English instruction, starting in the second grade.

The Sami (incorrectly called Lapp) people have their own language, which is distantly related to Finnish.

LODGING

The lodgings we list are the cream of the crop in each price category. We always list the facilities that are available—but we don't specify whether they cost extra: When pricing accommodations, always ask what's included and what costs extra.

In the larger cities, lodging ranges from first-class business hotels run by SAS, Sheraton, and Scandic to good-quality tourist-class hotels, such as RESO, Best Western, Scandic Budget, and Sweden Hotels, to a wide variety of single-entrepreneur hotels. In the countryside, look for independently run inns and motels. In Norway, *fjellstuer* or *pensjonat;*. Before you leave home, **ask your travel agent about discounts** (☞ Hotels, *below*), including summer hotel checks for Best Western, Scandic, and Inter Nor hotels, a summer Fjord pass in Norway, and enormous year-round rebates at SAS hotels for travelers over 65. All EuroClass (business class) passengers can get discounts of at least 10% at SAS hotels when they book through SAS.

Two things about hotels usually surprise North Americans: the relatively limited dimensions of Scandinavian beds and the generous size of Scandinavian breakfasts. Scandinavian double beds are often about 60 inches wide or slightly less, close in size to the U.S. queen size. King-size beds (72 inches wide) are difficult to find and, if available, require special reservations.

Older hotels may have some rooms described as "double," which in fact have one double bed plus one foldout sofa big enough for two people. This arrangement is occasionally called a combi-room but is being phased out.

Many older hotels, particularly the country inns and independently run smaller hotels in the cities, do not have private bathrooms. Ask ahead if this is important to you.

Scandinavian breakfasts resemble what many people would call lunch, usually including breads, cheeses, marmalade, hams, lunch meats, eggs, juice, cereal, milk, and coffee. Generally, the farther north you go, the larger the breakfasts become. Breakfast is usually included in hotel rates.

Make reservations whenever possible. Even countryside inns, which usually have space, are sometimes packed with vacationing Europeans.

Ask about high and low seasons when making reservations, since different countries define their tourist seasons differently. Some hotels lower prices during tourist season, whereas others raise them during the same period.

Assume that hotels operate on the European Plan (EP, with no meals) unless we specify that they use the Continental Plan (CP, with a Continental breakfast daily), Modified American Plan (MAP, with breakfast and dinner daily), or the Full American Plan (FAP, with all meals).

HOME EXCHANGES

If you would like to exchange your home for someone else's **join a home-exchange organization,** which will send you its updated listings of available exchanges for a year and will include your own listing in at least one of them. It's up to you to make specific arrangements.

➤ EXCHANGE CLUBS: **HomeLink International** (✉ Box 650, Key West, FL 33041, ☎ 305/294–7766 or 800/638–3841, FAX 305/294–1448; $93 per year). **Intervac U.S.** (✉ Box 590504, San Francisco, CA 94159, ☎ 800/756–4663, FAX 415/435–7440; $83 for catalogues).

CAMPING

For camping information and a list of sites, contact local tourist offices or the Norwegian Automobile Federation. For a list of vandrerhjem in Norway, contact Norske Vandrerhjem.

➤ CONTACTS: **Norwegian Automobile Federation** (✉ Storgt. 2, 0155, Oslo 1, ☎ 22/34–14–00). **Norske Vandrerhjem** (✉ Dronningensgt. 26, 0154 Oslo, ☎ 22/13–93–00, FAX 22/13–93–50).

HOSTELS

No matter what your age you can **save on lodging costs by staying at hostels.** In some 5,000 locations in more than 70 countries around the world, Hostelling International (HI), the umbrella group for a number of national youth-hostel associations, offers single-sex, dorm-style beds and, at many hostels, couples rooms and family accommodations. Membership in any HI national hostel association, open to travelers of all ages, allows you to stay in HI-affiliated hostels at member rates (one-year membership is about $25 for adults; hostels run about $10–$25 per night). Members also have priority if the hostel is full; they're eligible for discounts around the world, even on rail and bus travel in some countries.

➤ ORGANIZATIONS: **Australian Youth Hostel Association** (✉ 10 Mallett St., Camperdown, NSW 2050, ☎ 02/9565–1699, FAX 02/9565–1325). **Hostelling International—American Youth Hostels** (✉ 733 15th St. NW, Suite 840, Washington, DC 20005, ☎ 202/783–6161, FAX 202/783–6171). **Hostelling International—Canada** (✉ 400–205 Catherine St., Ottawa, Ontario K2P 1C3, ☎ 613/237–7884, FAX 613/237–7868). **Youth Hostel Association of England and Wales** (✉ Trevelyan House, 8 St. Stephen's Hill, St. Albans, Hertfordshire AL1 2DY, ☎ 01727/855215 or 01727/845047, FAX 01727/844126). **Youth Hostels Association of New Zealand** (✉ Box 436, Christchurch, New Zealand, ☎ 03/379–9970, FAX 03/365–4476). Membership in the U.S. $25, in Canada C$26.75, in the U.K. £9.30, in Australia $44, in New Zealand $24.

HOTELS

Norway offers Inn Checks, or prepaid hotel vouchers, for accommodations ranging from first-class hotels to country cottages. These vouchers, which must be purchased from travel agents or from the Scandinavian Tourist Board (☞ Visitor Information, *below*) before departure, are sold individually and in packets for as many nights as needed and offer savings of up to 50%. Most countries also offer summer bargains for foreign tourists. For further information about Scandinavian hotel vouchers, contact the Scandinavian Tourist Board.

ProSkandinavia checks can be used in 430 hotels across Scandinavia (excluding Iceland) for savings up to 50%, for reservations made usually no earlier than 24 hours before arrival, although some hotels allow earlier bookings. One check costs about $40 U.S. Two checks will pay for a double room at a hotel, one check for a room in a cottage. The checks can be bought at many travel agencies in Scandinavia or ordered

from **ProSkandinavia** (✉ Nedre Slottsgate 13, N-0157 Oslo, Norway, ☎ 47–22/42–50–06, FAX 47–22/42–06–57, www.proskandinavia.com). All hotels listed have private bath unless otherwise noted.

➤ TOLL-FREE NUMBERS: **Adams Mark** (☎ 800/444/2326). **Baymont Inns** (☎ 800/428–3438). **Best Western** (☎ 800/528–1234). **Choice** (☎ 800/221–2222). **Clarion** (☎ 800/252–7466). **Colony** (☎ 800/777–1700). **Comfort** (☎ 800/228–5150). **Days Inn** (☎ 800/325–2525). **Doubletree and Red Lion Hotels** (☎ 800/222–8733). **Embassy Suites** (☎ 800/362–2779). **Fairfield Inn** (☎ 800/228–2800). **Forte** (☎ 800/225–5843). **Four Seasons** (☎ 800/332–3442). **Hilton** (☎ 800/445–8667). **Holiday Inn** (☎ 800/465–4329). **Howard Johnson** (☎ 800/654–4656). **Hyatt Hotels & Resorts** (☎ 800/233–1234). **Inter-Continental** (☎ 800/327–0200). **La Quinta** (☎ 800/531–5900). **Marriott** (☎ 800/228–9290). **Le Meridien** (☎ 800/543–4300). **Nikko Hotels International** (☎ 800/645–5687). **Omni** (☎ 800/843–6664). **Quality Inn** (☎ 800/228–5151). **Radisson** (☎ 800/333–3333). **Ramada** (☎ 800/228–2828). **Renaissance Hotels & Resorts** (☎ 800/468–3571). **Ritz-Carlton** (☎ 800/241–3333). **Sheraton** (☎ 800/325–3535). **Sleep Inn** (☎ 800/753–3746). **Westin Hotels & Resorts** (☎ 800/228–3000). **Wyndham Hotels & Resorts** (☎ 800/822-4200).

MAIL

The letter rate for Norway is NKr 4, NKr 5 for the other Nordic countries, NKr 6 for Europe, and NKr 7 for outside Europe for a letter weighing up to 20 grams (¾ ounce).

MONEY MATTERS

Costs are high in Norway, where so many things must be imported. You can **reduce the cost of food by planning.** Breakfast is often included in your hotel bill; if not, you may wish to buy fruit, sweet rolls, and a beverage for a picnic breakfast. Electrical devices for hot coffee or tea should be bought abroad, though, to conform to the local current. **Opt for a restaurant lunch instead of dinner,** since the latter tends to be significantly more expensive. Instead of beer or wine, **drink tap water**—liquor can cost four times the price of the same brand in a store—but do specify tap water, as the term "water" can refer to soft drinks and bottled water, which are also expensive. Throughout Norway, the tip is included in the cost of your meal.

Cup of coffee, from NKr 14 in a cafeteria to NKr 25 or more in a restaurant; a 20-pack of cigarettes, NKr 60; a half-liter of beer, NKr 40–NKr 50; the smallest hot dog (with bun plus *lompe*—a flat Norwegian potato bread—mustard, ketchup, and fried onions) at a convenience store, NKr 20; cheapest bottle of wine from a government store, NKr 60; the same bottle at a restaurant, NKr 120–NKr 200; urban transit fare in Oslo, NKr 15; soft drink, from NKr 20 in a cafeteria to NKr 35 in a better restaurant; sandwich at a cafeteria, NKr 40–Nkr 50; 1½-km (1-mi) taxi ride, NKr 40–NKr 60 depending on time of day.

In most of Scandinavia, liquor and strong beer (over 3% alcohol) can be purchased only in state-owned shops, at very high prices, during weekday business hours, usually 9:30 to 6 and in some areas on Saturdays until mid-afternoon. Weaker beers and ciders are usually available in grocery stores in Scandinavia.

Prices throughout this guide are given for adults. Substantially reduced fees are almost always available for children, students, and senior citizens. For information on taxes, *see* Taxes, *below*.

ATMS

➤ ATM LOCATIONS: **Cirrus** (☎ 800/424–7787).

CREDIT CARDS

Throughout this guide, the following abbreviations are used: AE, American Express; DC, Diner's Club; MC, MasterCard; and V, Visa.

CURRENCY

The unit of currency in Norway is the *krone* (plural: *kroner*), which translates as "crown," written officially as NOK. Price tags are seldom marked

this way, but instead read "Kr" followed by the amount, such as Kr 10. (In this book, the Norwegian krone is abbreviated NKr.) One krone is divided into 100 *øre*, and coins of 50 øre and 1, 5, 10, and 20 kroner are in circulation. Bills are issued in denominations of 50, 100, 200, 500, and 1,000 kroner. In winter 2000, the exchange rate was NKr 7.96 to U.S. $1, NKr 12.94 to £1, and NKr 5.48 to C$1. **Since rates fluctuate daily, you should check them at the time of your departure.**

CURRENCY EXCHANGE

For the most favorable rates, **change money through banks.** Although ATM transaction fees may be higher abroad than at home, ATM rates are excellent because they are based on wholesale rates offered only by major banks. You won't do as well at exchange booths in airports or rail and bus stations, in hotels, in restaurants, or in stores. To avoid lines at airport exchange booths **get a bit of local currency before you leave home.**

➤ EXCHANGE SERVICES: **International Currency Express** (☎ 888/842–0880 on East Coast; 888/278–6628 on West Coast). **Thomas Cook Currency Services** (☎ 800/287–7362 for telephone orders and retail locations).

TRAVELER'S CHECKS

Do you need traveler's checks? It depends on where you're headed. If you're going to rural areas and small towns, go with cash; traveler's checks are best used in cities. Lost or stolen checks can usually be replaced within 24 hours. To ensure a speedy refund, buy your own traveler's checks—don't let someone else pay for them: irregularities like this can cause delays. The person who bought the checks should make the call to request a refund.

OUTDOOR ACTIVITIES AND SPORTS

Norway is a sports lover's paradise. Close to 100 recreational and competitive sports are recognized in Norway, each with its own national association, 57 of which are affiliated with the **Norges Idrettsforbund** (Norwegian Confederation of Sports, ✉

Hauger Skolevei 1, 1351 Rud, ☎ 67/15–46–00). The tourist board's Norway brochure, which lists sporting- and active-holiday resources and contacts, is a more helpful starting point for visitors.

BIKING

Most cities have marked bike and ski routes and paths. Bicycling on country roads away from traffic is a favorite national pastime, but as most routes are hilly, this demands good physical condition. All cyclists are required to wear protective helmets and use lights at night. You can rent a bike and get local maps through any local tourist board.

Den Norske Turistforening (DNT, ⊠ Box 1963 Vika, 0125 Oslo 1, ☎ 22/82–28–01, FAX 22/83–24–78) provides inexpensive lodging for cyclists planning overnight trips. You can also contact the helpful **Syklistenes Landsforening** (⊠ Storgt. 23C, 0028 Oslo 4, ☎ 22/41–50–80) for general information and maps, as well as the latest weather conditions.

BIRD-WATCHING

Northern Norway contains some of northern Europe's largest bird sanctuaries and teems with fantastic numbers of seabirds, even eagles. For organized tours, contact **Borton Overseas** (☎ 800/843–0602) or the Norwegian Tourist Board.

CANOEING

There are plenty of lakes and streams for canoeing in Norway, as well as rental facilities. Contact **Norges Padlerforbund** (⊠ Hauger Skolevei 1, 1351 Bærum, ☎ 67/15–46–00) for a list of rental companies and regional canoeing centers.

DIVING

Diving is very well organized and popular in Norway, especially on the west coast. There are few restrictions regarding sites—special permission is required to dive in a harbor, and diving near army installations is restricted. Contact **Norges Dykkforbund** (⊠ Hauger Skolevei 1, 1351 Baerum, ☎ 67/15–46–00) for a list of diving centers.

FISHING

To fish, you'll have to buy an annual or weekly fishing tax card at the post office and a local license from the sporting-goods store nearest the fishing site. Live bait is prohibited, and imported tackle must be disinfected before use.

HANG GLIDING

The mountains and hills of Norway provide excellent take-off spots. However, winds and weather conspire to make conditions unpredictable. For details on local clubs, regulations, and equipment rental, contact **Norsk Aeroklubb** (⊠ Tollbugt. 3, 0152 Oslo, ☎ 23/10–29–00).

RAFTING

Rafting excursions are offered throughout Norway. For more information, contact **Norwegian Wildlife and Rafting** (⊠ 2680 Vågå, ☎ 61/23–87–27), who operate guided two-day expeditions with accommodation and transport provided.

SAILING

Contact **Norges Seilforbund** (⊠ Hauger Skolevei 1, 1351 Bærum, ☎ 67/56–85–75) about facilities around the country.

SKIING

The **Skiforeningen** (⊠ Kongevn. 5, 0390 Oslo 3, ☎ 22/92–32–00) provides national snow-condition reports.

SPORTS FOR PEOPLE WITH DISABILITIES

Norway encouraged active participation in sports for people with disabilities long before it became popular elsewhere and has many Special Olympics medal winners. **Beitostølen Helsesportsenter** (⊠ 2953 Beitostølen, ☎ 61/34–08–00) has sports facilities for the blind and other physically challenged people as well as training programs for instructors. Sports offered include skiing, hiking, running, and horseback riding. For more information call **Norges Funksjonshemmede Idrettsforbund** (⊠ Hauger Skolevei 1, 1351 Bærum, ☎ 67/15–46–00).

SMART TRAVEL TIPS A TO Z

PACKING

Bring a folding umbrella and a lightweight raincoat, as it is common for the sky to be clear at 9 AM, rainy at 11 AM, and clear again in time for lunch. **Pack casual clothes,** as Norwegians tend to dress more casually than their Continental brethren. If you have trouble sleeping when it is light or are sensitive to strong sun, **bring an eye mask and dark sunglasses;** the sun rises as early as 4 AM in some areas, and the far-northern latitude causes it to slant at angles unseen elsewhere on the globe. **Bring bug repellent** if you plan to venture away from the capital cities; large mosquitoes can be a real nuisance on summer evenings throughout Norway.

In your carry-on luggage **bring an extra pair of eyeglasses or contact lenses** and **enough of any medication you take** to last the entire trip. You may also want your doctor to write a spare prescription using the drug's generic name, since brand names may vary from country to country. In luggage to be checked, **never pack prescription drugs or valuables.** To avoid customs delays, carry medications in their original packaging. And don't forget to copy down and carry addresses of offices that handle refunds of lost traveler's checks.

CHECKING LUGGAGE

How many carry-on bags you can bring with you is up to the airline. Most allow two, but not always, so make sure that everything you carry aboard will fit under your seat, and get to the gate early. Note that if you have a seat at the back of the plane, you'll probably board first, while the overhead bins are still empty.

If you are flying internationally, note that baggage allowances may be determined not by piece but by weight—generally 88 pounds (40 kilograms) in first class, 66 pounds (30 kilograms) in business class, and 44 pounds (20 kilograms) in economy.

Airline liability for baggage is limited to $1,250 per person on flights within the United States. On international flights it amounts to $9.07 per pound or $20 per kilogram for checked baggage (roughly $640 per 70-pound bag) and $400 per passenger for unchecked baggage. You can buy additional coverage at check-in for about $10 per $1,000 of coverage, but it excludes a rather extensive list of items, shown on your airline ticket.

Before departure **itemize your bags' contents** and their worth, and label the bags with your name, address, and phone number. (If you use your home address, cover it so that potential thieves can't see it readily.) Inside each bag **pack a copy of your itinerary.** At check-in **make sure that each bag is correctly tagged** with the destination airport's three-letter code. If your bags arrive damaged or fail to arrive at all, file a written report with the airline before leaving the airport.

PASSPORTS & VISAS

When traveling internationally **carry a passport even if you don't need one** (it's always the best form of ID), and **make two photocopies of the data page** (one for someone at home and another for you, carried separately from your passport). If you lose your passport promptly call the nearest embassy or consulate and the local police.

ENTERING NORWAY

All U.S. citizens, even infants, need only a valid passport to enter Norway for stays of up to three months.

PASSPORT OFFICES

The best time to apply for a passport or to renew is during the fall and winter. Before any trip, check your passport's expiration date, and, if necessary, renew it as soon as possible.

➤ AUSTRALIAN CITIZENS: **Australian Passport Office** (☎ 131–232).

➤ CANADIAN CITIZENS: **Passport Office** (☎ 819/994–3500 or 800/567–6868).

➤ NEW ZEALAND CITIZENS: **New Zealand Passport Office** (☎ 04/494–0700 for information on how to apply; 04/474–8000 or 0800/225–050 in New Zealand for information on applications already submitted).

➤ U.K. CITIZENS: **London Passport Office** (☎ 0990/210–410) for fees and documentation requirements and to request an emergency passport.

➤ U.S. CITIZENS: **National Passport Information Center** (☎ 900/225–5674; calls are 35¢ per minute for automated service, $1.05 per minute for operator service).

SENIOR-CITIZEN TRAVEL

To qualify for age-related discounts **mention your senior-citizen status up front** when booking hotel reservations (not when checking out) and before you're seated in restaurants (not when paying the bill). When renting a car ask about promotional car-rental discounts, which can be cheaper than senior-citizen rates.

TRAIN TRAVEL

Travelers over 60 can buy a **Senior-Rail Card** for about $27 in Norway. It gives 30% discounts on train travel in 21 European countries for a whole year from purchase.

➤ EDUCATIONAL PROGRAMS: **Elderhostel** (✉ 75 Federal St., 3rd fl., Boston, MA 02110, ☎ 877/426–8056, ℻ 877/426–2166). **Interhostel** (✉ University of New Hampshire, 6 Garrison Ave., Durham, NH 03824, ☎ 603/862–1147 or 800/733–9753, ℻ 603/862–1113).

SHOPPING

Prices in Norway are never low, but quality is high, and specialties are sometimes less expensive here than elsewhere. Norwegian fur is just one of the items to look for.

STUDENTS IN NORWAY

➤ STUDENT IDS & SERVICES: **Council on International Educational Exchange** (CIEE, ✉ 205 E. 42nd St., 14th fl., New York, NY 10017, ☎ 212/822–2600 or 888/268–6245, ℻ 212/822–2699) for mail orders only, in the U.S. **Travel Cuts** (✉ 187 College St., Toronto, Ontario M5T 1P7, ☎ 416/979–2406 or 800/667–2887) in Canada.

TAXES

VALUE-ADDED TAX (V.A.T.)

One way to beat high prices is to **take advantage of tax-free shopping.**

Throughout Scandinavia, you can make major purchases free of tax if you have a foreign passport. Ask about tax-free shopping when you make a purchase for $50 (about £32) or more. When your purchases exceed a specified limit (which varies from country to country), you receive a special export receipt. Keep the parcels intact and take them out of the country within 30 days of purchase. When you leave the last EU country visited, you can obtain a refund of the V.A.T. (called *moms* all over Scandinavia) in cash from a special office at the airport, or, upon arriving home, you can send your receipts to an office in the country of purchase to receive your refund by mail. Citizens of EU countries are not eligible for the refund. In Norway, for non-EU tourists, the refund is about 11–18% for purchases over NKr300.

The V.A.T. is a hefty 23% on all purchases except books in Norway; it is included in the prices of goods. All purchases of consumer goods totaling more than NKr 308 (approximately $40) for export by nonresidents are eligible for value-added tax refunds. Carry your passport when shopping to prove you are a nonresident.

Shops subscribing to "Norway Tax-Free Shopping" provide customers with vouchers, which they must present together with their purchases on departure to receive an on-the-spot refund of 11–18% of the tax.

Shops that do not subscribe to this program have slightly more detailed forms, which must be presented to the Norwegian Customs Office along with the goods to obtain a refund by mail. This refund is closer to the actual amount of the tax. For information on the tax-free system, call ☎ 67/14–99–01.

It's essential to have both the forms and the goods available for inspection upon departure. Make sure the appropriate stamps are on the voucher or other forms before leaving the country.

Note: Tax-free sales of alcohol, cigarettes, and other luxury goods has been abolished among EU countries, with the Scandinavian countries among the last to adopt these regula-

SMART TRAVEL TIPS A TO Z

tions. The Aland islands, however, are not part of the EU customs union and allows tax-free sales for ferries in transit through its ports. All Sweden–Finland ferry routes now pass through the islands, de facto continuing the extremely popular tax-free sales for tourists. Air travel to the Scandinavia EU member states (Sweden, Finland, Denmark), as well as Norway, no longer allows tax-free sales.

Europe Tax-Free Shopping is a V.A.T. refund service that makes getting your money back hassle-free. E.T.S. is Europe-wide and has 90,000 affiliated stores. In participating stores, **ask for the E.T.S. refund form** (called a Shopping Cheque). As is true for all customs forms, when leaving the European Union you get them stamped by the customs official. Then you take them to the E.T.S. counter and they will refund your money right there in cash, by check, or a refund to your credit card. All that convenience will cost you 20%—but then it's done.

➤ VAT REFUNDS: **Global Refund** (✉ 707 Summer St., Stamford, CT 06901, ☎ 800/566–9828).

TAXIS

Even the smallest villages have some form of taxi service. Towns on the railroad normally have taxi stands just outside the station. All city taxis are connected with a central dispatching office, so there is only one main telephone number, the taxi central. Look in the telephone book under "Taxi" or "Drosje."

TELEPHONES

The telephone system in Norway is modern and efficient; international direct service is available throughout the country. Phone numbers consist of eight digits throughout the country.

Public telephones are of two types. Push-button phones, which accept NKr 1, 5, and 10 coins (some accept NKr 20 coins), are easy to use: lift the receiver, listen for the dial tone, insert the coins, dial the number, and wait for a connection. The digital screen at the top of the box indicates the amount of money in your "account."

You can also purchase **Tellerskritt** (phone cards) at **Narvesen** and **Norsk Tipping** shops and kiosks. Cards come in Nkr 22, NKr 65, and NKr 150 units and can be used in the green public card telephones, as can major credit cards.

Both types of telephones have warning signals (short pips) indicating that the purchased time is almost over.

COUNTRY & AREA CODES

The country code for Norway is 47. When dialing a Norwegian number from abroad, drop the initial 0 from the local area code.

There are no longer city codes in Norway, except in that numbers in each city start with the same two-digit prefix, such as 22 (Oslo) and 55 (Bergen). You have to dial all eight digits whether or not you're in the city. Telephone numbers starting with the prefix 82 cost extra.

DIRECTORY ASSISTANCE AND OPERATOR INFORMATION

Dial 180 for information for Norway and the other Scandinavian countries, 181 for other international telephone numbers.

INTERNATIONAL CALLS

Dial the international access code, 00, then the country code, and number. All telephone books list country code numbers, including the United States and Canada (1), Great Britain (44), New Zealand (64), and Australia (61). For operator-assisted calls, dial 117 for national calls and 115 for international calls. All international operators speak English. You can contact U.S. operators from Norway by dialing local access codes.

AT&T, MCI, and Sprint access codes make calling long distance relatively convenient, but you may find the local access number blocked in many hotel rooms. First ask the hotel operator to connect you. If the hotel operator balks ask for an international operator, or dial the international operator yourself. One way to improve your odds of getting connected to your long-distance carrier is to travel with more than one company's calling card (a hotel may block Sprint, for example, but not MCI). If all else fails call from a pay phone.

➤ ACCESS CODES: **AT&T USADirect** (☎ 800/19011 Norway). **MCI Call USA** (☎ 800/19912 Norway). **Sprint Express** (☎ 050/12877, 800/19877 Norway). **WorldPhone** (☎ 800/19912)

LOCAL CALLS

Local calls cost NKr 3 or NKr 5 from a pay phone.

LONG-DISTANCE CALLS

All eight digits are required when dialing in Norway, both for local and long-distance calls. Rates vary according to distance and time of day. Toll-free numbers beginning with "800" or "810" are also common, especially among travel-related organizations.

TIPPING

Tipping is kept to a minimum in Norway because service charges are added to most bills. It is, however, handy to have a supply of NKr 5 or 10 coins for less formal service. Tip only in local currency.

Room service usually has a service charge included already, so tipping is discretionary. Round off a taxi fare to the next round digit, or tip anywhere from NKr 5 to NKr 10, a little more if the driver has been helpful. All restaurants include a service charge, ranging from 12% to 15%, in the bill. It is customary to add an additional 5% for exceptional service, but it is not obligatory. Maître d's are not tipped, and coat checks have flat rates, usually NKr 10 per person.

TOURS & PACKAGES

On a prepackaged tour or independent vacation everything is prearranged so you'll spend less time planning—and often get it all at a good price.

BOOKING WITH AN AGENT

Travel agents are excellent resources. But it's a good idea to collect brochures from several agencies because some agents' suggestions may be influenced by relationships with tour and package firms that reward them for volume sales. If you have a special interest **find an agent with expertise in that area;** ASTA (☞

Travel Agencies, *below*) has a database of specialists worldwide.

Make sure your travel agent knows the accommodations and other services of the place they're recommending. Ask about the hotel's location, room size, beds, and whether it has a pool, room service, or programs for children, if you care about these. Has your agent been there in person or sent others whom you can contact?

Do some homework on your own, too: Local tourism boards can provide information about lesser-known and small-niche operators, some of which may sell only direct.

BUYER BEWARE

Each year consumers are stranded or lose their money when tour operators—even large ones with excellent reputations—go out of business. So **check out the operator.** Ask several travel agents about its reputation, and try to **book with a company that has a consumer-protection program.** (Look for information in the company's brochure.) In the United States, members of the National Tour Association and United States Tour Operators Association are required to set aside funds to cover your payments and travel arrangements in case the company defaults. It's also a good idea to choose a company that participates in the American Society of Travel Agents' Tour Operator Program (TOP); ASTA will act as mediator in any disputes between you and your tour operator.

Remember that the more your package or tour includes the better you can predict the ultimate cost of your vacation. Make sure you know exactly what is covered, and **beware of hidden costs.** Are taxes, tips, and transfers included? Entertainment and excursions? These can add up.

➤ TOUR-OPERATOR RECOMMENDATIONS: **American Society of Travel Agents** (☞ Travel Agencies, *below*). **National Tour Association** (NTA, ✉ 546 E. Main St., Lexington, KY 40508, ☎ 606/226–4444 or 800/682–8886). **United States Tour Operators Association** (USTOA, ✉ 342 Madison Ave., Suite 1522, New York,

SMART TRAVEL TIPS A TO Z

NY 10173, ☎ 212/599–6599 or 800/468–7862, FAX 212/599–6744).

TRAIN TRAVEL

Traveling from Britain to Norway by train is not difficult and takes 20 to 24 hours. The best connection leaves London's Victoria Station (☎ 020/7928–5100), connecting at Dover with a boat to Oostende, Belgium. From Oostende there are overnight connections to Copenhagen, from where there are express and overnight connections on to Oslo. Call **Rail Europe** (☎ 0990/848–848) for further information.

NSB, the Norwegian State Railway System, has five main lines originating from the Oslo S Station. Train tickets can be purchased in railway stations or from travel agencies. NSB has its own travel agency in Oslo (✉ Stortingsgt. 28, ☎ 22/83–88–50). The longest train runs north to Trondheim, then extends onward as far as Fauske and Bodø. The southern line hugs the coast to Stavanger, whereas the western line crosses some famous scenic territory on the way to Bergen. An eastern line to Stockholm links Norway with Sweden, while another southern line through Gothenburg, Sweden, is the main connection with continental Europe. Narvik, north of Bodø, is the last stop on Sweden's Ofot line, the world's northernmost rail system, which runs from Stockholm via Kiruna. It is possible to take a five-hour bus trip between Bodø and Narvik to connect with the other train.

NSB trains are clean, comfortable, and punctual. Most have special compartments for travelers with disabilities and for families with children younger than two years of age. First- and second-class tickets are available. Both seat and sleeper reservations are required on express and overnight trains. Reserve a few days ahead in the summer, during major holidays, and for Friday and Sunday trains.

Discounted fares include family, student, senior-citizen (including not-yet-senior spouses), and off-peak "mini" fares, which must be purchased a day in advance. NSB gives student discounts only to foreigners studying at Norwegian institutions.

DISCOUNT PASSES

Norway participates in the following rail programs: EurailPass (and its flexipass variations), Eurail Drive, ScanRail Pass, Scanrail 'n Drive, InterRail, and Nordturist Card. A Norway Rail Pass is available for three, four, and five days of unlimited rail travel for nonresidents within Norway. The ticket is sold in the United States through ScanAm (✉ 933 Rte. 23, Pompton Plains, NJ 07444, ☎ 800/545–2204). Prices are approximately $175 for four days in second class; $197 for five days within one month in second class. First-class rail passes are about 30% higher. Low-season prices are offered October through April. Rail passes do not guarantee that you will get seats on the trains you want to ride, and seat reservations are sometimes required, particularly on express trains. You will also need reservations for overnight sleeping accommodations.

CUTTING COSTS

A number of special discounted trips are available, including the InterRail Pass, which is available for European residents of all ages, and the Eurail-Pass, sold in the United States only. **Consider a Scanrail Pass,** available for travel in Norway for both first- and second-class train travel: you may have five days of unlimited travel in a 15-day period ($222 first-class/$176 second-class); 10 days of unlimited travel in a month ($354/$248); or one month of consecutive day unlimited train travel ($516/$414). With the Scanrail Pass, you also enjoy travel bonuses, including free or discounted ferry, boat, and bus travel and a Hotel Discount Card that allows 10–30% off rates for select hotels June–August. Passengers 12–25 can **buy Scanrail Youth Passes** ($167 first-class/$132 second-class, five travel days in 15 days; $266/$213 for 10 travel days in a month; $387/$311 for one month of unlimited travel). Those over 55 can **take advantage of the Scanrail 55+ Pass,** which offers the travel bonuses of the Scanrail Pass and discounted travel ($198 first-class/$157 second-class, five days; $315/$253 10 days; $459/$368 one month). Buy Scanrail passes through Rail Europe and travel agents.

For car and train travel, price the Scanrail'n Drive Pass: in 15 days you can get five days of unlimited train travel and three days of car rental (choice of three car categories) with unlimited mileage in Norway. You can purchase extra car rental days and choose from first- or second-class train travel. Rates for two adults (compact car $315 first-class/$275 second-class), are considerably lower (about 25%) than for single adults.

In Norway, you can **use EurailPasses,** which provide unlimited first-class rail travel, in all of the participating countries, for the duration of the pass. If you plan to rack up the miles, get a standard pass. These are available for 15 days ($522), 21 days ($678), one month ($838), two months ($1,188), and three months ($1,468). Eurail- and EuroPasses are available through travel agents and Rail Europe.

In addition to standard EurailPasses, **ask about special rail-pass plans.** Among these are the Eurail YouthPass (for those under age 26), the Eurail SaverPass (which gives a discount for two or more people traveling together), a Eurail FlexiPass (which allows a certain number of travel days within a set period), the Euraildrive Pass, and the EuroPass Drive (which combines travel by train and rental car).

Whichever pass you choose, remember that you must **purchase your pass before you leave** for Europe.

Many travelers assume that rail passes guarantee them seats on the trains they wish to ride. Not so. You need to **book seats ahead even if you are using a rail pass**; seat reservations are required on some European trains, particularly high-speed trains, and are a good idea on trains that may be crowded—particularly in summer on popular routes. You will also need a reservation if you purchase sleeping accommodations.

► WHERE TO BUY RAIL PASSES: **Rail Europe** (⊠ 226–230 Westchester Ave., White Plains, NY 10604, ☎ 914/682–5172 or 800/438–7245; 2087 Dundas East, Suite 105, Mississauga, Ontario L4X 1M2, ☎ 416/602–4195). **DER Tours** (⊠ Box 1606, Des Plaines, IL 60017, ☎ 800/

782–2424, ℻ 800/282–7474). **CIT Tours Corp.** (⊠ 342 Madison Ave., Suite 207, New York, NY 10173, ☎ 212/697–2100 or 800/248–8687, or 800/248–7245 in western U.S.).

TRANSPORTATION WITHIN NORWAY

The southern part of Norway is fairly compact—all major cities are about a day's drive from each other. The distances make themselves felt on the way north, where Norway becomes narrower as it inches up to and beyond the Arctic Circle and hooks over Sweden and Finland to touch Russia. It is virtually impossible to visit the entire country from one base.

TRAVEL AGENCIES

A good travel agent puts your needs first. Look for an agency that has been in business at least five years, emphasizes customer service, and has someone on staff who specializes in your destination. In addition **make sure the agency belongs to a professional trade organization.** The American Society of Travel Agents (ASTA), with 27,000 agents in some 170 countries, is the largest and most influential in the field. Operating under the motto "Integrity in Travel," it maintains and enforces a strict code of ethics and will step in to help mediate any agent-client disputes if necessary. ASTA also maintains a Web site that includes a directory of agents. Note that if a travel agency is also acting as your tour operator, *see* Buyer Beware *in* Tours & Packages, *above.*

► LOCAL AGENT REFERRALS: American Society of Travel Agents (ASTA, ☎ 800/965–2782 24-hr hot line, ℻ 703/684–8319, www.astanet.com). **Association of British Travel Agents** (⊠ 68–271 Newman St., London W1P 4AH, ☎ 020/7637–2444, ℻ 020/7637–0713). **Association of Canadian Travel Agents** (⊠ 1729 Bank St., Suite 201, Ottawa, Ontario K1V 7Z5, ☎ 613/521–0474, ℻ 613/521–0805). **Australian Federation of Travel Agents** (⊠ Level 3, 309 Pitt St., Sydney 2000, ☎ 02/9264–3299, ℻ 02/9264–1085). **Travel Agents' Association of New Zealand** (⊠ Box 1888, Wellington 10033, ☎ 04/499–0104, ℻ 04/499–0786).

SMART TRAVEL TIPS A TO Z

VISITOR INFORMATION

➤ SCANDINAVIAN TOURIST BOARD:
U.S.: **Scandinavian Tourist Board** (⊠ *655 3rd Ave., New York, New York 10017-5617,* ☎ *212/949–2333, 212/ 885–9700,* ℻ *212/983–5260, 212/ 885–9710).*

U.K.: **Norwegian Tourist Board** (⊠ *5 Lower Regent St., London SW1Y 4LR,* ☎ *020/7839–6255,* ℻ *020/ 7839–6014).*

➤ U.S. GOVERNMENT ADVISORIES: **U.S. Department of State** (⊠ *Overseas Citizens Services Office, Room 4811 N.S., 2201 C St. NW, Washington, DC 20520;* ☎ *202/647–5225 for interactive hot line; 301/946–4400 for computer bulletin board;* ℻ *202/ 647–3000 for interactive hot line);* enclose a self-addressed, stamped, business-size envelope.

WEB SITES

Do **check out the World Wide Web** when you're planning. You'll find everything from up-to-date weather forecasts to virtual tours of famous cities. Fodor's Web site www.fodors. com, is a great place to start your online travels.

FERRY OPERATORS

Color Line (www.colorline.com), **Fjord Line** (www.fjordline.com), **ScandLines** (www.scandlines.com), **Scandinavian Seaways** (www.scansea.com), **Silja Line** (www.silja.com), **Smyril Line** (www.smyril-line.fo), **Stena Line** (www.stenaline.dk), **Viking Line** (www.vikingline.fi).

NORWEGIAN RESOURCES

Tourism information (general English-speaking information, www.norway.org;

general information, www.tourist.no; Oslo information, www.oslopro.no).

WHEN TO GO

The Norwegian tourist season peaks in June, July, and August, when daytime temperatures are often in the 70s (21°C to 26°C) and sometimes rise into the 80s (27°C to 32°C). In general, the weather is not overly warm, and a brisk breeze and brief rainstorms are possible anytime. Nights can be chilly, even in summer.

Visit in summer if you want to experience the delightfully long summer days. In June, the sun rises at 4 AM and sets at 11 PM and daylight lasts even longer farther north, making it possible to continue your sightseeing into the balmy evenings. Many attractions extend their hours during the summer, and many shut down altogether when summer ends. Fall, spring, and even winter are pleasant, despite the area's reputation for gloom. The days become shorter quickly, but the sun casts a golden light not seen farther south. On dark days, fires and candlelight will warm you indoors.

The Gulf Stream warms the western coast of Norway, making winters in these areas similar to those in London. Even the harbor of Narvik, far to the north in Norway, remains ice-free year-round. Away from the protection of the Gulf Stream, however, northern Norway experiences very cold, clear weather that attracts skiers.

CLIMATE

The following are average daily maximum and minimum temperatures for Oslo.

➤ FORECASTS: **Weather Channel Connection** (☎ *900/932–8437), 95¢ per minute from a Touch-Tone phone.*

OSLO

Jan.	28F	– 2C	May	61F	16C	Sept.	60F	16C
	19	– 7		43	6		46	8
Feb.	30F	– 1C	June	68F	20C	Oct.	48F	9C
	19	– 7		50	10		38	3
Mar.	39F	4C	July	72F	22C	Nov.	38F	3C
	25	– 4		55	13		31	– 1
Apr.	50F	10C	Aug.	70F	21C	Dec.	32F	0C
	34	1		54	12		25	– 4

FESTIVALS AND SEASONAL EVENTS

➤ JAN.: In Tromsø, the **Northern Lights Festival** celebrates the return of daylight with classical and contemporary performances by notable Norwegian and international musicians. The **Tromsø International Film Festival,** Norway's largest and the world's most northerly such festival, presents a cutting-edge program of films from around the world.

➤ FEB.: Lillehammer's **Winter Festival** is a cultural affair including music, theater, and art exhibitions. The **Røros Fair** in the town of Røros (designated as Cultural Heritage Landmark by UNESCO) has been an annual tradition since 1854. The 21st of February is **His Majesty King Harald's birthday.**

➤ FEB. 20–MAR. 2: The **Nordic World Ski Championships** in Trondheim is the biggest event celebrating Trondheim's 1,000th-year anniversary.

➤ MAR.: Europe's largest dogsledding competition, the **Finnmark Race,** follows old mail routes across Finnmarksvidda. The **Birkebeiner Race** commemorates a centuries-old cross-country ski race from Lillehammer to Rena. In Oslo, the **Holmenkollen Ski Festival** features Nordic skiing events as well as breathtaking ski-jumping feats.

➤ MAR.–APR.: The **Karasjok Easter Festival** features a variety of concerts, theater performances, art exhibits, snowmobile rallies, husky dog and reindeer races.

➤ MAY 17: **Constitution Day** brings out every Norwegian flag and crowds of marchers for parades and celebrations throughout the country.

➤ MAY: The **Grete Waitz Race** is a 5-km (3-mi), women-only race in Oslo. The festivities of the annual **Bergen International Festival,** customarily opened by the king, include dance, music, and theater performances.

➤ MAY 30–JUNE 8: Trondheim's 1,000-year anniversary is in full swing during the city's **Festival Week.**

➤ JUNE 23: **Midsummer Night,** called *Sankt Hans Afton,* is celebrated nationwide with bonfires, fireworks, and outdoor dancing. Meet fellow Norwegian Americans and Norwegians at the annual **Emigration Festival** in Stavanger. The **North Norway Cultural Festival** in Harstad features a feast of cultural activities, including performance art, exhibitions, music, theater, and youth events.

➤ JULY: The plays, exhibitions, concerts, and historic walking tours of the **Kristin Festival** pay tribute to *Kristin Lavransdatter,* the novel by Nobel prize–winning Sigrid Undset; they are held at Jorund Farm, the site of Liv Ullmann's movie based on the same novel. More than 400 jazz musicians participate in the popular **Molde International Jazz Festival.**

➤ JULY: Jazzaholics and international stars descend on Norway's west coast for the **Molde International Jazz Festival.** The festival is one of the longest-established jazz festivals in Europe. As well as theater performances and art exhibitions, there are over 50 free-of-charge concerts. The **Bislett Games** attract leading international track and field athletes to the Bislett Stadium in Oslo.

➤ AUG.: You'll find Scandinavian and international folk music, folk dancing, and folk songs at the **Telemark International Folk Music Festival** in the town of Bø in Telemark, as well as jazz and blues concerts. The **Peer Gynt Festival** in Gudbrandsdalen brings art exhibits, children's activities, and open-air theater performances of Henrik Ibsen's *Peer Gynt*—as well as Edvard Grieg's music. The **International Chamber Music Festival** stages classical concerts at venues in and around Stavanger.

➤ LATE AUG.: The **Norwegian Food Festival** awards the Norwegian Championship in cooking, seminars, and lectures. The **International Ibsen Stage Festival** gets underway in Oslo, with stars from overseas participating.

➤ SEPT.: The **Oslo Marathon** stretches 42 km (26 mi) through the streets of Oslo. For art lovers, the annual **Høstutstillingen** (Fall Exhibition) at Kunstnernes Hus (the Artists' House) is worth a visit.

➤ DEC. 10: The **Nobel Peace Prize** is awarded—by invitation only—in Oslo.

1 DESTINATION: NORWAY

NORWEGIAN LANDSCAPES

JUST NORTH OF LILLEHAMMER lives a Norwegian family on the banks of Mjøsa Lake. Every year they pack their bags and drive to their holiday retreat, where they bask in the warmth of the long, northern sun for four full weeks—then they pack up and drive the 300 ft back home again.

Norwegians have a deep attachment to, pride in, and reverence for their great outdoors. Whether in the verdant dales of the interior, the brooding mountains of the north, or the fjords and archipelagoes of the coast, their ubiquitous *hytter* (cabins or cottages) dot even the most violent landscapes. It's a question of perspective: to a Norwegian, it's not a matter of whether to enjoy the land, but how to enjoy it at this very moment.

In any kind of weather, blasting or balmy, inordinate numbers are out of doors, to fish, bike, ski, and hike, and, intentionally or not, strike the pose many foreigners regard as larger-than-life Norwegian: ruddy-faced, athletic, reindeer-sweatered. Everybody—from cherubic children to hardy senior citizens—are bundled up for just one more swoosh down the slopes, one more walk through the forest.

Although Norway is a modern, highly industrialized nation, vast areas of the country (up to 95%) remain forested or fallow, and Norwegians intend to keep them that way—in part by making it extremely difficult for foreigners, who may feel differently about the land, to purchase rural property.

When discussing the size of their country, Norwegians like to say that if Oslo remained fixed and the northern part of the country were swung south, it would reach all the way to Rome. Perched at the very top of the globe, this northern land is long and rangy, 2,750 km (1,705 mi) in length, with only 4.4 million people scattered over it—making it the least densely populated land in Europe after Iceland.

Thanks to the Gulf Stream, the coastal regions enjoy a moderate, temperate climate in winter whereas the interior has a more typical northern climate, with winter temperatures dipping far below zero.

Norwegians are justifiably proud of their ability to survive the elements. The first people to appear on the land were reindeer hunters and fisherfolk who were migrating north, following the path of the retreating ice. By the Bronze Age, settlements began to appear, and, as rock carvings show (and modern schoolchildren are proud to announce), the first Norwegians began to ski—purely as a form of locomotion—some 4,000 years ago.

The Viking Age has perhaps left the most indelible mark on the country. The Vikings' travels and conquests took them west to Iceland, England, Ireland (they founded Dublin in the 840s), and North America, and east to Kiev and as far as the Black Sea. Though they were famed as plunderers, their craftsmanship and fearlessness are revered by Norwegians today, who place ancient Viking ships in museums, cast copies of thousand-year-old silver designs into jewelry, and adventure across the seas in sailboats to preserve the memory of their forefathers' courage.

Harald I, better known as Harald the Fairhaired, swore he would not cut his hair until he united Norway, and in the 9th century he succeeded in doing both. But a millennium passed between that great era and Norwegian independence. Between the Middle Ages and 1905, Norway remained under the rule of either Denmark or Sweden, even after the constitution was written in 1814.

The 19th century saw the establishment of the Norwegian identity and a blossoming of culture. This romantic period produced some of the nation's most famous individuals, among them composer Edvard Grieg, dramatist Henrik Ibsen, expressionist painter Edvard Munch, polar explorer Roald Amundsen, and explorer-humanitarian Fridtjof Nansen. Vestiges of nationalist lyricism spangle the buildings of the era with Viking dragonheads and scrollwork, all of which symbolize the rebirth of the Viking spirit.

Faithful to their democratic nature, Norwegians held a referendum to choose a king in 1905, when independence from Sweden became reality. Prince Carl of Denmark became King Haakon VII. His baby's name was changed from Alexander to Olav, and he, and later his son, presided over the kingdom for more than 85 years. When King Olav V died in January 1991, the normally reserved Norwegians stood in line for hours to write in the condolence book at the Royal Palace. Rather than simply sign their names, they wrote personal letters of devotion to the man they called the "people's king." Thousands set candles in the snow outside the palace, transforming the winter darkness into a cathedral of ice and flame.

Harald V, Olav's son, is now king, with continuity assured by his own young-adult son, Crown Prince Haakon, who graduated from the University of California Berkeley in 1999. Norwegians continue to salute the royal family with flag-waving and parades on May 17, Constitution Day, a spirited holiday of independence that transforms Oslo's main boulevard, Karl Johans Gate, into a massive street party as people of all ages, many in national costume, make a bee-line to the palace.

During both world wars, Norway tried to maintain neutrality. World War I brought not only casualties and a considerable loss to the country's merchant fleet but also financial gain through the repurchase of major companies, sovereignty over Svalbard (islands near the North Pole), and the reaffirmation of Norway's prominence in international shipping. At the onset of World War II, Norway once again proclaimed neutrality and appeared more concerned with Allied mine-laying on the west coast than with national security. A country of mostly fisherfolk, lumber workers, and farmers, it was just beginning to realize its industrial potential when the Nazis invaded. Five years of German occupation and a burn-and-retreat strategy in the north finally left the nation ravaged. True to form, however, the people who had been evacuated returned to the embers of the north to rebuild their homes and villages.

In 1968 oil was discovered in the North Sea, and Norway was transformed from a fishing, subsistence farming, and shipping outpost to a highly developed industrial nation. Though still committed to a far-reaching social system, Norway developed in the next 20 years into a wealthy country, with a per capita income and standard of living among the world's highest, as well as long life expectancy.

Stand on a street corner with a map, and a curious Norwegian will show you the way. Visit a neighborhood, and within moments you'll be the talk of the town. As a native of Bergen quipped, "Next to skiing, gossip is a national sport." With one foot in modern, liberal Scandinavia and the other in the provincial and often self-righteous countryside, Norway, unlike its Nordic siblings, is clinging steadfastly to its separate and distinct identity within Europe. Famous for its social restrictiveness—liquor may not be served before 3 PM (and never on Sunday), and violence, even among cartoon characters, is closely monitored—Norway is determined to repel outside interference, so much so that a national referendum in November 1994 chose to reject membership in the European Union (EU). Thanks to Norway's oil supply—which has resulted in a strong economy and widespread affluence—no threat to its isolation has occurred. However, Norway is aware of its place in a wider Europe and is mirroring and implementing EU requirements and directives.

–Updated by Daniel Cash and Roderick Craig

NEW AND NOTEWORTHY

As 2000 approached, Norway's economy was in full swing thanks to a resurgence in oil prices. Despite Norway's Euroskepticism—and some say because of it—the country's future has never looked better. Unemployment is low and the standard of living high. The boom is thanks in large part to the discovery, between 1995 and 1997, of at least 20 new oil and gas fields in the Norwegian sector of the North Sea. For travelers, the burgeoning economy means more museums to visit and better services, since the government tends to invest in tourism and educational projects. Hotels and restaurants remain expensive, however, so be prepared.

Norway's longtime ex–Prime Minister, Gro Harlem Brundtland, took on the leadership of the World Health Organization (WHO) in Geneva in 1998, but she remains a much-loved figure in her home country. A hard act to follow, she was succeeded by the Labor Party's Thorbjorn Jagland, who had lost the 1997 elections to a coalition led by the Christian Democrats. Kjell Mange Bondevik is now Prime Minister and is enjoying widespread popularity after making a rapid recovery after a mild nervous breakdown.

Meanwhile, North Americans just can't get enough of the fjords, according to the Norwegian Tourist Board. They make up a substantial proportion of Norway's steadily increasing number of foreign visitors. In 1999, the tourist board also reported that Norway is becoming a hip destination for affluent tourists from southern Europe, particularly Spain and Italy, who are escaping hot summers for the clear air and refreshing temperatures of the North.

WHAT'S WHERE

Norway, roughly 400,000 square km (155,000 square mi), is about the same size as California. Approximately 30% of this long, narrow country is covered with clear lakes, lush forests, and rugged mountains. Western Norway, bordered by the Norwegian Sea and the Atlantic Ocean, is the fabled land of the fjords—few places on earth can match the power and splendor of this land. The magnificent Sognefjord, the longest inlet in western Norway, is only one of many fjords found here, including the Hardangerfjord, Geirangerfjord, Lysefjord, and Nordfjord.

Bergen, often hailed as the "Fjord Capital of Norway," is the second-largest city in the country. The cobblestone streets, well-preserved buildings at the Bryggen, and seven mountains that surround the city all add to its storybook charm.

Eastern Norway, bordered by Sweden, and by Finland and Russia to the north, is punctuated by rolling hills, abundant valleys, and fresh lakes—much more subdued than the landscape of the west. Near Gudbrandsdalen (Gudbrands Valley) you'll find Lillehammer, the site of the 1994 Winter Olympics. Almost directly south, rising from the shores of the Oslofjord, is the capital of Norway—Oslo. With a population of about a half million, Oslo is a friendly, manageable city.

If you follow the coast south, you'll come to Kristiansand, one of Sørlandet's (the Southland's) leading cities. Sørlandet is known for its long stretches of unspoiled, uncrowded beach. Stavanger, farther west, is one of the most cosmopolitan cities in Scandinavia—its oil and gas industry draws people from around the globe.

Halfway between Oslo and Bergen lies Hardangervidda (Hardanger Plateau), Norway's largest national park. At the foot of the plateau is Geilo, one of the country's most popular ski resorts. Almost directly north is the bustling city of Trondheim.

From here, a thin expanse of land stretches up to the Nordkapp (North Cape). Known as the Land of the Midnight Sun (the display of the northern lights in the winter is pretty amazing, too), this region is marked with exquisite landscapes: glaciers, fjords, and rocky coasts. Narvik, a major Arctic port, is the gateway to the Lofoten Islands, where puffins and penguins march about. Even farther north is one of Norway's major universities, Tromsø, the lifeline to settlements and research centers at the North Pole. At the very top of Norway is the county of Finnmark, where many Sami (native Laplanders) live. Access to the area is primarily through Hammerfest, Europe's northernmost city, where the sun is not visible from November 21 to January 21, but is uninterrupted May 17 through July 29.

PLEASURES AND PASTIMES

Beaches

Many Norwegians enjoy beaches in the summer, but low water temperatures, from 14°C to 18°C (57°F to 65°F), are enough to deter all but the most hardy visitors from getting into the water. Those around Mandal in the south and Jaeren's Ogna, Brusand, and Bore, closer to Stavanger, are the country's best, with fine white sand. However, all along the Oslo Fjord are good beaches too. The western fjords are warmer and calmer than the open beaches of the south—although they have rock, and not sand, beaches—and inland freshwater lakes are chillier still than Gulf Stream–warmed fjords. Topless bathing is common, and there are nude beaches all along the coast.

Dining

Eating is a cultural element of Norwegian society. The Norwegians pride themselves on gracious entertaining and lavish dinner parties using their finest silver and glassware. Dining out in Norway is expensive, so many weekend nights are spent at the houses of friends and relatives enjoying long, candlelit dinners with lively conversation and oftentimes countless glasses of wine. (The BYOB—Bring Your Own Bottle—policy is common in Norway because alcohol prices are so high.) However, eating out at restaurants is still popular, especially in cities like Oslo and Stavanger. In these larger areas, the dining scene is thriving. Until lately, fine restaurants were invariably French, and fine food usually meant meat. Now, in addition to the old reliable restaurants that serve traditional Norwegian dishes, you'll find spots that serve everything from tapas and ostrich to Thai curries and Japanese sushi.

Some Norwegian chefs are responding to competition from foreign foods by taking greater pride in their native cuisine. Today seafood and game are favored over beef and veal. Fish, from common cod and skate to the noble salmon, have a prominent place in the new Norwegian kitchen. Norwegian lamb, full of flavor, continues to be popular, and game, from birds to moose and reindeer, is prepared with sauces made from the wild berries that comprise their diet.

Desserts, too, often feature fruit and berries. Norwegian strawberries and raspberries ripen in the long, early summer days and are sweeter and more intense than those grown farther south. Red and black currants are also used. Two berries native to Norway are *tyttebær* (lingonberries), which taste similar to cranberries but are much smaller, and *molter* (cloudberries), which look like orange raspberries but have an indescribable taste. These wild berries grow above the tree line and are a real delicacy. Molter are often served as *moltekrem* (in whipped cream) as a dessert, whereas tyttebær preserves often accompany traditional meat dishes.

For centuries, Norwegians regarded food as fuel, and their dining habits still bear traces of this. *Frokost* (breakfast) is a fairly big meal, usually with a selection of crusty bread, jams, herring, cold meat, and cheese. *Geitost* (a sweet, caramel-flavored whey cheese made wholly or in part from goats' milk) and Norvegia (a Norwegian Gouda-type cheese) are on virtually every table. They are eaten in thin slices, cut with a cheese plane or slicer—a Norwegian invention—on buttered wheat or rye bread.

Lunsj (lunch) is simple and usually consists of *smørbrød* (open-faced sandwiches). Most businesses have only a 30-minute lunch break, so unless there's a company cafeteria, people bring their lunch from home. Big lunchtime buffet tables, *koldtbord*, where one can sample most of Norway's special dishes all at once, are primarily for special occasions and visitors.

Middag (dinner), the only hot meal of the day, is early—from 1 to 4 in the country, 3 to 7 in the city—so many cafeterias serving home-style food close by 6 or 7 in the evening. In Oslo it's possible to get dinner as late as midnight at certain dining establishments, especially in summer. You'll probably find that most restaurants in Oslo usually stop serving dinner around 10 PM.

Traditional, home-style Norwegian food is stick-to-the-ribs fare, served in generous portions and blanketed with gravy. One of the most popular meals is *kjøttkaker* (meat cakes), which resemble small Salisbury steaks, served with boiled potatoes, stewed cabbage, and brown gravy. Almost as popular are *medisterkaker* (mild pork sausage patties), served with brown gravy and caraway-seasoned sauerkraut, and *reinsdyrkaker* (reindeer meatballs), served with cream sauce and lingonberry jam. Other typical meat dishes include *fårikål,* a great-tasting lamb and cabbage stew, and *steik* (roast meat), always served well done. Fish dishes include poached *torsk* (cod) or *laks* (salmon), served with a creamy sauce called Sandefjord butter; *seibiff,* fried pollack and onions; and *fiskegrateng,* something between a fish soufflé and a casserole, usually served with carrot slaw.

Norway is known for several eccentric, often pungent fish dishes, but these are not representative—both *rakørret* and *raklaks* (fermented trout and salmon) and *lutefisk* (dried cod soaked in lye and then boiled) are acquired tastes, even for natives. These dishes are often served at holidays, accompanied by the national drink, *akevitt* (sometimes spelled aquavit), a schnapps-like liquor that is made from potatoes and caraway seeds.

Traditional desserts include *karamellpudding* (crème caramel) and *rømmegrøt* (sour-cream porridge served with cinnamon sugar) and a glass of *saft* (raspberry juice). Rømmegrøt—a typical farm dish—tastes very much like warm cheesecake batter. It's often served with *fenalår* (dried leg of mutton) and *lefsekling*, a thin tortilla-like pancake made with sour cream and potatoes, buttered, and coated with sugar. Christmastime brings with it a delectable array of light, sweet, and buttery pastries. The *bløtkake* (layered cream cake with custard, fruit, and marzipan) is a favorite for Christmas and special occasions but can be purchased in bakeries year-round.

CATEGORY	COST*
$$$$	over NKr450
$$$	NKr300–NKr450
$$	NKr150–NKr300
$	under NKr150

per person for a three-course meal, including tax and 12½% service charge

Fishing

Whether it's fly-fishing in western rivers or deep-sea fishing off the northern coast, Norway has all kinds of angling possibilities.

Hiking

Seemingly, one of the most common expressions in the Norwegian language is *gå på tur*, or go for a walk. Every city has surrounding trails where Norwegians usually spend a good part of their weekends hiking and strolling. Many of the trails have cabins where hikers can rest, eat, and even spend the night. Den Norske Turistforening (☞ Hiking *in* Smart Travel Tips A to Z) and affiliated organizations administer cabins and tourist facilities in the central and northern mountainous areas of the country and will arrange group hikes.

Lodging

Norway is a land of hard beds and hearty breakfasts. Hotel standards in Norway are high, and even the simplest youth hostels provide good mattresses with fluffy down comforters and clean showers or baths. Breakfast, usually served buffet style, is almost always included in the room price at hotels, whereas hostels often charge extra for the morning meal.

Norway has a good number of hotel chains, with many offering repeat-visit discount passes. Radisson SAS, which is a division of the airline, has a number of luxury hotels designed for the business traveler. Many are above the Arctic Circle and are the "only game in town." Rica and Quality hotels, also luxury chains, have expanded extensively in the past few years. Best Western, Golden Tulip Rainbow, Scandic, and Choice Hotels International are moderate-price chains, found in most major towns. The most interesting and distinctive hotel chain is Comfort Home Hotels (Swedish owned), which has successfully converted existing historic buildings into modern functional establishments in the middle price range. All Comfort Home Hotels provide an evening meal and free beer—they are Norway's best buy.

The Farmer's Association operates simple hotels in most towns and cities. These reasonably priced accommodations usually have "-heimen" as part of the name, such as Bondeheimen in Oslo. The same organization also runs cafeterias serving traditional Norwegian food, usually called Kaffistova. All of these hotels and restaurants are alcohol-free. Rustic cabins and campsites are also available everywhere, as well as some independent hotels.

In the Lofoten and Vesterålen islands, *rorbuer*, fishing cottages that have been converted into lodgings or modern versions of these simple dwellings, are the most popular form of accommodation. These rustic quayside cabins, with minikitchens, bunk beds, living rooms, and showers, are reasonably priced, and they give a unique experience of the region. *Sjøhus* (sea houses) are larger, usually two- or three-storied buildings similar to rorbuer.

Norway has more than 100 youth hostels, but in an effort to appeal to vacationers of all ages, the name has been changed to *vandrerhjem* (travelers' home). Norwegian hostels are among the best in the world, squeaky clean and with excellent facilities. Rooms sleep from two to six, and many have private showers. You don't have to be a member, but members get discounts, so it's worth joining. Membership can be arranged at any vandrerhjem, or you can buy a coupon book good for seven nights, which includes the membership fee. Linens are usually rented per night, so it's a good idea to bring your own—if you haven't, you can buy a *lakenpose* (sheet sleeping bag) at travel-gear or many department stores and at most vandrerhjem (☞ Lodging *in* Smart Travel Tips A to Z).

Norway has more than 500 inspected and classified campsites, many with showers, bathrooms, and hookups for electricity. Most also have cabins or chalets to rent by the night or longer.

CATEGORY	MAJOR CITIES*	OTHER AREAS*
$$$$	over NKr1,300	over NKr1,000
$$$	NKr1,000–NKr1,300	NKr850–NKr1,000
$$	NKr800–NKr1,000	NKr650–NKr850
$	under NKr800	under NKr650

All prices are for a standard double room, including service and 23% VAT.

Orienteering

One of Norway's most popular mass-participation sports is based on running or hiking over territory with a map and compass to find control points marked on a map. Special cards can be purchased at sports shops to be punched at control points found during a season. It's an enjoyable, inexpensive family sport.

Shopping

Almost no one leaves Norway without buying a hand-knit sweater. Although the prices for these sweaters may seem high, the quality is outstanding. The classic knitting designs, with snowflakes and reindeer, are still best-sellers and can be bought at most *Husfliden* (homecraft) outlets and specialty souvenir stores, whereas more modern sweaters, made of combinations of brightly colored yarns, can be purchased from yarn shops.

Given the Norwegians' affection for the outdoors, an abundance of high-quality sports gear and outerwear is available. Good buys include Helly-Hansen rain gear, insulated boots, and the *supertrøye*, a gossamer-thin, insulated undershirt.

Handicraft lovers will marvel at Norway's goods. You'll find embroidered cloth, handmade pewter and wrought-iron candlesticks, hand-dipped candles, handblown glass, and hand-turned wood bowls, spoons, and platters made of birch roots, decorated with *rosemaling* (intricate painted or carved floral folk-art designs). Although your visit may be in June, this is a great place to stock up on your Christmas goods. All Husfliden stores and many gift shops sell Christmas ornaments handmade from straw and wood shavings. *Juleduk* (Christmas tablecloths) with typical Norwegian themes are for sale year-round at embroidery shops. Other, more offbeat, items include *ostehøvler* (cheese slicers) and *kransekakeformer*, graduated forms for making almond ring cakes. If you're looking for Norwegian recipes, you may want to seek out Arne Brimi's cookbook—*A Taste of Norway*. It's sold in most bookstores.

Silver is a good buy in Norway, especially with the value-added tax refund (☞ Taxes *in* Smart Travel Tips A to Z). Norwegian silver companies produce a wide range of distinctive patterns. Although the price of Norwegian silver is competitive, at 830 parts to 1,000 (compared with the standard 925 parts in sterling), it's not as pure as English or American silver. However, some will argue that it's stronger.

Unfortunately, Norwegian rustic antiques may not be exported. Even the simplest corner shelf or dish rack valued at $50 is considered a national treasure if it is known to be more than 100 years old. However, you'll find that there are some really good replicas of old Norwegian farm furniture available.

Skiing

As the cradle of skiing, Norway has made a major contribution to the world of winter sports. In 1994 the Winter Olympics were held in Lillehammer, which, along with other Norwegian resorts, regularly hosts World Cup competitions and world skiing championships. In addition to downhill and cross-country, the 100-year-old Telemark style is also popular across the country. It involves a characteristic deep-knee bend in the turns and heavy boots attached to the skis only at the toe. Cross-country skiing is a great way to see Norway's nature; it requires only basic equipment, and rentals are readily available. Most every city has lit trails for evening skiing. Norway's skiing season lasts from November to Easter. But winter's not the only time for skiing in Norway—you may want to try summer skiing on a glacier.

GREAT ITINERARIES

Norway is long and narrow, bordered by Sweden to the east, and jagged coastline to the west. The west coast is carved by deep, dramatic fjords, and small coastal villages dot the shores in between. Bergen, the country's second largest city, is touted as the capital of the West Coast.

Norway's official capital, Oslo, is in the east, only a few hours from the Swedish border. The coast, from Oslo around the southern tip of the country up to Stavanger, is filled with wide beaches and seaside communities. North of here, in Norway's central interior, the country is blanketed with mountains that sculpt the landscape, creating dramatic valleys and plateaus. Moving north, the land becomes wild and untouched. Outside the north's two main cities, Trondheim and Tromsø, the land seems to stretch for miles, which it actually does—into the Arctic Circle and up to the Russian border. We describe each of these regions in its own section below.

What sets Norway apart from other European countries is not so much its cultural tradition or its internationally renowned museums as its spectacular natural beauty. What other world capital has subway service to the forest, or lakes and hiking trails within city limits as Oslo does? Although it takes only a few days to briefly explore Oslo and its environs, a full week or more would allow for more leisurely explorations of Norway's stunning countryside, including its fjords, plateaus, mountains, and valleys.

If You Have 5 Days

Oslo, Norway's capital, makes a good starting point since most flights to Nor-

way arrive here. Spend your first two days exploring **Oslo.** Take it easy the first day and explore the downtown area—meander on Karl Johans Gate, see Akershus Castle and the Kvadraturen, and walk through Vigelands (Frogner) Park. On day two, head out to Bygdøy and visit the area's museums—the Folkemuseum is a must. On the third day, depart for Bergen by train. This six-hour trip across Norway's interior allows you to see some of the country's spectacular scenery, including **Hardangervidda.** When you get to **Bergen,** check into your hotel and head to Bryggen for dinner. Here along Bergen's wharf you'll see some of the city's oldest and best-preserved buildings. Spend your fourth day exploring Bergen. If you have time, head out to Troldhaugen, which was composer Edvard Grieg's house for 22 years; it's a half-day trip from Bergen's center. Spend your last night in Bergen, and on the fifth day, fly back to Oslo.

If You Have 10 Days

Spend your first four days following the tour above. On your fifth day, take the day trip **Norway in a Nutshell** (☞ Guided Tours *in* Smart Travel Tips A to Z), which is a bus-train-boat tour that takes you through some of western fjord country. Spend your fifth night in Bergen, and on your sixth day, fly to **Tromsø,** which is north of the Arctic Circle. Spend the rest of the day touring Tromsø. Overnight here, and on your seventh day, rent a car and head for **Alta.** If you arrive early enough, visit the Alta Museum. Spend the night in Alta, and on the eighth day, continue your voyage, driving farther on to **Hammerfest,** the world's northernmost town. Overnight in Hammerfest, and the next day, take an excursion up the treeless tundra of the **Nordkapp** (North Cape). Return to Hammerfest, and on your last day, fly back to Oslo via Alta.

When to Tour Norway

To experience the endless days of the Midnight Sun, the best time to visit Norway is mid-May to late July. Hotels, museums, and sights are open and transportation is beefed up. If you decide to travel in May, try to be in Norway on the 17th, or *Syttende Mai,* Norway's Constitution Day, when flag-waving Norwegians bedecked in national costumes, or *bunader,* fill the streets.

Autumn weather is quite unpredictable. The days can be cool and crisp, or wet and cold. However, the Gulf Stream, which flows along the Norwegian coast, keeps the weather surprisingly mild for such a high latitude.

Norway in winter is a wonderland of snow-covered mountains glowing under the northern lights, and few tourists are around to get in your way (although many tourist sights are closed). The days may seem perpetually dark, and November through February can seem especially dreary. If it's skiing you're interested in, plan your trip for March or April, as there's usually still plenty of snow left. Take note that during the week of Easter, many Norwegians head for the mountains, so it's hard to get accommodations, and cities are virtually shut down—even grocery stores close.

FODOR'S CHOICE

Flavors

★ **Bagatelle, Oslo.** One of the best restaurants in Europe showcases the French culinary treatment of fresh Norwegian ingredients by internationally known owner-chef Eyvind Hellstrøm. $$$$

★ **Refsnes Gods, Moss.** Chef Katrine Bjørnstad continues her predecessor Erwing Stocker's French twist to traditional Norwegian seafood to create what some call the best fare in Norway. $$$

Comforts

★ **Ambassadeur, Oslo.** Hand-picked antiques, china tea sets, and tapestries in the salon only hint at the sweet, individual styles of the rooms with monikers like "Roma" and "Osa." $$$–$$$$

★ **Frogner House, Oslo.** Sitting inconspicuously amid rows of other turn-of-the-century townhouses, Frogner is cozily dressed in pastels and abundant lace coverings. $$$–$$$$

★ **Clarion Admiral Hotel, Bergen.** Right on the water across the harbor from Bryggen, this former dockside warehouse–cum geometric Art Nouveau hotel dates from 1906. $$–$$$

★ **Kvikne's Hotel, Balestrand.** This huge wooden gingerbread house at the edge of the Sognefjord has been a landmark since 1915, when the area became popular with wealthy British tourists. $$

Castles and Churches

★ **Akershus Slott, Oslo.** Parts of this historic fortress, on the brow of the fjord, date to the 1300s.

Museums

★ **Munchmuseet, Oslo.** Edvard Munch, who painted *The Scream,* bequeathed thousands of his works to Oslo upon his death in 1944.

★ **Norsk Folkemuseum, Bygdøy, Oslo.** Some 140 structures from all over the country have been reconstructed on the museum grounds.

Special Moments

★ Eating dinner in a Sami tent, with your reindeer parked outside

★ Having a drink by the light of the midsummer sun at the North Cape

★ People-watching along Oslo's Karl Johans Gate during the 17th of May (Constitution Day) celebrations

★ Admiring the monumental sculptures in Oslo's Vigeland Park

BOOKS AND VIDEOS

One of the greatest influences on 20th-century drama is the Norwegian poet and dramatist Henrik Ibsen, best known for his works *A Doll's House* (1879) and *Hedda Gabler* (1890). In the 20th century, three Norwegian novelists have won the Noble Prize in Literature: Bjørnstjerne Bjørnson in 1903; Knut Hamsun in 1920 for his novel *Another Growth of the Soil* (Vintage), a story of elemental existence in rural Norway; and Sigrid Undset in 1928 for her masterpiece *Kristin Lavransdatter.* This trilogy, a landmark among historical novels, gives rich insight into 14th-century Scandinavia.

Jostein Gaarder is one of Norway's modern-day writers. His book *Sophie's World* (Berkley Publishing, 1997) explores the history of philosophy through a young Norwegian's eyes.

A History of the Vikings (Oxford University Press, 1984) recounts the story of the aggressive warriors and explorers who during the Middle Ages influenced a large portion of the world, extending from Constantinople to America. Gwyn Jones's lively account makes learning the history enjoyable.

Living in Norway (Abbeville Press, 1993) is a glossy depiction of Norwegian interior design.

In 1995, Liv Ullmann directed the epic film *Kristin Lavransdatter,* an adaptation of Sigrid Undset's trilogy set in 14th-century Norway.

2 OSLO

What sets Oslo apart from other European cities is not so much its cultural traditions or its internationally renowned museums as its simply stunning natural beauty. What other world capital has subway service to the forest, or lakes and hiking trails within city limits? But Norwegians will be quick to remind you that Oslo—with thriving theaters, vibrant nightlife, and more—is as cosmopolitan as any world capital. And like other major metropolises, Oslo also has modern architectural monstrosities, traffic problems, and even a bit of urban sprawl.

ALTHOUGH IT IS ONE OF THE WORLD'S largest capital cities in area, Oslo has only 500,000 inhabitants. Nevertheless, in recent years the city has taken off: shops are open later; cafés, pubs, and restaurants are crowded at all hours; and theaters play to full houses every night of the week.

Even without nightlife, Oslo has a lot to offer—parks, water, trees, hiking, and skiing trails (2,600 km/1,600 mi in greater Oslo), and above all, spectacular views. Starting at the quays opposite City Hall, right at the edge of the Oslo Fjord, the city sprawls up the sides of the mountains that surround it, providing panoramic vistas from almost any vantage point but no definable downtown skyline. A building spree in the late 1980s and early '90s has added a number of modern towers, particularly in the area around the Central Railway Station, which clash painfully with the neoclassical architecture in the rest of the city.

Oslo has been Norway's center of commerce for about 500 years, and most major Norwegian companies are based in the capital. The sea has always been Norway's lifeline to the rest of the world: the Oslo Fjord teems with activity, from summer sailors and shrimpers to merchant ships and passenger ferries heading for Denmark and Germany. It is an old city, dating from the mid-11th century. The city has actually burned down 14 times since its creation, and was all but destroyed by a fire in 1624, when it was redesigned and renamed Christiania by Denmark's royal builder, King Christian IV. During the mid-19th century, and under the influence of the Swedish king, Karl Johan, who ruled the newly united Kingdom of Norway and Sweden, the grand axis—named after himself—was constructed. Karl Johans Gate has been at the center of city life ever since. An act of Parliament finally changed the city's name back to Oslo, its original Viking name, in 1925.

EXPLORING OSLO

Karl Johans Gate, starting at Oslo Sentralstasjon (Oslo Central Station, also called Oslo S Station) and ending at the Royal Palace, forms the backbone of downtown Oslo. Many of Oslo's museums and historic buildings lie between the parallel streets of Grensen and Rådhusgata. Just north of the center of town is a historic area with a medieval church and old buildings. West of downtown is Frogner, the residential area closest to town, with embassies, fine restaurants, antiques shops, galleries, and the Vigeland sculpture park. Farther west is the Bygdøy Peninsula, with five interesting museums and a castle. Northwest of town is Holmenkollen, with beautiful houses, a famous ski jump, and a restaurant. On the east side, where many new immigrants live, are the Munch Museum and the botanical gardens.

Numbers in the text correspond to numbers in the margin and on the Oslo map.

Downtown: The Royal Palace to City Hall

Although the entire city region is huge (454 square km/175 square mi), downtown Oslo is compact, with shops, museums, historic sights, restaurants, and clubs concentrated in a small, walkable center—brightly illuminated at night.

A Good Walk

Oslo's main promenade, Karl Johans Gate, runs from **Slottet** ① through town. Walk down the incline, and to your left you will see three yellow buildings of the old **Universitet** ②—today they are used only by the law school. Murals painted by Edvard Munch decorate the interior walls of these buildings. Around the corner from the university on Universitetsgata is the **Nasjonalgalleriet** ③, which contains hundreds of Norwegian, Scandinavian, and European works, including Munch's famous painting *The Scream*. Back-to-back with the National Gallery, across a parking lot, is a big cream-brick Art Nouveau–style building housing the **Historisk Museum** ④, whose collection of Viking artifacts is impressive. Continue along Frederiksgate to the university and cross Karl Johans Gate to the **Nationalteatret** ⑤ and Studenterlunden Park. This impressive building is not only the national theater, but a popular meeting place—many buses stop out front, and the T-bane (subway) is right beside it.

Walk past the Lille Grensen shopping area and once again cross Karl Johans Gate to see **Stortinget** ⑥, the Norwegian Parliament. Then go back to Stortingsgata. From here, turn left on Universitetsgata, and walk through a cul-de-sac–type area toward the water to reach the redbrick **Rådhuset** ⑦, a familiar landmark with its two block towers, dedicated during Oslo's 900th-year jubilee celebrations in 1950. After visiting Rådhuset, end your tour with an *øl* (beer) or mineral water at one of the many outdoor cafés at Aker Brygge (☞ Dining, *below*).

TIMING

The walk alone should take no more than two hours. If you happen to be at the Royal Palace midday, you might catch the changing of the guard, which happens every day at 1:30. Note that many museums are closed on Mondays.

Sights to See

❹ **Historisk Museum** (Historical Museum). Intricately carved *stav kirke* (wood church) portals and other Viking and medieval artifacts are on display here. There's an exhibition about the Arctic, as well as Asian and African ethnographic exhibits. ⊠ *Frederiksgt. 2*, ☎ *22/85–99–12.* 🖼 *Free.* ☉ *Mid-May–mid-Sept., Tues.–Sun. 11–3; late Sept.–early May, Tues.–Sun. noon–3.*

❸ **Nasjonalgalleriet** (The National Gallery). Many Scandinavian impressionists are represented here in Norway's official art museum. Some impressive fjord and moonlight scenes by Norwegian artists such as Christian Krogh and J. C. Dahl fill the walls of the 19th- and early 20th-century Norwegian rooms. The gallery also has an extensive Munch collection. ⊠ *Universitetsgt. 13*, ☎ *22/20–04–04.* 🖼 *Free.* ☉ *Mon., Wed., Fri., and Sat. 10–6; Thurs. 10–8; Sun. 11–4.*

❺ **Nationalteatret** (National Theater). In front of this neoclassical theater, built in 1899, are statues of Norway's great playwrights, Bjørnstjerne Bjørnson and Henrik Ibsen, author of *A Doll's House, Hedda Gabler,* and *The Wild Duck.* Most performances are in Norwegian, so you may just want to take a guided tour of the interior. Guided tours may be arranged by appointment, for about NKr 300 for up to 10 persons. ⊠ *Stortingsgt. 15*, ☎ *22/00–14–00.*

★ ❼ **Rådhuset** (City Hall). The redbrick exterior of Oslo's City Hall may seem dull compared with the marble-floored interior, whose murals and frescoes are bursting with color. Many sculptures outside, as well as murals inside, reflect the artistic climate in Norway in the 1930s—socialist modernism in its highest form. Much of the adornment depicts not only daily life but also Viking gods and Norwegian literary figures. This may be the only City Hall in the world with a sculpture of a prostitute; it's on the east side of the building facing the fjord. The Nobel Peace Prize has been handed out in the Main Hall since 1990. ⊠ *Rådhuspl.*, ☎ *22/86–16–00.* 🖼 *NKr 15.* ☉ *May–Aug., Mon.–Sat. 9–5, Sun.*

Oslo

KEY

AE American Express Office

i Tourist Information

— Rail Lines

Frogner Park

BYGDØY

Frognerkilen

Langvikbukta

Aker Brygge

0 _____ 1 mile
0 _____ 1 km

N

Akershus Slott og Festning, **11**
Astrup Fearnley Museet for Moderne Kunst, **10**
Fram-Museet, **26**
Gamle Aker Kirke, **14**
Gamlebyen, **16**
Historisk Museum, **4**
Holmenkollbakken, **22**
Kon-Tiki Museum, **27**
Kunstindustri-museet, **15**
Munchmuseet, **13**

Museet for Samtidskunst, **9**
Nasjonalgalleriet, **3**
Nationalteatret, **5**
Norges Hjemmefront Museum, **12**
Norsk Folkemuseum, **24**
Oscarshall Slott, **23**
Oslo Domkirke, **8**
Oslo Ladegård, **18**
Rådhuset, **7**
St. Halvards Kirke, **17**

Slottet, **1**
Stortinget, **6**
Tryvannstårnet, **21**
Universitet, **2**
Vigelandsparken, **19**
Vigelandsmuseet, **20**
Vikingskiphuset, **25**

Seilduksgt.
Helgesens gt.
Helgesens gt.
Grüners gt.
Sofienberggt.
Nordregt.
Møllerveien
Akerselva
Maridalsveien
Ullevålsveien
Akersbakken

Vår
Frelsers
Gravlund

14

Collets gt.
Waldemar Thranes gt.

Parkveien
Piestredet
Holbergs gate
Pilestredet

Wessels gt.
Nordahl Bruns gt.
St. Olavsgt.
15
Akersveien
Damstredet

Hausmanns gt.
Trondheimsveien
Jens Bjelkes gt.

Drammensveien

1

Frederiks gate
Universitetsgt.
4
3
2
Karl
5
Johans
Gate
AE
6
Stortingsgt.
AE
R. Admundsens gt.
Nedre Vollgt.
Rosenkrantz' Gt.
Henrik Ibsens
Gate
Akersgata
Grubbe
Grensen

Møllergt.
Torggt.
Youngs-
torget
Storgt.
Brugt.
Oslo
Spektrum

Urtegt.
Norbygt.
Tøyengt.
13

17

Munkedamsveien
7
i
Rådhusgt.

Stortorvet
8
Basarhallene

Oslo City

Lakkegata
Grønlandsleiret

16
Gamlebyen

Dokkveien

Nedre Slotsgt.
Prinsens gt.
Tollbugata
Dronningens gt.
Kirkegata
Skippergt.
Fred Olsens gt.
Strandgt.

Central
Station
Nylandsveien
Schweigaards gt.

Pipervika

Akershusstranda
12
11
9
Revier str.
Mynt gt.
10

Kongens Gate
Skippergt.

Bjørvika
Akerselva
Bispevika
Bispegt.

St. Halvards
Plass
18
Minne-
parken

SØRENGA

Oslofjorden

Mosseveien
Oslo gt.
Ekebergsletta

noon–5; Sept.–Apr., Mon.–Sat. 9–3:30, Sun. noon–5. Guided tours year-round, weekdays 10, noon, and 2.

★ ❶ **Slottet** (The Royal Palace). The neoclassical palace, completed in 1848, is closed to visitors, but the garden is open to the public. An equestrian statue of Karl Johan, king of Sweden and Norway from 1818 to 1844, stands in the square in front of the palace.

❻ **Stortinget** (The Norwegian Parliament). Built in the middle of the 19th century, this classic building is perched on the top of a small hill. At night, the steps here become a great spot for people-watching. When Parliament is in session, the public gallery is open to curious onlookers. ⊠ *Karl Johans Gt. 22,* ☎ *22/31–30–50.* 🎫 *Free.* ☉ *Guided tours on weekdays, July–Aug.; Sat., Sept.–June.*

❷ **Universitetet** (The University). The great hall of the center building is decorated with murals by Edvard Munch, such as *The Sun,* whose penetrating rays over a fjord give a whole new meaning to the notion of daylight. It was the site of the Nobel Peace Prize award ceremony until 1989. The hall still receives other notable visitors, such as Salman Rushdie, who showed up almost unannounced in 1995. ⊠ *Aulaen, Karl Johans Gt. 47,* ☎ *22/85–97–11* 🎫 *Free.* ☉ *July, weekdays 10:45–2.*

Kvadraturen and Akershus Castle

The Kvadraturen is the oldest part of Oslo still standing. In 1624, after the town of Oslo burned down for the 14th time, King Christian IV renamed the city Christiania and moved it from the area that is today south of Oslo S Station, called Gamlebyen (☞ *below*), and rebuilt it adjacent to the Akershus fortress. The king decreed that houses were to be built in stone or brick instead of wood—in order to prevent future fires. He also built a stone wall around the newly rebuilt city to protect it from his enemies, the Swedes.

A Good Walk

The Kvadraturen area, which includes Akershus Slott, is bound on the east side of the fortress by Skippergata and on the north side by Karl Johans Gate between Oslo Domkirke and Stortorvet. The boundary follows Øvre Vollgata around to the other side of the fortress. Kvadraturen translates roughly as "square township," which refers to the area's geometrically ordered streets. Be aware that the streets around Skippergata and Myntgata are known as a mini–red-light district. The area, however, is not dangerous.

Start at Stortorvet, Oslo's main square. On the right of the square is **Oslo Domkirke** ⑧, completed in 1697. Take a look inside—artists have been contributing to the cathedral's richly decorated interior since the 18th century. Behind the cathedral is a semicircular arcade called Kirkeristen, or **Basarhallene**, housing many artisans' small shops.

From the cathedral, follow Kirkegata left past Karl Johan to the **Museet for Samtidskunst** ⑨, which is housed in the 1902 Bank of Norway building. Take some time to view the museum's contemporary works, especially the ones by Norwegian artists. From the museum, take the side street Revierstredet to Dronningensgate, where you'll come across a building that does not seem to fit in with its 17th-century neighbors. Designed and built in the early 1990s, this brick and steel office building houses the **Astrup Fearnley Museet for Moderne Kunst** ⑩. This stop is a must for modern-art lovers.

Take Dronningensgate back to Rådhusgata and turn left. As you go up the street, notice the 17th-century building at 11 Rådhusgata. It houses the celebrated restaurant Statholdergården (☞ Dining, *below*). This was the home of the "statholder," the official representative from Copenhagen when Norway was under Danish rule.

Continue on Rådhusgata until you reach the corner of Nedre Slottsgate. The yellow building you see was the old city hall; now it's the 1850's Gamle Raadhus (☞ Dining, *below*) restaurant. Diagonally across Rådhusgata in the two 17th-century buildings are an art gallery and an artsy café. The building that houses Kafé Celcius was one of the first buildings erected in Christian IV's town. It has had many functions, first as a schoolhouse and eventually as a military hospital and then the living quarters of a mayor.

Turn left on Akersgata and walk alongside the grassy hill to the entrance of **Akershus Slott og Festning** ⑪, the central element of Christian IV's Kvadraturen. It's a slight climb, but the views from the top are worth it. The castle became the German headquarters during the occupation of Norway in World War II, and many members of the Resistance were executed on the castle grounds. Their memorial has been erected at the site, across the bridge at the harbor end of the castle precinct. In a building next to the castle, at the top of the hill, is the **Norges Hjemmefront Museum** ⑫.

Walk back to Rådhusgata to see another interesting building, **Skogbrand Insurance** (Rådhusgt. 23B). Architects Jan Digerud and Jon Lundberg have won awards for their innovative 1985 vertical addition to this 1917 building. Once you have your fill of history and architecture, you can get in touch with something a bit more corporeal at the **Emanuel Vigelands Museet,** which displays artistic erotica created by the brother of the celebrated sculptor Gustav Vigeland. To get here, turn right on any of the streets along Rådhusgata back to Karl Johans and take the T-bane (T-bane is short for *tunnelbane,* which is an underground railway, or subway) line 1 from Nationalteatret station, in the direction of Frognerseteren, and get off at Slemdal, one of Oslo's hillside residential neighborhoods.

TIMING

The walk alone should take at least three hours. Combined with museum visits and breaks, the itinerary could take up more than half a day. Akershus Festning will take at least half an hour. Astrup Fearnley is open afternoons only; and the Teatermuseet is open only a few days a week. Try to do this tour during daylight hours, catching late-afternoon sun from atop the Akershus grounds. Also note that the T-bane ride to the Emanuel Vigeland Museet in Slemdal takes about 15 minutes and that the museum is open only on Sunday afternoons.

Sights to See

⑪ **Akershus Slott og Festning** (Akershus Castle and Fortress). The oldest part of the castle was built in 1299. Today some of the building is used for state occasions, but a few rooms, including the chapel, are open to the public. ⊠ *Akershus Slott, Festningspl.,* ☎ *22/41–25–21.* ⊠ *Grounds and concerts free; castle NKr20.* ◷ *Grounds daily 6 AM–9 PM; concerts, mid-May–mid-Oct., Sun. at 2; castle May–mid-Sept., Mon.–Sat. 10–4, Sun. 12:30–4. Guided tours May–Sept., Mon.–Sat. 11, 1, and 3; Sun. 1 and 3.*

⑩ **Astrup Fearnley Museet for Moderne Kunst** (Astrup Fearnley Museum for Modern Art). Shiny marble floors and white and gray walls (whose colors may change with the exhibitions) provide a neutral and elegant background for a series of fascinating and often disturbing works. Spacious exhibition rooms lead to a glassed-in sculpture garden with Niki de St. Phalle's sparrow and several other oversize 20th-century figures. ⊠ *Dronningens Gt. 4,* ☎ *22/93–60–60.* ⊠ *NKr 40.* ◷ *Tues., Wed.,*

*and Fri. noon–4, weekends noon–5; Thurs. noon–7. Guided tours
weekends at 1.*

OFF THE   **EMANUEL VIGELANDS MUSEET –** Although he never gained the fame of
BEATEN PATH   his brother Gustav, the creator of Vigeland Park, the younger Emanuel is
                 an artist of some notoriety. His alternately saucy, natural, and downright
                 erotic frescoes make even the sexually liberated Norwegians blush. ⊠
                 Grimelundsvn. 8, ☎ *22/14–93–42.* ⊠ *Free.* ⊗ *Sun. noon–4.*

❾ **Museet for Samtidskunst** (The Museum of Contemporary Art). The building, a good example of Norwegian Art Nouveau architecture, houses
a fine collection of international and Norwegian contemporary works
in small rooms. ⊠ *Bankpl. 4,* ☎ *22/33–58–20.* ⊠ *Free.* ⊗ *Tues.–Wed.,
Fri. 10–5, Thurs. 10–8, Sat. 11–4, Sun. 11–5. Guided tours by appointment only.*

⓬ **Norges Hjemmefront Museum** (Norwegian Resistance Museum). Winding hallways take you through a series of audiovisual displays docu-
menting events that took place during the German occupation (1940–
45). ⊠ *Norges Hjemmefrontmuseum, Akershus Festning,* ☎ *23/09–
31–38.* ⊠ *NKr 20.* ⊗ *Mid-Apr.–mid-June and Sept., Mon.–Sat. 10–
4, Sun. 11–4; mid-June–Aug., Mon.–Sat. 10–5, Sun. 11–5; Oct.–mid-
Apr., Mon.–Fri. 10–3, weekends 11–4.*

❽ **Oslo Domkirke** (Oslo Cathedral). In the 19th century, the fire department operated a fire lookout point from the bell tower here, which you
can visit today. This dark-brown brick structure has been Oslo's main
church since the 17th century. Inside is an intricately carved Baroque
pulpit and a five-story organ. Built in 1697, the church underwent extensive renovations before reopening in the summer of 1997 to cele-
brate its 300th anniversary. ⊠ *Stortorvet 1,* ☎ *22/41–27–93.* ⊠ *Free.*
⊗ *Weekdays 10–4.*

NEED A   **Pascal** (⊠ Tollbugt. 11, ☎ 22/42–11–19), a Parisian patisserie inside
BREAK?   an old-fashioned Norwegian *konditori* (café) serves enormous croissants
                 and pastries with French coffee. Look for the little angels baking
                 bread—they're painted on the ceiling.

East, North, and South of Downtown:
Munch Museum, Damstredet, and Gamlebyen

The Munch Museum is east of the city center in Tøyen, an area in which
Edvard Munch spent many of his years in Oslo. The Tøyen district has
a much different feel than Oslo's cushy west side—it's simpler and more
industrial. West of Tøyen, just north of the city center, is the quiet, old-
fashioned district of Damstredet, its quaint streets lined with artisans'
shops. If you're a die-hard history buff, you'll probably enjoy the last
half of this tour through Gamlebyen. However, if this is your first time
in Oslo and you have a limited amount of time, you may want to end
your tour at the Kunstindustrimuseet. Gamlebyen, south of the city center, is somewhat off the beaten track, and although the area is interesting, some of the ruins are barely discernible.

A Good Walk

Start by taking any T-bane from the city center to Tøyen, where **Munchmuseet** ⓭ sits on a hill near the **Botanisk Hage,** a quiet oasis of plants
and flowers. Munch's family lived in a house in the neighborhood during part of his life. After visiting the museum, head back toward the
city center. Take the T-bane toward Sentrum and get off at Stortinget.

Head down Karl Johans Gate and take a right onto Akersgata. Follow it past the offices of *Aftenposten*, Norway's leading daily paper. As you head up the hill, you will see a huge rotund building, **Deichmanske Bibliotek,** the city's library. When you reach St. Olavs Church, veer gently to the right on Akersveien. You may want to take a detour down **Damstredet** when you come to it—it's one of the city's oldest streets. Afterward, continue back along Akersveien. **Vår Frelsers Gravlund** (Our Savior's Graveyard), where you can seek out the gravestones of many famous Norwegians who are buried here, including Ibsen and Munch, will be on your left. At the graveyard's northeastern corner is **Gamle Aker Kirke** ⑭, the city's only remaining medieval church.

On the other side of the cemetery, follow Ullevålsveien down the hill to the corner of St. Olavs Gate and Akersgata, where you'll find the **Kunstindustrimuseet** ⑮. The museum has a superb furniture collection.

If history and archaeology interest you, visit **Gamlebyen** ⑯, the old town, on the south side of Oslo S Station. South of here on Oslo Gate is St. Halvards Plass. During the 13th century, the area near St. Halvards Plass was the city's ecclesiastical center. Still intact are the foundations of **St. Halvards Kirke** ⑰, dating from the early 12th century. Some other ruins, including Korskirke and Olavs Kloster, lie in **Minneparken.** Nearby on Bispegata is **Oslo Ladegård** ⑱, a restored Baroque-style mansion that sits on the site and foundations of a 13th-century Bishop's Palace.

The oldest traces of human habitation in Oslo are the 5,000-year-old carvings on the runic stones near **Ekebergsletta Park.** They are across the road from the park on Karlsborgveien and are marked by a sign reading FORTIDSMINNE. To reach the park, walk south on Oslo Gate until it becomes Mosseveien. The park will be on your right. Here is a good spot to rest your feet and end your tour.

TIMING

The Munchmuseet will take up most of the morning, especially if you take a guided tour. The second half of the tour, from Gamlebyen to Ekebergsletta, is a perfect way to spend a summer Sunday afternoon. Things are quiet, and locals tend to stroll around this area when the weather is nice.

Sights to See

⑭ **Gamle Aker Kirke** (Old Aker Church). Oslo's medieval stone basilica has undergone many changes since it was constructed around 1100. ✉ *Akersvn. 26,* ☎ *22/69–35–82.* ✇ *Free.* ☉ *Tues. 2–4, Wed.–Sat. noon–2, Sun. 9–11.*

⑯ **Gamlebyen** (The Old City). This area contains the last remains of medieval Oslo. Today it's the largest homogeneous archaeological site found in any capital city in Scandinavia. To get here, go back to Stortorvet and take *trikk* (as the Norwegians fondly call the streetcars) 18, marked "Ljabru," from Stortorvet to St. Halvards Plass (you can also take trikk 19 from Nationalteatret). Contact Oslo Byantikvar (☎ 22/20–85–80), the Antiquities Department of Oslo, for information on guided tours of the area, or ask at the Norway Information Center for the self-guided tour brochure, a *Guide to Gamlebyen,* by Morten Krogstad and Erik Schia.

⑮ **Kunstindustrimuseet** (Museum of Applied Art). Clothes worthy of any fairy tale, including Queen Maud's jewel-encrusted coronation gown from 1904, are displayed here in the museum's Royal Norwegian Costume Gallery. There are also extensive collections of industrial designs and arts and crafts. ✉ *St. Olavs Gt. 1,* ☎ *22/03–65–40.* ✇ *NKr 25.* ☉ *Tues.–Fri. 11–3, weekends noon–4.*

Minneparken. Oslo was founded by Harald Hårdråde ("Hard Ruler") in 1048, and the earliest settlements were near what is now Bispegata, a few blocks behind Oslo S Station. Ruins are all that are left of the city's former spiritual center: the **Korskirke** (Cross Church, ✉ Egedes Gate 2), a small stone church dating from the end of the 13th century; and **Olavs Kloster** (Olav's Cloister, ✉ St. Halvards Plass 3), built around 1240 by Dominican monks (✉ Entrance at Oslo Gt. and Bispegt). Call the Oslo Bymuseum (Oslo City Museum, ☎ 22/43–06–45), which also contains arts and objects tracing the city's history, for guided tours.

★ ⑬ **Munchmuseet** (Munch Museum). Edvard Munch, one of Scandinavia's leading artists, bequeathed an enormous collection of his work (about 1,100 paintings, 4,500 drawings, and 18,000 graphic works) to the city when he died in 1944. The works languished in warehouses for nearly 20 years, until the city built a museum to house them in 1963. For much of his life Munch was a troubled man, and his major works, dating from the 1890s, with such titles as *The Scream* and *Vampire*, reveal his angst, but he was not without humor. His extraordinary talent as a graphic artist emerges in the print room, with its displays of lithograph stones and woodblocks. ✉ *Tøyengt. 53,* ☎ *22/67–37–74.* 🎫 *NKr 50.* ☉ *June–mid-Sept., daily 10–6; mid-Sept.–May, Tues., Wed., Fri., Sat. 10–4, Thurs. and Sun. 10–6.*

⑱ **Oslo Ladegård.** The original building, a 13th-century Bispegård (Bishop's Palace), burned down in the 1624 fire, but its old vaulted cellar was not destroyed. The present mansion was restored and rebuilt in 1725; it now belongs to the city council and contains scale models of 16th- to 18th-century Oslo. ✉ *St. Halvards Pl., Oslogt. 13,* ☎ *22/19–44– 68.* 🎫 *NKr 20.* ☉ *May–Sept.; guided tours on Wed. at 6, Sun. at 1.*

⑰ **St. Halvards Kirke** (St. Halvard's Church). This medieval church, named for the patron saint of Oslo, remained the city's cathedral until 1660. St. Halvard became the city's patron saint when his murdered body was found floating in the Drammensfjord, despite the presence of a heavy stone around his neck. He had been trying to save a pregnant woman from three violent pursuers when they caught and murdered him along with her. ✉ *Minneparken, entrance at Oslogt. and Bispegt.*

Frogner, Majorsturen, and Holmenkollen

One of the city's most stylish neighborhoods, Frogner combines old-world Scandinavian elegance with contemporary European chic. Most of the pastel-and-white buildings in the area were constructed in the early years of this century. Many have interesting wrought-iron work and sculptural detail. Terribly hip boutiques and galleries coexist with embassies and ambassadors' residences on the streets near and around Bygdøy Allé. Holmenkollen, the hill past Frogner Park, features miles of ski trails—and more beautiful homes of the affluent.

A Good Walk

Catch the No. 12 "Majorstuen" trikk from Nationalteatret on the Drammensveien side of the Royal Palace. You can also take the No. 15 from Aker Brygge.

Opposite the southwest end of the palace grounds is the triangular **U.S. Embassy**, designed by Finnish-American architect Eero Saarinen and built in 1959. Look to the right at the corner of Drammensveien and Parkveien for a glimpse of the venerable **Nobel Institute.** Since 1905 these stately yellow buildings have been the secluded setting where the five-member Nobel Committee decides who will win the Nobel Peace Prize. The 15,000-volume library is open to the public.

Stay on the trikk and ride to Frogner Park or walk the seven short blocks. To walk, follow Balders Gate to Arno Bergs Plass, with its central fountain. Turn left on Gyldenløves Gate until you reach Kirkeveien. Turn right past the Dutch Embassy, and cross the street at the light. Frogner Park, also called Vigelandspark interchangeably, is just ahead.

Walk through the front gates of the park and toward the monolith ahead: you are entering **Vigelandsparken** ⑲. There's nothing anywhere else in the world quite like this stunning sculpture garden designed by one of Norway's greatest artists, Gustav Vigeland, who is, oddly, virtually unknown to the rest of the world. Across from the park, you can study the method to his madness at **Vigelandsmuseet** ⑳.

After you leave the park, continue on Kirkeveien to the Majorstuen underground station. Here you have two options: you can take a walk down Bogstadveien, look at the shops, explore the Majorstuen area, and then take the Holmenkollen line of the T-bane to Frognerseteren; or you can skip the stroll down Bogstadveien and head right up to Holmenkollen. The train ride up the mountain passes some stunning scenery. If you have brought your children, you may want to make a detour at the first T-bane stop, Frøen, and visit the **Barnekunstmuseet.**

Continue on the T-bane to the end of the line. This is Frognerseteren—where city dwellers disappear to on winter weekends. The view of the city here is spectacular. The **Tryvannstårnet** ㉑ has an even better panoramic view of Oslo. Downhill is **Holmenkollbakken** ㉒, where Norway's most intrepid skiers prove themselves every February during the Holmenkollen Ski Festival.

TIMING

This is a good tour for Monday, since the museums mentioned are open, unlike most others in Oslo. You will need a whole day for both neighborhoods since there is some travel time involved. The trikk ride from the city center to Frogner Park is about 15 minutes; the T-bane to Frognerseteren is about 20. You're no longer in the compact city center, so distances between sights are greater. The walk from Frognerseteren is about 15 minutes and is indicated with signposts. Try to save Holmenkollen with its magnificent views for a clear day. Summer hours for museums and lookout points are extended because the days are so long. In the spring, though, go before the sun starts to set.

If you want to see Norwegians younger than two years old on skis, a winter Sunday in Frognerseteren is your best bet. Frogner Park has some skiers and sledders, and families flock to Holmenkollen for Sunday ski school.

Sights to See

Ⓒ **Barnekunstmuseet** (Children's Art Museum). The museum was the brainchild of Rafael Goldin, a Russian immigrant who has collected children's drawings from more than 150 countries. ✉ *Lille Frøensvn. 4,* ☎ *22/46–85–73.* ✆ *NKr 40.* ☉ *Mid-June–mid-Aug., Tues.–Thurs. and Sun. 11–4; mid-Aug.–mid-Dec. and late Jan.–mid-June, Tues.–Thurs. 9:30–2, Sun. 11–4.*

★ ㉒ **Holmenkollbakken** (Holmenkollen Ski Museum and Ski Jump). Oslo's ski jump holds a special place in the hearts of Norwegians. The 1892 jump was rebuilt for the 1952 Winter Olympics and is still used for international competitions. At the base of the jump, turn right, past the statue of the late King Olav V on skis, to enter the museum. It displays equipment from the Fritjof Nansen and Roald Amundsen polar voyages and a model of a ski maker's workshop. You can also climb (or ride the elevator) to the top of the jump tower. ⊠ *Kongevn. 5,* ☎ *22/92–32–64.* ◨ *NKr 60.* ◔ *June–Aug., daily 9–8; Apr.–May and Sept., daily 10–5; Oct.–Mar., daily 10–4.*

㉑ Tryvannstårnet (Tryvann's Tower). The view from Oslo's TV tower encompasses 36,000 square ft of hills, forests, cities, and several bodies of water. You can see as far as the Swedish border to the east and nearly as far as Moss to the south. ⊠ *Voksenkollen,* ☎ *22/14–67–11.* ◨ *NKr 35.* ◔ *May and Sept., daily 10–5; June–Aug., daily 10–6; Oct.–Apr., daily 10–4*

㉒ Vigelandsmuseet. This small museum displays many of the plaster models for the Vigeland Park sculptures, the artist's woodcuts and drawings, and mementos of his life. ⊠ *Nobelsgt. 32,* ☎ *22/54–25–30.* ◨ *NKr 30.* ◔ *May–Sept., Tues.–Sat. 10–6, Sun. noon–7; Oct.–Apr., Tues.–Sat. noon–4, Sun. noon–6.*

★ **㉑ Vigelandsparken** (Frogner Park). This park, formally called Frogner Park, contains more than 50 copper statues by sculptor Gustav Vigeland, hence the moniker Vigelandspark. Vigeland began his career as a wood-carver, and his talent was quickly appreciated and supported by the townspeople of Oslo. In 1921 they provided him with a free house and studio, in exchange for which he began to chip away at his life's work, which he would ultimately donate to the city. He worked through World War II and the German occupation, and after the war the work was unveiled to the combined enchantment and horror of the townsfolk. Included was the 470-ton monolith that is now the highlight of the park. Look for the park's most beloved sculpture—an enraged baby boy stamping his foot and scrunching his face in fury. Known as *Sinnataggen* (The Really Angry One), this ball of rage has been filmed, parodied, painted red, and even stolen from the park.

The grassy grounds of Vigelandspark are a living part of the city—people walk dogs on the green and bathe chubby babies in the fountains, and they jog, ski, and sunbathe throughout. The park complex also includes the Olso Bymuseum (☞ *above*), a swimming pool (☞ Outdoor Activities and Sports, *below*), an ice rink and skating museum (☎ *22/43–49–20*), several playgrounds, and an outdoor restaurant—Herregårdskroen—where you can have anything from a buffet lunch to a three-course dinner. ⊠ *Middlethunsgt.* ◨ *Park entrance free.*

Bygdøy

Oslo's most important historic sights are concentrated on Bygdøy Peninsula, as are several beaches, jogging paths, and the royal family's summer residence.

A Good Walk
The most pleasant way to get to Bygdøy, from May to September, is to catch a ferry from the Rådhuset. Times vary, so check with Nortra (☞ Visitor Information *in* Oslo A to Z, *below*) for schedules. Another alternative is to take Bus 30, marked "Bygdøy," from Stortingsgata at Nationalteatret along Drammensveien to Bygdøy Allé, a wide avenue lined with chestnut trees. The bus passes Frogner Church and several embassies on its way to Olav Kyrres Plass, where it turns left, and soon left again, onto the peninsula. The royal family's current summer residence, actually just a big white frame house, is on the right. Get off at the next stop, Norsk Folkemuseum. The pink castle nestled in the trees is **Oscarshall Slott** ㉓, once a royal summer palace.

Next is the **Norsk Folkemuseum** ㉔, which consists of some 150 structures from all over the country that have been reconstructed on site. Around the corner to the right is the **Vikingskiphuset** ㉕, one of Norway's most famous attractions, which houses some of the best-preserved remains of the Viking era found yet.

Follow signs on the road to the **Fram-Museet** ㉖, an A-frame structure in the shape of a traditional Viking boathouse, which houses the famed *Fram* polar ship as well as artifacts from various expeditions. Across the parking lot from the Fram-Museet is the older **Kon-Tiki Museum** ㉗, with Thor Heyerdahl's famous raft, along with the papyrus boat *Ra II*. You can get a ferry back to the City Hall docks from the dock in front of the Fram-Museet. Before heading back to Oslo, you may want to have a snack at **Lanternen Mat og Vinhus**, which overlooks the entire harbor.

If your kids are squirming to break out of the museum circuit, entertain the thought of a trip to **VikingLandet,** an attraction park that stages the more peaceful aspects of the Vikings' existence, from farming to burial mounds. You can combine the excursion with a trip to Tusen-Fryd, an amusement park next door.

TIMING

Block out a day for Bygdøy. You could spend at least half a day at the Folkemuseum alone. Note that the museums on Bygdøy tend to be open daily but close earlier than their counterparts that close Mondays.

The HMK trip to VikingLandet is an afternoon trip, so count on spending half a day. It takes between 10 and 20 minutes to reach the park from downtown Oslo by bus. If you decide to go on your own from Oslo S Station, you might want to spend the whole day playing in both parks.

Sights to See

★ ○ ㉖ **Fram-Museet.** The *Fram* polar ship takes up almost every inch of this museum, which was constructed around it. The *Fram* was built in 1892 by Scottish-Norwegian shipbuilder Colin Archer. Fridtjof Nansen led the first *Fram* expedition, across the ice surrounding the North Pole; the ship's most famous voyage took Roald Amundsen to Antarctica, the first leg of his successful expedition to the South Pole in 1911. ⊠ *Bygdøynes,* ☎ *22/43–83–70.* ☞ *NKr 25.* ○ *June–Aug., daily 9–5:45; May and Sept., daily 10–4:45; Mar.– Apr. and Oct.–Nov., daily 11–3:45; Dec.–Feb., weekends 11–3:45.*

★ ○ ㉗ **Kon-Tiki Museum.** The museum celebrates Norway's most famous 20th-century explorer. Thor Heyerdahl made a voyage in 1947 from Peru to Polynesia on the *Kon-Tiki,* a balsa raft, to confirm his theory that the first Polynesians originally came from Peru. The *Ra II* sailed from Morocco to the Caribbean in 1970. ⊠ *Bygdøynesvn. 36,* ☎ *22/ 43–80–50.* ☞ *NKr 30.* ○ *Apr.–May and Sept., daily 10:30–5; June–Aug., daily 9:30–5:45; Oct.–Mar., daily 10:30–4.*

★ ○ ㉔ **Norsk Folkemuseum** (Norwegian Folk Museum). You'll get a bird's-eye view of the entire country with imaginative exhibitions, 153 authentic houses, and tour guides in traditional garb. The **Gol Stavkirke** (Gol Stave Church), constructed around 1200, is one of the most important buildings here. In summer and on weekends year-round, guides demonstrate various home crafts, such as weaving tapestries, sewing national costumes, and baking flatbread. Indoor collections in the main building include toys, dolls and dollhouses, a Sami (Lapp) collection, national costumes, and Ibsen's actual study. On one side of this museum is a reconstructed 19th-century village, with shops and houses.

The museum puts on a summer calendar of special events, including daily activities from folk dancing to concerts. ✉ *Museumsvn. 10,* ☎ *22/12-36-66.* 🖭 *NKr 50.* ☉ *Mid-Oct.–mid-May, Mon.–Sat. 11–3, Sun. 11–4, mid-May–mid-June, daily 10–5, mid-June–Aug., daily 10–6.*

㉓ Oscarshall Slott. This eccentric neo-Gothic palace, built in 1852 for King Oscar I, served as a site for picnics and other summer pursuits. It now houses Norwegian art, including works by Tidemand and Gude. ✉ *Oscarshallvn.,* ☎ *22/43-77-49.* 🖭 *NKr 15.* ☉ *Mid-May–mid-Sept., Tues., Thurs., and Sun. noon–4.*

㊦ VikingLandet. Norway's foremost theme park on the Viking Age takes you back 1,000 years to experience daily life as a Viking. You can combine the trip with a visit to **Norgesparken Tusenfryd,** Oslo's amusement park. There are carnival rides, a roller coaster with a loop, and a water slide. There's a separate entrance fee, but both parks are under the same management. HMK provides an afternoon bus excursion from Norway Information Center (☞ Guided Tours *in* Oslo A to Z, *below).* There's also a shuttle bus that departs from Oslo Bussterminalen Galleriet, the city's main train station, which is right by Oslo S Station. ✉ *Both parks: Vinterbro,* ☎ *64/97-64-97.* 🖭 *Combined ticket NKr 195.* ☉ *Early June–mid-Aug., daily 10:30–7; May and late Aug., weekends 10:30–7.*

★ **㉕ Vikingskiphuset.** Norway's claim to fame centers on its incorrigible Viking explorers, and this museum celebrates their fascinating culture. The building resembles a cathedral on the outside, and inside the feeling of reverence is very real. It's hard to believe that the three ships on display, all found buried along the Oslo Fjord, are nearly 1,200 years old. Viking elites wanted to make sure their dead were well equipped for life after death, so they buried them in long ships with all the necessities, which sometimes included a servant. The discoverers of the *Oseberg* even found wood, leather, and woolen textiles intact. The richly carved *Oseberg,* thought to have been the burial chamber for Queen Åse, is the most decorative, whereas the *Gokstad* is a functional longboat, devoid of ornament. Items found with the ships, including tools, household goods, and a tapestry, are also on view. ✉ *Huk Aveny 35,* ☎ *22/43-83-79.* 🖭 *NKr 30.* ☉ *May–Aug., daily 9–6; Sept., daily 11–5; Apr. and Oct., daily 11–4; Nov.–Mar., daily 11–3.*

DINING

Food was once an afterthought in Oslo, but not anymore. The city's chefs are winning contests worldwide. Norwegian cuisine, based on products from the country's pristine waters and lush farmland, is now firmly in the culinary spotlight. Menus change daily, weekly, or according to the season in many of Oslo's finer restaurants. With a steady rise in immigration to Norway, Oslo has also seen a recent influx of Asian eateries, many located in the comparatively affordable Grunerløkka District.

In Oslo, average food is expensive, and excellent food doesn't necessarily cost more—it's just a matter of knowing where to go. If you visit Oslo in summer, head for Aker Brygge, the wharf turned shopping area. Hundreds of café-goers vie for the sun and the view at the fjord-side outdoor tables. Aker Brygge is also a good place to buy shrimp, an activity that heralds the coming of summer for many locals. If you don't want to buy them fresh off the boat, order them at one of the floating restaurants. Generally they come on a baguette or in a big bowl with mayonnaise and wedges of lemon on the side.

A good place to get a meal that won't cost more than your hotel room is the food court downstairs at Paléet Shopping Center, which is open daily 10–8. A bit pricier, and a lot snazzier than the fast-food bonanzas of most American malls, this food court has a variety of stands with international fare, ranging from Danish and Greek to American.

Many of the less expensive restaurants listed below are simply cafés, bars, and even sometimes discos. These types of establishments are becoming increasingly popular dining options as Oslo's twentysomething generation decides it likes to eat out. (Because of high prices, eating out is a huge luxury for most Norwegians.) Meals at these cheaper spots invariably include pasta dishes, shellfish, pizzas, and salads rather than lobsters and lamb chops. For a more exhaustive list of Oslo cafés, pick up a copy of *Café Guiden*, a glossy publication describing more than 100 spots in detail. It is available in most bars and cafés (☞ Cafés *in* Nightlife and the Arts, *below*).

Downtown: Royal Palace to the Parliament

$$$$ ✕ **D'Artagnan.** Diplomas, certificates, and prizes from all over the world
★ line the walls of this downtown *restaurant gastronomique,* which underwent a major renovation in 1999 in celebration of its 20th anniversary. Owner Freddie Nielsen, one of Norway's most celebrated restaurateurs, received both his education and inspiration in France, but do not expect diminutive nouvelle portions of cuisine. Only the famished should embark upon the seven-course Grand Menu. The saffron-poached pike with asparagus is a good way to start a meal, and the boned fillet of salmon with dill lobster-cream sauce is delectable. The veal is so tender you can cut it with your fork. The dessert cart is loaded with jars of fruit preserved in liqueurs, which are served with sorbets and ice creams. ⊠ *Øvre Slottsgt. 16,* ☎ *22/41–50–62. AE, DC, MC, V. Closed Sun. and mid-July–mid-Aug. No lunch Jan.–Aug.*

$$$ ✕ **Babette's Gjestehus.** French chef Dominic Choaqa and his friendly staff make their guests feel welcome at this tiny restaurant hidden in the shopping arcade by City Hall. Bright blue walls, starched white tablecloths, and lace curtains against paned windows contribute to the rustic, homey feel. The food is Scandinavian with a French twist. Try the garlic-marinated rack of lamb in rosemary sauce or panfried breast of duck with creamed spring cabbage. Dishes vary according to season but are always well prepared. ⊠ *Rådhuspassasjen, Roald Amundsensgt. 6,* ☎ *22/41–64–64. Reservations essential. AE, DC, MC, V. Closed Sun. No lunch.*

$$$ ✕ **Theatercafeen.** This Oslo institution, on the ground floor of the Hotel
★ Continental (☞ Lodging, *below*), is *the* place to see and be seen. Built in 1900, the last Viennese-style café in northern Europe retains its Art Nouveau character. The menu is small and jumbled, with starters and main dishes interspersed; the only hint of the serving size is the price column. Pastry chef Robert Bruun's *konfektkake* (a rich chocolate cake) and apple tart served with homemade ice cream are reasons enough to visit. ⊠ *Stortingsgt. 24–26,* ☎ *22/82–40–50. AE, DC, MC, V.*

$$ ✕ **Dinner.** Though its bland name belies this restaurant's outstanding
★ Szechuan-style cuisine, this is the place in Oslo for Chinese food. The four-course Peking duck is a specialty. Don't bother with the others. ⊠ *Stortingsgt. 22,* ☎ *22/42–68–90. AE, DC, MC, V. No lunch.*

$$ ✕ **A Touch of France.** Just downstairs from D'Artagnan (☞ *above*), Freddie Nielsen's clean, inviting wine bistro is straight out of Paris. The French ambience is further accented by the waiters' long, white aprons, the Art Nouveau decor, old French posters, and closely packed tables. The tempting menu includes a steaming hot bouillabaisse. ⊠ *Øvre Slottsgt. 16,* ☎ *22/42–56–97. AE, DC, MC, V.*

26

Oslo Dining and Lodging

KEY

- **AE** American Express Office
- **i** Tourist Information
- — Rail Lines

Dining

A Touch of France, **31**
Babette's Gjestehus, **19**
Bagatelle, **10**
Brasserie 45, **25**
Café Sjakk Matt, **16**
Clodion Art Café, **2**
Coco Chalet, **34**
D'Artagnan, **31**
De Fem Stuer, **3**
Den Grimme Ælling, **26**

Det Gamle Raadhus, **35**
Dinner, **18**
Dionysos Taverna, **40**
Engebret Café, **37**
Feinschmecker, **6**
Frognerseteren, **4**
Hos Thea, **9**
Kaffistova, **32**
Kastanjen, **7**
Klosteret, **33**

Lofoten Fiskerestaurant, **15**
Markveien Mat og Vinhus, **41**
Maud's, **17**
Palace Grill, **11**
Restaurant Le Canard, **5**
Statholdergaarden, **36**
Theatercafeen, **20**

Lodging

Ambassadeur, **13**
Bristol, **28**
Frogner House, **12**
Gabelshus, **8**
Grand Hotel, **23**
Haraldsheim, **42**
Holmenkollen Park Hotel Rica, **3**
Hotel Continental, **20**
Hotel Karl Johan, **27**
Hotell Bondeheimen, **32**
Munch, **30**

Radisson SAS
Park Royal, **1**

Radisson SAS Plaza
Hotel Oslo, **39**

Radisson SAS
Scandinavia Hotel, **24**

Rainbow Cecil, **22**

Rainbow
Gyldenløve, **14**

Rainbow Hotel
Stefan, **29**

Rica Victoria, **21**

Royal Christiania, **38**

$ ✕ **Brasserie 45.** Overlooking the fountain on Karl Johans Gate, this brasserie serves a dependable meal in an elegant Scandinavian setting, complete with candlelight, red walls, and shiny wooden floors. Prices of these tempting dishes are quite reasonable, with main courses averaging about NKr 80; consider the hearty lasagna or fettuccine. Salted fillet of reindeer is one of the more intriguing starters. ⊠ *Karl Johans Gt. 45 (upstairs),* ☎ *22/41–34–00. AE, DC, MC, V.*

$ ✕ **Café Sjakk Matt.** This popular spot between Vika and Karl Johan is one of the many bars that serve decent food. They've made dining a specialty, but you do still have to order at the bar. A variety of pita sandwiches and melts, ratatouille, quiche, and the house specialty—lasagna—are some of what's on the menu. Hot dishes usually come with salad and nutty Norwegian bread. The place has a modern Scandinavian feel: dozens of candles, potted plants, and shiny floors. ⊠ *Haakon VII's Gt. 5,* ☎ *22/83–41–56. AE, DC, MC, V.*

$ ✕ **Den Grimme Ælling.** Dane Bjarne Hvid Pedersen's smørbrød are the best buy in town: lots of meat, fish, or cheese on a small piece of bread. This popular Copenhagen-style restaurant in the food court at Paleet also has daily dinner specials, such as homemade *hakkebøf* (Danish Salisbury steak) with gravy, onions, and potatoes. ⊠ *Paleet, Karl Johans Gt. 41B,* ☎ *22/42–47–83. No credit cards.*

$ ✕ **Kaffistova.** Norwegian country cooking is served, cafeteria style, at this downtown restaurant. Everyday specials include soup and a selection of entrées, including a vegetarian dish. Kjøttkaker (meat cakes) served with creamed cabbage is a Norwegian staple, and the steamed salmon with Sandefjord butter is as good here as in places where it costs three times as much. Low-alcohol beer is the strongest drink served. ⊠ *Rosenkrantz' Gt. 8,* ☎ *22/42–99–74. AE, DC, MC, V.*

$ ✕ **Vegeta.** Near the Nationalteatret bus and trikk station, this no-smoking restaurant is a popular spot for hot and cold vegetarian meals and salads. The all-you-can-eat specials offer top value. ⊠ *Munkedamsvn. 3B,* ☎ *22/83–40–20. AE, DC, MC, V.*

Kvadraturen and Aker Brygge

$$$$ ✕ **Statholdergaarden.** Award-winning chef Bent Stiansen is currently the shining star of Norwegian haute cuisine. As a result, it is hard to get a table here—especially around Christmastime—so plan early. The five-course gastronomic menu changes daily. You can also order directly from the à la carte menu. Try one of the imaginative appetizers, such as smoked duck breast with fried goat cheese and pine-nut salad. Specialties include salmon mousse and other fish delicacies. This restaurant, in a building that dates back to 1640, is in the heart of Oslo's oldest standing neighborhood. ⊠ *Rådhusgt. 11,* ☎ *22/41–88–00. Reservations essential. Jacket and tie. AE, DC, MC, V. Closed Sun. and 3 wks in July.*

$$$ ✕ **Engebret Café.** This somber, old-fashioned restaurant at Bankplassen was a haunt for bohemian literati at the turn of the century. The more formal dinner menu includes traditional Norwegian staples, such as *lutefiske* (fish calcified to jelly) and *pinne-kjott* (sticks of meat), which lamb steamed over branches of birch. For a real taste of Norway, try traditional *smalahove* (sheep's head). Many Norwegian families consider it a treat to visit the restaurant during *Juletide* (Christmastime) so book early. ⊠ *Bankplassen 1,* ☎ *22/33–66–94. AE, DC, MC, V.*

$$-$$$ ✕ **Lofoten Fiskerestaurant.** With all windows overlooking the water at Aker Brygge, this is Oslo's quintessential fish restaurant. All types of fish, from salmon to cod to monkfish, are served fresh and cooked in a variety of sauces, from house bouillabaisse to classic wine or saffron sauce. The clientele is well-heeled, and the elegant wood-paneled

interior brings to mind a vintage Scandinavian cruise ship. Try to get an outdoor table in summer: you take advantage of a cheaper menu as well as late-evening sunlight on the fjord. Service can be slow busy evenings, but it's definitely worth the wait. ⊠ *Stranden 75 Brygge*, ☎ *22/83–08–08. AE, DC, MC, V.*

$$ ✕ **Det Gamle Raadhus.** This restaurant in the former ci is famous for its lutefisk, a Scandinavian specialty made fro fish that has been soaked in lye and then poached. However, nu here does allow ample choice for the less daring. Favorites i let of veal with pickled mushrooms, Parmesan, and arugula, a n with mushrooms and fennel. This is Oslo's oldest restaurant, d 41. ⊠ *Nedre Slottsgt. 1*, ☎ *22/42–01–07. AE, DC, MC, V.* n.

$$ ✕ **Maud's.** The regional Norwegi here are so traditional that they seem exotic to some Nor ty folk who left the nest long ago. Specialties include medi op sirloin from India and grilled steak of fatted calf. ⊠ *Vest ssen. 1*, ☎ *22/83–72–28. AE, DC, MC, V. Closed Sun.*

$ ✕ **Coco Chalet.** Best for its homemade cakes and pies, Coco Chalet is moving in world of affordable haute cuisine. The Asian-inspired menu f a delectable chicken breast with vegetables julienne. The din m of this restaurant in Oslo's oldest neighborhood feels some e a haunted mansion: white tablecloths bedeck the tables at al rs of the day, spooky candelabras sit on the mantle, and the m emale staff wears black uniforms with white aprons and collar *Øvre Slottsgt. 8*, ☎ *22/33–32–66. AE, DC, MC, V.*

East of D town

✕ **Klosteret.** This popular east-side eatery's name means "the cloisters." Its not-so-medieval dining room is downstairs in a spacious cellar with a rounded brick ceiling. Wacky iron candelabras sprouting from red walls like thorny branches and stark steel-backed chairs work in perfect harmony with the gold-bedecked saints and Christ childs that adorn the walls. The handwoven menus are sheathed in monastic hymnal pages and recite a liturgy of appealing meat and fish dishes, plus a daily vegetarian option. Main courses are often served atop sautéed leafy greens, a refreshing alternative to the more traditional Norwegian *kinakål*, a white lettuce-cabbage. Take a taxi. ⊠ *Fredensborgvn. 13*, ☎ *22/20–66–90. AE, DC, MC, V. Closed Sun. and 3–4 wks in July.*

$$$ ✕ **Markveien Mat og Vinhus.** This artsy food and wine house in the heart of the Grunerløkka district serves fresh French-inspired cuisine. The atmosphere is relaxed and the clientele is bohemian. Paintings cover the yellow walls, and the tables are black and somber. As most touristy spots in Oslo lie in the *Vest* (west), a trip to the *Øst* (east) will give you a chance to see how the other side lives. ⊠ *Torvbakkgt. 12 (entrance on Markvn. 57)*, ☎ *22/37–22–97. AE, DC, MC, V. Closed Sun.*

$$ ✕ **Dionysos Taverna.** Nicola Murati warmly welcomes guests to this
★ unpretentious little Greek restaurant, where a bouzouki trio performs Thursday through Sunday. The hors d'oeuvre platter, comprising stuffed grape leaves, meatballs, feta cheese, tomatoes, and cucumbers, is a meal in itself. The tzatziki, souvlaki, and moussaka are authentically prepared, as are the more unusual casseroles, such as *exohiko* (lamb baked with red wine, tomatoes, and onions). ⊠ *Calmeyersgt. 11*, ☎ *22/60–78–64. AE, MC, V. No lunch.*

Frogner and Majorstuen

$$$$ ✕ **Bagatelle.** One of Oslo's best restaurants is a short walk from
★ downtown. Paintings by contemporary Norwegian artists accent the otherwise subdued interior, but the food is the true show here. Inter-

nationally known chef-owner Eyvind Hellstrøm's cuisine is modern Norwegian with French overtones. The three-, five-, and seven-course menus change daily. Consider grilled pike poached with wild mushrooms in a riesling sauce. Bagatelle has a wine cellar to match its food. ⊠ *Bygdøy Allé 3,* ☎ *22/44–63–97. Jacket required. AE, DC, MC, V. Closed Sun., late summer, Easter, and Christmastime. No lunch.*

$$$$ ✕ **Feinschmecker.** The name is German, but the food is modern Scandinavian. The atmosphere is friendly and intimate, with green rattan chairs, yellow tablecloths, and floral draperies. Owners Lars Erik Underthun, one of Oslo's foremost chefs, and Bengt Wilson, one of Scandinavia's leading food photographers, make sure the food looks as good as it tastes. For an excellent seafood dish, try the peppered baby halibut with asparagus, leaf spinach, and beans in a crayfish sauce. ⊠ *Balchensgt. 5,* ☎ *22/44–17–77. Reservations essential. AE, DC, MC, V. Closed Sun. and last 3 wks of July. No lunch.*

$$$ ✕ **Hos Thea.** An old-fashioned–looking gem with blue-and-beige decor,
★ this restaurant has only 36 seats. It's at the beginning of Embassy Row, a short distance from downtown. Owner Sergio Barcilon, originally from Spain, is one of the pioneers of the new Scandinavian cooking. The small menu offers four or five choices in each category, but every dish is superbly prepared, from the duck baked in salt to rack of lamb with a mustard sauce. Noise and smoke levels can be high late in the evening. ⊠ *Gabelsgt. 11, entrance on Drammensvn.,* ☎ *22/44–68–74. Reservations essential. AE, DC, MC, V. No lunch.*

$$$ ✕ **Palace Grill.** This tiny dining spot across from the Royal Palace has won its way into the ranks of the hip on the Oslo restaurant scene. You can sip a beer in the adjoining cowboy rock-and-roll bar while you wait for one of about eight tables. Don't let the "grill" part confuse you: it may be relaxed, but it's far from fast food. The Norwegian ingredients of the French-inspired menu, which is written on a hanging chalkboard, change daily. If you've had your fill of reindeer in Norway, you can still take a glimpse at the exotic sauces. Try the chicken leg with eggplant and sweet green shallot sauce if it's on the menu. ⊠ *Solligt. 2 (just off Dramensveien),* ☎ *22/56–14–02. Reservations not accepted. AE, DC, MC, V. Closed Sun. and 1 month in summer.*

$$$ ✕ **Restaurant Le Canard.** Undoubtedly one of Oslo's plushest locales, this oasis in Frogner is brimming with eclectic antiques, Oriental rugs, chandeliers, and Baroque paintings. It is housed in a looming brick mansion with spires and wrought-iron decorations that was built at the turn of the century. The main dining room is spread throughout the first floor's rooms and color-coded salons; upstairs is reserved for private parties. In summer you can dine on the small terrace. The specialty is, of course, duck, from sautéed breast of duck with horseradish and a cognac sauce to duck roasted in honey. The wine cellar holds more than 2,000 bottles. ⊠ *Pres. Harbitzgt. 4,* ☎ *22/43–40–28. AE, DC, MC, V. Closed Sun. No lunch in winter.*

$$ ✕ **Kastanjen.** This casual Frogner bistro, named after the chestnut trees
★ that line the street, is the kind every neighborhood needs. The style of food is new traditional—modern interpretations of classic Norwegian dishes. Be sure to check out the warmly lit downstairs lounge for before or after-dinner drinks. ⊠ *Bygdøy Allé 18,* ☎ *22/43–44–67. AE, DC, MC, V. Closed Sun. and 2 wks in July.*

$ ✕ **Clodion Art Café.** A bright blue facade and cartoons of the suns, stars, and moon adorn the entrance to this trendy Frogner café. Not an inch of the place is left unpainted, and the curvy, colorful couches will make you want to stay all day. Meals here are light but always tasty. The menu changes daily but typically offers a spicy vegetable-and-chicken dish. ⊠ *Bygdøy Allé 63, entrance on Thomas Heftyes Gt.,* ☎ *22/44–97–26. AE, DC, MC.*

Holmenkollen

$$$$ ✕ **De Fem Stuer.** Near the famous Holmenkollen ski jump, in the his-
★ toric Holmenkollen Park Hotel, this restaurant has first-rate views and
food. Chef Frank Halvorsen's modern Norwegian dishes have strong
classic roots. Well worth trying is the three-course "A Taste of Norway" meal. ⊠ *Holmenkollen Park Hotel, Kongevn. 26,* ☎ *22/92–27–
34. Jacket and tie. AE, DC, MC, V.*

$$ ✕ **Frognerseteren.** Just above the Holmenkollen ski jump, this restau-
rant, specializing in fish and venison, looks down on the entire city and
is probably the most famous in Oslo. Be sure not to miss the house
specialty—scrumptious apple cake. The upstairs room has the same
view as the more expensive panoramic veranda, and there is also an
outdoor café. Take the Holmenkollbanen to the end station and then
follow the signs downhill to the restaurant. ⊠ *Hollmenkollvn. 200,*
☎ *22/14–05–50. DC, MC, V.*

LODGING

Most hotels are centrally located, a short walk from Karl Johans Gate,
and often between the Royal Palace and the central railway station.
The newest hotels are in the area around Oslo S Station, at the bot-
tom end of Karl Johan. For a quiet stay, choose a hotel in either
Frogner or Majorstuen, elegant residential neighborhoods just minutes
from downtown.

Oslo usually has enough hotel rooms to go around, but it's always a
good idea to reserve a room at least for the first night of your stay, es-
pecially if you will be arriving late. Otherwise, the hotel accommoda-
tions office at Oslo S Station (☞ Visitor Information *in* Oslo A to Z,
below) is open from 8 AM to 11 PM and can book you in anything from
a luxury hotel to a room in a private home for a fee of NKr 20. Usu-
ally there are last-minute discount rooms.

Lodging in the capital is expensive. Prices for downtown accommo-
dations are high, even for bed-and-breakfasts, although just about all
hotels have weekend, holiday, and summer rates (25% to 50% re-
ductions). Taxes and service charges, unless otherwise noted, are in-
cluded. Breakfast is usually included also, but be sure to ask before
booking your room.

You can cut your lodging costs considerably—and get more for your
money than with summer or weekend rates—by buying an Oslo Pack-
age in advance. This combines an Oslo Card (☞ Getting Around *in*
Oslo A to Z, *below*) with discounted room rates at almost all of Oslo's
better hotels. Contact local agents of the Scandinavian Tourist Board
for more information and reservations. In the United States or Canada,
call **Scanam World Tours** (☎ 973/835–7070, FAX 973/835–3030); in Aus-
tralia, the **Mansions Travel Service** (☎ 61/7–229–5631, FAX 61/7–221–
9731); in the United Kingdom, **Scantours UK** (☎ 020/744–839–2927,
FAX 020/744–839–4327).

If you want to rent an apartment, contact **B&B Oslo Apartments** (⊠
Stasjonsvn. 13, Blommenholm, 1300 Sandvika, ☎ 67/54–06–80, FAX
67/54–09–70), which is open weekdays 8:30–4. Most are in Bærum,
15 minutes from downtown Oslo, and about 20 are in Skøyen, a
grassy suburban area, closer to both the airport and the center. All are
no more than a 10-minute walk from public transport.

Downtown: Royal Palace to the Parliament

$$$$ 🏨 **Grand Hotel.** Right in the center of town on Karl Johans Gate, the
★ Grand has been Oslo's premier hotel since it opened in 1874. Ibsen
used to start his mornings with a brisk walk followed by a stiff drink
at the Grand Café in the company of journalists. Munch was also a
regular guest, and since his time the Grand has hosted many famous
people and all recipients of the Nobel Peace Prize. Many Norwegians
check in on Constitution Day, May 17, in order to have a room overlooking the parades. The lobby only hints at the style and flair of the
rooms. Even standard rooms are large, looking more like guest quarters in an elegant house than hotel rooms. Those in the newer wing
are smaller, cheaper, and not as nice. The hotel's restaurant, Julius
Fritzner, is considered one of Oslo's most elegant dining establishments.
☒ *Karl Johans Gt. 31, 0159,* ☎ *22/42–93–90,* FAX *22/42–12–25. 287
rooms, 50 suites. 3 restaurants, 3 bars, indoor pool, sauna, health club,
meeting rooms. AE, DC, MC, V.*

$$$$ 🏨 **Hotel Continental.** An elegant turn-of-the-century facade has put the
★ Continental on Norway's historic-preservation list. Its location—across
from Nationalteatret and next door to a high concentration of cafés,
clubs, and cinemas—is perfect for both vacationers and business travelers. The Brockmann family, owners since 1900, have succeeded in
combining the rich elegance of the Old World with modern living. Munch
graphics from the family's own collection adorn the walls. Antique furniture and shiny white porcelain fixtures add a distinctive touch to the
rooms. Theatercafeen (☞ Dining, *above*) is a landmark, and the newest
addition, Lipp, a restaurant-café-bar-nightclub, is among Oslo's "in"
places. Dagligstuen (The Sitting Room) is a wonderful place in which
to start or end the evening with an appetizer or nightcap. ☒ *Stortingsgt.
24–26, 0161,* ☎ *22/82–40–00,* FAX *22/42–96–89. 140 rooms, 23 suites.
3 restaurants, 2 bars. AE, DC, MC, V.*

$$$$ 🏨 **Radisson SAS Scandinavia Hotel.** Oslo's established business hotel,
built in 1974, has some competition but can still hold its own. Simple, elegant rooms come in different styles: art deco, Italian, Asian, Continental, Scandinavian, and—predictably, for a hotel run by an
airline—69 high-tech business-class rooms. The lower-level shopping
arcade has stylish clothing and leather-goods shops. The SAS is across
the street from the palace grounds; downtown is a few blocks downhill. ☒ *Holbergs Gt. 30, 0166,* ☎ *22/11–30–00,* FAX *22/11–30–17. 496
rooms, 3 large suites. 2 restaurants, 2 bars, pool, health club, nightclub, dance club, business services. AE, DC, MC, V.*

$$$ 🏨 **Bristol.** The Bristol caters to people who want a dignified hotel in
the center of town. The immense lobby lounge was decorated in the
1920s with an intricate Moorish theme and feels more like Fez than
Scandinavia. Nevertheless, it is a tribute to style, and the piano bar is
one of Oslo's best. The rooms do not necessarily reflect the lobby's lush-
ness: small and comfortable, they have all the amenities of modern Scan-
dinavia. Upgraded in early 1999, the hotel has a new fitness center with
sauna, solarium, and Jacuzzi. ☒ *Kristian IV's Gt. 7, 0164,* ☎ *22/82–
60–00,* FAX *22/82–60–01. 250 rooms, 10 suites. 3 restaurants, 3 bars, sauna,
health club, nightclub, convention center. AE, DC, MC, V.*

$$$ 🏨 **Hotel Karl Johan.** The late-19th-century Karl Johan, once known
as the Nobel, is elegant: one look at the wrought-iron railing and
stained-glass windows that line the circular staircase will make you feel
you're in 19th-century Paris. The lobby's hardwood floors are shiny
and covered with Oriental rugs and velvety navy carpet; fabrics are gold
and navy striped; and Old English caricatures hang on the off-white
walls. Every room has a different Norwegian treasure, but the feel is

sophisticated, not rustic. Its location, next door to the Grand, couldn't be better, and the hotel claims to have a set of regulars who prefer it to its overshadowing neighbor. If you're sensitive to noise, ask for a room away from Rosenkrantz' Gate, where bar hoppers and night-clubbers boogie until the wee hours. ⊠ *Karl Johans Gt. 33, 0162,* ☎ *22/42–74–80,* FAX *22/42–05–19. 112 rooms, 1 suite. Restaurant, bar. AE, DC, MC, V.*

$$$ ⊞ **Rainbow Hotel Stefan.** This hotel makes every aspect of a stay here a positive experience, from hot drinks for late arrivals to breakfast tables complete with juice boxes and plastic bags for packing a lunch (request this service in advance). The top-floor lounge has books and magazines in English. The Stefan's kitchen is famous for creating the best buffet lunch in town. ⊠ *Rosenkrantz' Gt. 1, 0159,* ☎ *22/42–92–50,* FAX *22/33–70–22. 138 rooms. Restaurant, library, meeting rooms. AE, DC, MC, V.*

$$$ ⊞ **Rica Victoria.** This modern business hotel occupies one of the city center's taller buildings, giving some top-floor rooms glimpses of Oslo's rooftops. The rooms, built around a center atrium, are elegant and very stylish, furnished with Biedermeier reproductions, brass lamps, and paisley-print textiles in bold reds and dark blues. Rooms with windows on the atrium may be claustrophobic for some but colorful and fun for others. ⊠ *Rosenkrantz' Gt. 13, 0160,* ☎ *22/42–99–40,* FAX *22/41–06–44. 199 rooms, 5 suites. Restaurant, bar. AE, DC, MC, V.*

$$ ⊞ **Hotell Bondeheimen.** Founded in 1913 for country folk visiting the city, Bondeheimen, which means "farmers' home," still gives discounts to members of Norwegian agricultural associations. The interior is simple, furnished with all the makings of a contemporary Norwegian country home. Cube-shape cushioned chairs, sofas, and solid tables are made of pine, and fabrics and carpets are dyed in farmers' colors: green, blue, yellow, and red. Modern Norwegian graphics hang on the walls, and bathrooms have rustic swigs of hay on the walls. The lobby has a small library of books on Norway, even some in English. Bondeheimen is affiliated with the country kitchen Kaffistova (☞ Dining, *above*). It is a good choice for families, but if you are looking for quiet, ask for a room in back. ⊠ *Rosenkrantz' Gt. 8 (entrance on Kristian IV's Gate), 0159,* ☎ *22/42–95–30,* FAX *22/41–94–37. 76 rooms. Cafeteria, sauna, library, meeting rooms. AE, DC, MC, V.*

$$ ⊞ **Rainbow Cecil.** This modern hotel, a block from Parliament, is
★ down the road from several other, more expensive hotels and is closer to the main drag than most. The second floor opens onto a plant-filled atrium, the hotel's activity center. In the morning it's a breakfast room, but in the afternoon it becomes a lounge, serving coffee, juice, and fresh fruit, with newspapers available in many languages. Many rooms face the atrium for the sake of peace and quiet, but others have a view of the Stortinget and its many passersby (where you'll get a better feel for the city). The hotel provides umbrellas for rainy days and claims to have the best air-conditioning in the city for those rare—but beloved—summer heat waves. ⊠ *Stortingsgt. 8, 0130,* ☎ *22/42–70–00,* FAX *22/42–26–70. 112 rooms, 2 suites. AE, DC, MC, V.*

East of Downtown

$ ⊞ **Haraldsheim.** Oslo's hilltop youth hostel is one of Europe's largest. Most of the rooms have four beds, and those in the new wing have showers. Bring your own sheets or rent them there. It is 6 km (almost 3 mi) from the city center—take trikk 10 or 11 (marked "Kjelsås") to Sinsen. Nonmembers of the International Youth Hostel organization and those older than 25 years pay a surcharge. ⊠ *Haraldsheimvn. 4, 0409,* ☎ *22/15–50–43,* ℻ *22/22–10–25. 264 beds. V.*

$ ⊞ **Munch.** This modern B&B, about a 10-minute walk from Karl Johans Gate, is unpretentious, well run, clean, and functional. The decent-size rooms are painted in pastels or blue with floral curtains. The lobby, with Chinese rugs and leather couches, contrasts with the rest of the hotel. ⊠ *Munchsgt. 5, 0165,* ☎ *22/42–42–75,* ℻ *22/20–64–69. 180 rooms. Breakfast room. AE, DC, MC, V.*

Frogner, Majorstuen, and Holmenkollen

$$$$ ⊞ **Holmenkollen Park Hotel Rica.** The magnificent 1894 building in the national romantic style commands an unequaled panorama of the city in a quiet and natural setting. It is worth a visit even if you don't lodge there, perhaps for a meal at its legendary restaurant, De Fem Stuer (☞ Dining, *above*). The rather ordinary guest rooms are in a newer structure behind it. The ice-covered snowflake sculpture in the lobby is appropriate for a hotel that's a stone's throw from the Holmenkollen ski jump. Ski and walking trails are just outside. ⊠ *Kongevn. 26, 0390,* ☎ *22/92–20–00,* ℻ *22/14–61–92. 221 rooms. 2 restaurants, bar, pool, sauna, cross-country skiing, health club, convention center. AE, DC, MC, V.*

$$$–$$$$ ⊞ **Ambassadeur.** Hidden behind a pale pink facade with wrought-iron
★ balconies in a stylish residential area near the Royal Palace, the Ambassadeur is a 15-minute walk from both downtown and Frogner Park. Originally built in 1889 as an apartment hotel, it still has a turn-of-the-century feel. The owner has hand-picked antiques, china tea sets, and tapestries for the small downstairs salon. The rooms are individually furnished according to themes. "Roma" rooms have canopy beds draped in pale taffeta and maps of old Rome on the walls. "Peer Gynt" rooms have Scandinavian landscape paintings and a Norwegian farmhouse feel. If it's a special occasion, request the pricey "Osa" suite. The painted wooden furniture, carved canopy bed, and exquisite printed fabrics could easily be on display at the Norwegian Folk Museum. The hotel's small, professional staff doesn't bother with titles because everyone does whatever task presents itself, from laundering a shirt on short notice to delivering room service. ⊠ *Camilla Colletts vei 15, 0258,* ☎ *22/44–18–35,* ℻ *22/44–47–91. 33 rooms, 8 suites. Bar, meeting room. AE, DC, MC, V.*

$$$–$$$$ ⊞ **Frogner House.** This elegant hotel opened in 1992 and receives mainly business clients, but welcomes independently traveling tourists looking for a quiet stay. The five-story redbrick and stone building went up in 1890 as an apartment house and now sits inconspicuously amid rows of other turn-of-the-century town houses. Dressed in pastels and abundant lace coverings, the rooms are spacious and insulated. Some have balconies, and many have views of the boutique-lined residential streets. ⊠ *Skovveien 8, 0257,* ☎ *22/56–00–56,* ℻ *22/56–05–00. 60 rooms, 8 suites. Meeting room. AE, DC, MC, V.*

$$ ⊞ **Gabelshus.** With only a discreet sign above the door, this ivy-covered brick house in a posh residential area is one of Oslo's most personal hotels. It's been owned by the same family for almost 50 years. The lounges are filled with antiques, some in the national romantic style, but the rooms are plain. It's a short walk to several of Oslo's best restaurants and a short trikk ride to the center of town. The Ritz Hotel, across the parking lot, is owned by the same family and takes the overflow. ⊠ *Gabels Gt. 16, 0272,* ☎ *22/55–22–60,* ℻ *22/44–27–30. 50 rooms (plus 42 rooms in Ritz). Restaurant. AE, DC, MC, V.*

$ ☖ **Rainbow Gyldenløve.** Nestled among the many shops and cafés on Bogstadveien, this hotel is one of the city's most reasonable. It is within walking distance of Vigeland Park, and the trikk stops just outside the door. ☎ *Bogstadvn. 20, 0355,* ☎ *22/60–10–90,* FAX *22/60–33–90. 169 rooms. Coffee shop. AE, DC, MC, V.*

Near Gardermoen Airport and Oslo S Station

$$$$ ☖ **Radisson SAS Plaza Hotel Oslo.** Northern Europe's largest hotel is a three-minute walk from Karl Johans Gate and just across from Oslo's central train station. A snazzy 33-story skyscraper in a city that has few, Oslo Plaza has become a part of the city's skyline. The Panorama Bar on the top floor is a popular spot for a cocktail; if you get a chance, peek inside the adjoining conference rooms, which afford great views of Oslo. ⊠ *Sonja Henies Pl. 3, 0134,* ☎ *22/17–10–00,* FAX *22/17–73–00. 673 rooms. 2 restaurants, bar, indoor pool, health club, convention center. AE, DC, MC, V.*

$$$$ ☖ **Royal Christiania.** It started out as bare-bones housing for 1952
★ Olympians. The original plain exterior has been retained, but inside it's a whole new luxury hotel, built around a central seven-story atrium. The emphasis here is on discreet comfort—the large rooms are decorated with soft-colored love seats and armchairs. ⊠ *Biskop Gunnerus' Gt. 3, 0106,* ☎ *23/10–80–100,* FAX *23/10–80–80. 451 rooms, 73 suites. 2 restaurants, 2 bars, indoor pool, health club, convention center. AE, DC, MC, V.*

$$$ ☖ **Radisson SAS Park Royal.** Oslo Gardermoen Airport's main hotel has an impressive stainless-steel, circular front and is located only 100 meters from the terminal building and railway station. There are excellent business facilities, including a business-class airline check-in, and a well-equipped sports center. ⊠ *Hotellvegen, Box 163, 2061, Gardermoen,* ☎ *63/93–30–00,* FAX *63/93–30–30. 350 rooms, 88 suites. Restaurant, bar, health club, business services, meeting rooms. AE, DC, MC, V.*

NIGHTLIFE AND THE ARTS

Nightlife

For the past few years Oslo has strived to be the nightlife capital of Scandinavia, although local government factions have talked about toughening laws on noise pollution and drinking. At any time of the day or night, people are out on Karl Johan, and many clubs and restaurants in the central area stay open until the wee hours. Still, strict zoning laws have prohibited the sale of anything harder than "light" beer after 2:30 AM, which means many nightclubs close their doors earlier than one would expect.

Night owls can pick up a copy of the free monthly paper *Natt og Dag* at almost any café, bar, or hip-looking shop. It lists rock, pop, and jazz venues and contains an "øl barometer," listing the city's cheapest and most expensive places for a beer—a necessary column in a city where a draft, on average, costs NKr 40 to 50. The listings are in Norwegian, but some ads are in English.

Many bars and nightclubs in Oslo have a minimum age, which will often give you a sense of who goes there. A minimum age of 18 will generally draw high schoolers, whereas 24 will draw young professionals.

Bars and Lounges

Barbeint (⊠ Drammensvn. 20, ☎ 22/43–87–88) is an ultrahip spot where students, media folk, and local celebrities from the fashionable

Frogner district convene on their way in from or out on the town. Avant-garde art adorns the walls, and the loud, cutting-edge music ranges from funk-metal and rock to rap. The trendiest twentysomethings imbibe the night away at **Beach Club** (✉ Aker Brygge, ☎ 22/83–83–82), a kitschy American hamburger joint with life-size stuffed fish on the walls and diner-style tables and booths. If you're more partial to lounging than drinking, try the English-style bar at the **Bristol Hotel** (✉ Kristian IV's Gt. 7, ☎ 22/82–60–00). **Børsen Online Café** (✉ Nedre Vollgt. 19, enter on Stortingsgt., ☎ 22/33–08–00) caters to the cyber crowd and the upwardly mobile. Adding to this theme, TV monitors display the drink prices, which fluctuate according to supply and demand. For variety, get an outdoor table at **Lorry** (✉ Parkvn. 12, ☎ 22/69–69–04), just over from the Royal Palace. Filled with a cast of grizzled old artists, the place advertises 204 brews, but don't be surprised if not all of them are in stock. For the serious beer connoisseur, **Oslo Mikro-bryggeriet** (✉ Bogstadvn. 6, ☎ 22/56–97–76) brews eight varieties of beer, including the increasingly popular Oslo Pils, on the premises. **Studenten Bryggeri** (✉ Karl Johans Gt. 45, ☎ 22/42–56–80), another microbrewery, is often packed with students and loud music as well.

Cafés

Many cafés are open for cappuccino and quiet conversation practically around the clock, and they're the cheapest eateries as well (☞ Dining, *above*). The **Broker Café** (✉ Bogstadvn. 27, ☎ 22/69–36–47) in Majorstuen has great pasta and salads and old, cushiony sofas on which to drink or dine. **Café Bacchus** (✉ Dronningensgt. 27, ☎ 22/33–34–30), in the old railroad offices by Oslo Domkirke, is tiny but serves a mean brownie. Background music is classical during the day, jazz into the night. **Clodion Art Café** (☞ Dining, *above*) is one of Oslo's hippest spots for coffee. Downtown, **Nichol & Son** (✉ Olavs Gt. 1, ☎ 22/83–19–60), a must for Jack Nicholson fans, is an amiable spot to relax with a newspaper. In the trendy area around Frogner and Homansbyen, try **Odion** (✉ Hegdehaugsvn. 34, ☎ 22/69–05–35) for Asian edibles. The Spanish-inspired **Tapas** (✉ Hegdehaugsvn. 22, ☎ 22/60–38–28) serves bowls of café au lait in the morning and aperitif-size chunks of potatoes, chorizo, and cheese later on.

Gay Bars

For information about gay and lesbian activities in Oslo, you can read *Blikk*, the gay newsletter, or call **LLH** (Landsforening for Lesbisk of Homofil Frigjøring, ☎ 22/36–19–48), the nationwide gay and lesbian liberation association. The main gay bar in town is **Club Castro** (✉ Kristian IV's Gt. 7, ☎ 22/41–51–08), which is renowned for its energetic dance floor. The **Backyard Cruising Bar** (✉ Theatergaten 3, ☎ 22/20–62–99) has an excellent top-floor restaurant. **Den Sorte Enke** (The Black Widow, ✉ Karl Johans Gt. 10, ☎ 22/33–23–01), Oslo's self-designated "gay-house," attracts a crowd of mainly younger men to dance the night away. **London Pub** (✉ C.J. Hambros Pl. 5, ☎ 22/70–87–00) has a top-floor piano bar with Sunday theme parties. **Potpurriet** (✉ Øvre Vollgt. 13, ☎ 22/41–14–40) organizes well-attended women's dance nights on the last Friday of each month.

Jazz Clubs

Norwegians love jazz. Every August, the **Oslo Jazz Festival** (✉ Tollbugt. 28, ☎ 22/42–91–20) brings in major international artists and attracts big crowds. Festivities commence with a Dixie-style parade, but all types of jazz are present and explained in free leaflets and newsletters everywhere. **Herr Nilsen** (✉ C.J. Hambros Pl. 5, ☎ 22/33–54–05) features some of Norway's most celebrated jazz artists in a Manhattanesque setting. There is live music three days a week and a jazz café on Saturday afternoons. **Oslo Jazzhus** (⊠ Stockholmsgt. 12, ☎ 22/38–59–63) is in an out-of-the-way location and is open only Thursday through Saturday, but the music is worth the journey. **Stortorvets Gjæstgiveri** (⊠ Grensen 1, ☎ 22/42–88–63) often presents New Orleans–style and ragtime bands and is known for its swinging dance nights.

Nightclubs

Most dance clubs open late, and the beat doesn't really start until around midnight. There's usually a minimum age, and the cover charge is around NKr 50. Oslo's beautiful people congregate at the elegant **Barock** (⊠ Universitetsgt. 26, ☎ 22/42–44–20). **Cosmopolite** (⊠ Industrigt. 36, ☎ 22/69–16–63) has a big dance floor and music from all over the world, especially Latin America. **Galleria** (⊠ Kristian IV's Gt. 12, ☎ 22/42–29–46), another hot spot, has a live jazz club, a disco, and a bar filling up its three art-bedecked floors. **Lipp** (⊠ Olav V's Gt. 2, ☎ 22/82–40–60) is extremely popular as a restaurant, nightclub, and bar. Most of the big hotels have discos that appeal to the over-30 crowd. **Smuget** (⊠ Rosenkrantz Gt. 22, ☎ 22/42–52–62) is an institution: live rock and blues every night except Sunday bring crowds who then flock to the in-house discotheque. Thursday is student disco night at **Snorre-Kompagniet** (⊠ Rosenkrantz' Gt. 11, ☎ 22/33–52–60), where the hip-hopping clientele is often still teenaged.

Rock Clubs

At Oslo's numerous rock clubs, the cover charges are low, the crowds young and boisterous, and the music loud. If your taste leans toward reggae and calypso, try the **Afro International Night Club** (⊠ Brennerivn. 5, ☎ 22/36–07–53), which has frequent Caribbean evenings. **Blue Monk** (⊠ St. Olavs Gt. 23, ☎ 22/20–22–90) has live music on Wednesdays, Fridays, and Saturdays—and the beer is surprisingly cheap. In the basement you'll find the boisterous Sub Pub, which airs punk and '80s classics. **Rockefeller/John Dee** (⊠ Torggt. 16, ☎ 22/20–32–32) features more alternative musical acts, like Nick Cave and Neil Finn. **Oslo Spektrum** (⊠ Sonia Henies Pl. 2, ☎ 22/05–29–00) is one of Norway's largest live-music venues. Just behind Oslo City shopping center, it attracts big names, such as Alanis Morissette and Rod Stewart.

The Arts

The monthly tourist information brochure *What's on in Oslo* lists cultural events in Norwegian, as does *Aftenposten,* Oslo's (and Norway's) leading newspaper, in its evening "Oslo Puls" section. The Wednesday edition of *Dagbladet,* Oslo's daily liberal tabloid, also gives an exhaustive preview of the week's events. Tickets to virtually all performances in Norway, from classical or rock concerts to hockey games, can be purchased at any post office. You can also call **Billet Service** (☎ 810–33–133) and pick up tickets at the post office later.

Art

Art galleries are cropping up all over town as a generation of young artists comes of age. Although much official Norwegian art is folk art, some of the newer artists take a more postmodern approach to their craft. Pick up a copy of *Listen,* a brochure that lists all current exhibitions.

Film

All films are shown in the original language with subtitles, except for some children's films, which are dubbed. You can buy tickets to any film showing at the box office of any of Oslo's cinemas, and you can reserve tickets by calling any cinema and leaving your phone number. Tickets cost NKr 60 and are discounted some days in summer. If you like alternative and classic films, try **Cinemateket** (✉ Dronningensgt. 16, ☎ 22/47–45–00), the city's only independent cinema.

Music

The **Norwegian Philharmonic Orchestra,** under the direction of Mariss Janssons, is among Europe's leading ensembles. Its house, **Konserthuset** (✉ Munkedamsvn. 14, ☎ 23/11–31–00), was built in 1977 in marble, metal, and rosewood. In the summer, folkloric dances are staged here twice a week. **Den Norske Opera** (✉ Storgt. 23, ☎ 22/42–94–75 for information; 815/44–488 to order tickets) and the ballet perform at Youngstorvet. The breathtaking **Gamle Logen** (✉ Grev Wedels Pl. 2, ☎ 22/33–44–70), Norway's oldest concert hall, often sponsors classical music series, especially piano music.

For a thoroughly Norwegian cultural experience, check out the **Norwegian Masters** (☎ 22/43–34–70), who play character monologues from Ibsen's *Peer Gynt* against a backdrop of Munch paintings and to the music of the beloved Grieg, who originally wrote music to accompany the Norwegian fable. The performance takes place in English, and its venue changes from year to year.

Theater

Nationalteatret (✉ Stortingsgt. 15, ☎ 22/00–14–00) performances are in Norwegian: bring along a copy of the play in translation, and you're all set. The biennial Ibsen festival, which features plays by the great dramatist in both Norwegian and English, is set for summer 2000 and 2002. **Det Norske Teater** (✉ Kristian IV's Gt. 8, ☎ 22/47–38–00) is a showcase for pieces in Nynorsk and guest artists from abroad.

OUTDOOR ACTIVITIES AND SPORTS

Surrounding Oslo's compact center are varied and unspoiled landscapes, including forests, farmland, and, of course, the fjord. Just 15 minutes north of the city center by tram is the **Oslomarka,** where locals ski in winter and hike in summer. The area is dotted with 27 small hytter, which are often available free of charge for backpackers on foot or on ski. These can be reserved through the **Norske Turistforening** (✉ Stortingsgt. 28, ☎ 22/82–28–00), which has maps of the *marka* (fields and land), surrounding Oslo as well. The **Oslo Archipelago** is also a favorite with sunbathing urbanites, who hop ferries to their favorite isles.

Aerobics

If you need a fitness fix, you can visit one of the many health studios around the city. Most have a "klippekort" system, which means you buy 10 hours' worth of fitness and they "klip," or punch, your card with each entry. The ever-popular **Trim Tram** (✉ Stranden 55, Aker Brygge, ☎ 22/83–66–50) offers myriad low- and high-intensity aerobics and step classes at reasonable rates. **Friskis & Svettis** (✉ Munkedamsvn. 17–18, ☎ 22/83–94–40) holds free aerobics classes on the green in Frogner Park. From mid-May to mid-August you can watch or join the hundreds of health-conscious Osloites huffing and puffing and rolling in the dirt. Call for times and intensity levels.

Beaches

Beaches are scattered throughout the archipelago and sun-loving Scandinavians pack every patch of sand during the long summer days to make up for lack of light in winter. The most popular beach is Paradisbukta at Huk (on the Bygdøy peninsula), which devotes one portion of the beach to nude bathers and the other to "clothed." To get there, follow signs along Huk Aveny from the Folk- and Viking Ship museums. You can also take Bus 30A, marked "Bygdøy," to its final stop.

Biking

Oslo is a bike-friendly city. There are many marked paths in and around town meant for bicycles and pedestrians, and cyclists are allowed to use sidewalks. (Note, however, that cars do not have to stop for bicycles the way they do for pedestrians at crosswalks.) One great ride starts at Aker Brygge and takes you along the harbor to the Bygdøy peninsula, where you can visit the museums or cut across the fields next to the royal family's summer house. Ask locals how to get to Huk, the peninsula's popular beach (☞ Beaches, *above*).

Den Rustne Eike (The Rusty Spoke, ⊠ Vestbanepl. 2, ☎ 22/44–18–80), just a few doors down from the Norway Information Center, rents bikes and equipment, including helmets. The store also offers five different sightseeing tours and has maps of the area for those braving it on their own. If you feel like roughing the terrain of the Holmenkollen marka (woods), you can rent mountain bikes from **Tomm Murstad Skiservice** (⊠ Tryvannsvn. 2, ☎ 22/13–95–00) in the summer. Just take T-bane 1 to Frognerseteren and get off at the Voksenkollen station. **Syklistenes Landsforening** (National Organization of Cyclists, ⊠ Stortingsgt. 23C, ☎ 22/41–50–80) sells books and maps for cycling holidays in Norway and abroad and gives friendly, free advice.

Fishing

A national fishing license (NKr 90, available in post offices) and a local fee (NKr 100 from local sports shops) are required to fish in the Oslo Fjord and the surrounding lakes. You can also fish throughout the Nordmarka woods area in a canoe rented from Tomm Murstad (☞ Biking, *above*). Ice fishing is popular in winter, but you'll have a hard time finding an ice drill—truly, you may want to bring one from home.

Golf

Oslo's international-level golf course, **Oslo Golfklubb** (⊠ Bogstad, 0740 Oslo 7, ☎ 22/50–44–02) is private, and heavily booked, but will admit members of other golf clubs (weekdays before 2 PM and weekends after 2 PM) if space is available. Visitors must have a handicap certificate of 20 or lower for men, 28 or lower for women. Fees range from NKr 275 to NKr 325.

Hiking and Running

Head for the woods surrounding Oslo, the marka, for jogging or walking; there are thousands of kilometers of trails, hundreds of them lit. Frogner Park has many paths, and you can jog or hike along the Aker River, but a few unsavory types may be about late at night or early in the morning. Or you can take the Sognsvann trikk to the end of the line and walk or jog along the Sognsvann stream. For walks or jogs closer to town, explore the stately residential area around Drammensveien west of the Royal Palace, which has paths leading to Bygdøy. The Norske Turistforening (☞ *above*) has many maps of trails around Oslo and can recommend individual routes.

Grete Waitz and Ingrid Kristiansen have put Norway on the marathon runners' map in recent years. On the last Saturday in May, a women's mini-marathon is held in Grete Waitz's name; hundreds of women flock to Oslo to enjoy a nice day—and usually night—out. **Norges Friidretts**

Forbund (⊠ Karl Johans Gt. 2, 0104 Oslo, ☎ 22/42–03–03) has information about local clubs and competitions.

Skiing

The **Skiforeningen** (⊠ Kongevn. 5, 0390 Oslo 3, ☎ 22/92–32–00) provides national snow-condition reports and can provide tips on the multitude of cross-country trails. They also offer cross-country classes for young children (3- to 7-year-olds), downhill for older children (7- to 12-year-olds), and both, in addition to Telemark-style and racing techniques, for adults.

Among the floodlit trails in the Oslomarka are the **Bogstad** (3½ km/2 mi), marked for the disabled and blind), the **Lillomarka** (about 25 km/15½ mi), and the **Østmarken** (33 km/20½ mi).

For downhill, which usually lasts from mid-December to March, there are 15 local city slopes as well as organized trips to several outside slopes, including **Norefjell** (☎ 32/14–94–00), 100 km (66 mi) north of the city, also available.

You can rent both downhill and cross-country skis from **Tomm Murstad Skiservice** (⊠ Tryvannsvn. 2, ☎ 22/13–95–00) at the Tryvann T-bane station. This is a good starting point for skiing; although there are but few downhill slopes in this area, a plethora of cross-country trails for every level of competence exist.

Swimming

Tøyenbadet (⊠ Helgesensgt. 90, ☎ 22/67–18–87) and **Frogner Park** (☎ 22/08–22–50) have large outdoor swimming pools that are open from mid-May through late August, depending on the weather (weekdays 7 AM–7:30 PM, weekends 10–5:30). Tøyenbadet also has an indoor pool that's open year-round. All pools cost NKr 40. Pools are free with the Oslo Card (☞ Getting Around, *below*).

SHOPPING

Oslo is the best place for buying anything Norwegian. Prices of handmade articles, such as knitwear, are controlled, making comparison shopping unnecessary. Otherwise shops have both sales and specials—look for the words *salg* and *tilbud*. Sales of seasonal merchandise, combined with the value-added tax refund, can save you more than half the original price. Norwegians do like au courant skiwear, so there are plenty of bargains in last season's winter sportswear.

Stores are generally open from 9 to 5 during the week, but they often close by 3 on Saturdays. Shopping malls and department stores are open later, until 8 during the week and 6 on weekends. Shops also stay open late Thursdays as well as on the first Saturday of the month, known as *super lørdag* (super Saturday) to enthusiastic shoppers. Only during the holiday season are stores open Sunday.

Several shopping districts stand out. From the city center, you can wander up the tree-lined Bygdøy Allé and poke around the fashionable **Frogner** area, which is brimming with modern and antique furniture stores, interior design shops, gourmet food shops, art galleries, haute couture, and a solid majority of Oslo's beautiful people. Stores of every ilk are crammed into the downtown area around **Karl Johans Gate,** where many shoppers flock. The concentration of department stores is especially high in this part of town. **Majorstuen** starts at the T-bane station with the same name and proceeds down Bogstadveien to the Royal Palace. Once you're off the main shopping street, a tiny smattering of independent shops and galleries cater to needs as obscure as your next safari hunt. **Vikaterrassen,** near Aker Brygge (☞ *below*), is a pleasant shopping street with small, exclusive stores. Its glass and concrete facade sits directly underneath a more magnificent building that houses Norway's Ministry of Foreign Affairs.

Department Stores

Christiania GlasMagasin (⊠ Stortorvet 9, ☎ 22/90–89–00) is an amalgam of shops under one roof rather than a true department store. Traditionally, families visit GlasMagasin at Christmastime, so the store is usually open on Sundays in December. The best buys are glass and porcelain. Christmas decorations reflecting Norway's rural heritage are easily packed. There is also a wide selection of pewter ware. **Steen & Strøm** (⊠ Kongens Gt. 23, ☎ 22/00–40–01), one of Oslo's first department stores, sells the usual: cosmetics, clothing, books, accessories. It also has a well-stocked outdoors floor.

Shopping Centers

Aker Brygge, Norway's first major shopping center, is right on the water across from the Tourist Information Office at Vestbanen. Shops are open until 8 most days, and some even on Sundays. **Oslo City** (⊠ Stenersgt. 1E, ☎ 22/17–09–92), at the other end of downtown, with access to the street from Oslo S Station, is the largest indoor mall, but the shops are run-of-the-mill, and the food is mostly fast. The elegant **Paleet** (⊠ Karl Johans Gt. 39–41, between Universitetsgt. and Rosenkrantz' Gt., ☎ 22/41–70–86) opens up into a grand atrium lined with supports of various shades of black and gray marble. There's a good bookstore and some high-end clothing shops on the main floor; the basement houses a food court. It's open 10–10 weekdays, 10–5 Saturdays.

Specialty Stores

Antiques
Norwegian rustic antiques cannot be taken out of the country, but just about anything else can with no problem. The Frogner district is dotted with antiques shops, especially Skovveien and Thomas Heftyes Gate between Bygdøy Allé and Frogner Plass. Deeper in the heart of the Majorstua district, Industrigate is famous for its good selection of shops. **Blomqvist Kunsthandel** (⊠ Tordenskiolds Gt. 5, ☎ 22/41–26–31) has a good selection of small items and paintings, with auctions six times a year. The rare volumes at **Damms Antiqvariat** (⊠ Tollbugt. 25, ☎ 22/41–04–02) will catch the eye of any antiquarian book buff, with books in English as well as Norwegian, which could be harder to find back home. **Esaias Solberg** (⊠ Dronningens Gt. 27, ☎ 22/42–41–08), behind Oslo Cathedral, has exceptional small antiques. **Kaare Berntsen** (⊠ Universitetsgt. 12, ☎ 22/20–34–29) sells paintings, furniture, and small items, all very exclusive and priced accordingly. **Marsjandisen** (⊠ Paléet, ☎ 22/42–71–68), nestled in the slickest of shopping centers, carries "merchandise" ranging from discontinued Hadeland glasses to letter openers and authentic World War II–era postcards, pins, and buttons. **West Sølv og Mynt** (⊠ Niels Juels Gt. 27, ☎ 22/55–75–83) has the largest selection of silver, both old and antique, in town.

Books
Bjørn Ringstrøms Antikvariat (⊠ Ullevålsvn. 1, ☎ 22/20–78–05), across the street from the Museum of Applied Art, has a wide selection of used books and records. **Erik Qvist** (⊠ Drammensvn. 16, ☎ 22/54–26–00), across from the Royal Palace, has an extensive English-

language selection. **Tanum Libris** (⌂ Karl Johans Gt. 37–41, ☎ 22/41–11–00) has scores of English-language books, ranging from travel guides to contemporary fiction.

Embroidery

Randi Mangen (⌂ Jacob Aalls Gt. 17, ☎ 22/60–50–59), near Majorstuen, sells only embroidery. **Husfliden** (☞ Handicrafts, *below*) sells embroidery kits, including do-it-yourself *bunader* (national costumes); traditional yarn shops also sell embroidery.

Food

Buy a smoked salmon or trout for a special treat. Most grocery stores sell vacuum-packed fish. **W. Køltzow** (⌂ Stranden 3, ☎ 22/83–00–70), at Aker Brygge, can pack fish for export.

Fur

Look for the Saga label for the best-quality farmed Arctic fox and mink. Other popular skins include Persian lamb and beaver. **Hansson** (⌂ Kirkevn. 54, ☎ 22/69–64–20), near Majorstuen, has an excellent selection of furs. **Studio H. Olesen** (⌂ Karl Johans Gt. 31, enter at Rosenkrantz' Gt., ☎ 22/33–37–50) has the most exclusive designs.

Furniture

Norway is well known for both rustic furniture and orthopedic yet well-designed chairs. **Tannum** (⌂ Stortingsgt. 28, ☎ 22/83–42–95) is a good starting point. Drammensveien and Bygdøy Allé have a wide selection of interior-design stores.

Glass, Ceramics, and Pewter

Abelson Brukskunst (⌂ Skovvn. 27, ☎ 22/55–55–94), behind the Royal Palace, is crammed with the best modern designs. The shops at **Basarhallene** behind the cathedral also sell glass and ceramics. If there's no time to visit a glass factory (☞ Chapter 3), department stores are the best option: **Christiania GlasMagasin** (⌂ Stortorvet 9, ☎ 22/90–89–00) stocks both European and Norwegian glass designs. **Lie Antikk & Kunsthandverk** (⌂ Hegdehaugsveien 27, ☎ 22/60–98–61) is a tiny shop at the bottom of Hegdehaugsveien that sells colorful wineglasses. **Norway Designs** (⌂ Stortingsgt. 28, ☎ 22/83–11–00) is probably the largest design-oriented store in Oslo and specializes in glass, metal, and ceramics crafted by Norwegian and Scandinavian folk artists. It also has trendy home appliances.

Handicrafts

Basarhallene, the arcade behind the cathedral, is also worth a browse for handicrafts made in Norway. **Format Kunsthandverk** (⌂ Vestbanepl. 1, ☎ 22/83–73–12) has beautiful, yet pricey, individual pieces (but you can buy a postcard to show your friends back home). **Heimen Husflid AS** (⌂ Rosenkrantz' Gt. 8, ☎ 22/41–40–50, enter at Kristian IV's Gt.) has small souvenir items and a specialized department for Norwegian national costumes. **Husfliden** (⌂ Møllergt. 4, ☎ 22/42–10–75), one of the finest stores with handmade goods in the country, has an even larger selection, including pewter, ceramics, knits, handwoven textiles, furniture, handmade felt boots and slippers, hand-sewn loafers, sweaters, national costumes, wrought-iron accessories, Christmas ornaments, and wooden kitchen accessories—all made in Norway.

Jewelry

Gold and precious stones are no bargain, but silver and enamel jewelry, along with reproductions of Viking pieces, are. Some silver pieces are made with Norwegian stones, particularly pink thulite. **David-Andersen** (⌂ Karl Johans Gt. 20, ☎ 22/41–69–55; Oslo City, ☎ 22/17–09–34) is Norway's best-known goldsmith, with stunning silver and gold designs. **ExpoArte** (⊠ Drammensvn. 40, ☎ 22/55–93–90), also a gallery, specializes in custom pieces and displays work of avant-garde Scandinavian jewelers. **Heyerdahl** (⊠ Roald Amundsensgt. 6, ☎ 22/41–59–18), near City Hall, is a good, dependable jeweler.

Knitwear and Clothing

Norway is famous for its handmade, multicolored ski sweaters, and even mass-produced (machine-knit) models are of top quality. The prices are regulated, so buy what you like when you see it. **Husfliden** (☞ Handicrafts, *above*) stocks handmade sweaters in the traditional style. **Mau-rtua** (⊠ Fr. Nansens Pl. 9, ☎ 22/41–31–64), near City Hall, has a huge selection of sweaters and blanket coats. **Oslo Sweater Shop** (⊠ SAS Scandinavia Hotel, Tullinsgt. 5, ☎ 22/11–29–22) has one of the city's widest selections. **Rein og Rose** (⊠ Ruseløkkvn. 3, ☎ 22/83–21–39), in the Vikaterassen strip, has extremely friendly salespeople and a good selection of knitwear, yarn, and textiles. **Siril** (⊠ Rosenkrantz' Gt. 23, ☎ 22/41–01–80), near City Hall, is a small shop with attentive staff. **William Schmidt** (⊠ Karl Johans Gt. 41, ☎ 22/42–02–88), founded in 1853, is Oslo's oldest shop specializing in sweaters and souvenirs.

Sportswear

Look for the ever-popular Helly-Hansen brand. The company makes everything from insulated underwear to rainwear, snow gear, and great insulated mittens. **Gresvig** (⊠ Storgt. 20, ☎ 22/17–39–80) is a little more expensive but has a good selection. **Sigmund Ruud** (⊠ Kirkevn. 57, ☎ 22/69–43–90) also has a comprehensive stock of quality sportswear.

Watches

For some reason, Swiss watches are much cheaper in Norway than in many other countries. **Bjerke** (⊠ Karl Johans Gt. 31, ☎ 22/42–20–44; Prinsensgt. 21, ☎ 22/42–60–50) has a large selection.

Street Markets

Although some discerning locals wonder where it procures its wares, the best flea market is on Saturday at **Vestkanttorvet,** near Frogner Park at Amaldus Nilsens Plass at the intersection of Professor Dahlsgate and Eckerberg Gate. Check the local paper for weekend garage sales, or *loppemarkeder,* held in schools.

OSLO A TO Z

Arriving and Departing

By Boat

Several ferry lines connect Oslo with the United Kingdom, Denmark, Sweden, and Germany. **Color Line** (☎ 22/94–44–00) sails to Kiel, Germany, and to Hirtshals, Denmark; **DFDS Scandinavian Seaways** (☎ 22/41–90–90) to Copenhagen via Helsingborg, Sweden; and **Stena Line** (☎ 23/17–90–00) to Frederikshavn, Denmark.

By Bus

The main bus station, **Oslo Bussterminalen Galleriet** (☎ 23/00–24–00), is across from the Oslo S Station. You can buy local bus tickets at the terminal or on the bus. Tickets for long-distance routes on **Nor-Way Bussekspress** (☎ 815/44–444, ⅎ 22/17–59–22) can be purchased here or at travel agencies. For local traffic information, call **Trafikanten** (☎ 22/17–70–30 or 177).

By Car

Route E18 connects Oslo with Göteborg, Sweden (by ferry between Sandefjord and Strömstad, Sweden); Copenhagen, Denmark (by ferry between Kristiansand and Hirtshals, Denmark); and Stockholm directly overland. The land route from Oslo to Göteborg is the E6. All streets and roads leading into Oslo have toll booths a certain distance from the city center, forming an "electronic ring." The toll is NKr 12 and was implemented to reduce pollution downtown. If you have the correct amount in change, drive through one of the lanes marked "Mynt." If you don't, or if you need a receipt, use the "Manuell" lane.

By Plane

SAS (☎ 810/03–300) is the main carrier, with both international and domestic flights. The main domestic carriers are **Braathens SAFE** (☎ 67/58–60–00) and **Widerøe** (☎ 67/11–14–60).

Other major airlines serving Gardermoen include **British Airways** (☎ 22/82–20–00), **Air France** (64/81–05–00), **Delta Air Lines** (☎ 22/41–56–00), **Finnair** (☎ 81/00–11–00), **Icelandair** (☎ 22/03–40–50), **KLM** (☎ 67/58–38–00), and **Lufthansa** (☎ 23/35–54–00).

Gardermoen Airport (☎ 63/97–84–90), 37 km (23 mi) north of the city, became Oslo's primary airport in October 1998, replacing the former international airport, Fornebu. Due to frequently poor area weather conditions, flights out of Gardermoen are often delayed by ice and fog. Always check ahead with your airline the status of your flight.

Between the Airport and Downtown: Gardermoen Airport is a 50-minute car ride via the E6 from Oslo's city center. From Oslo S Station, it's a 19-minute ride by Flytogen (express train), with six trains scheduled per hour (4:40 AM–1:16 AM).

Flybussen (☎ 815/44–444; NKr 65; *to Oslo* weekdays and Sun. 7:30 AM–11:30 PM, Sat. 7:30 AM–11 PM; *to Gardermoen* weekdays 6 AM–9:40 PM, Sat. 6 AM–7:40 PM, Sun. 6 AM–9:50 PM) departs from its terminal under Galleri Oslo shopping center every 10–15 minutes and reaches Gardermoen approximately 40 minutes later. Another bus departs from the SAS Scandinavia Hotel. Between the two buses, there are stops at the central train station as well as at Stortinget, Nationaltheatret, and near Aker Brygge. There is also a bus that departs Galleri Oslo for Gardermoen daily; the trip takes about 40 minutes. Call for specific departure times.

There is a taxi line at the front of the airport. By taxi the trip takes about 50 minutes and is extremely expensive, upwards of 600 Kroner (US $100), so try to catch the Express Train. All taxi reservations should be made through the **Oslo Taxi Central** (☎ 22/38–80–90; dial 1 for direct reservation) no less than 20 minutes before pickup time.

By Train

Long-distance trains arrive at and leave from **Oslo S Station** (☎ 22/17–14–00), whereas most suburban commuter trains use **Nationaltheatret** or **Oslo S.** Commuter cars reserved for monthly pass holders are marked with a large black "M" on a yellow circle. Trains marked "C," or InterCity, offer such upgraded services as breakfast and "office cars" with phones and power outlets, for an added fee.

Getting Around

Most public transportation starts running by 5:30 AM, with the last run just after midnight. On weekends there's night service on certain routes. Tickets on all public transportation within Oslo cost NKr 20 with a one-hour transfer, whereas tickets that cross communal boundaries have different rates. It pays to buy a pass or a multiple-travel card, which includes transfers. A one-day *dags kort* (day card) costs NKr 40, and a seven-day pass costs NKr 130. A *flexikort*, available at post offices, tourist information offices, T-bane stations, and on some routes for NKr 110, is good for eight trips by subway, bus, or trikk (tram) with one-hour transfers. Oslo Sporveier operates most modes of transport in the city, including tram, bus, underground, train, and boat. **Trafikanten** (✉ Jernbanetorget, ☎ 22/17–70–30 or 177), the information office for public transportation, is open weekdays 7 AM–11 PM, weekends 8 AM–11 PM.

The **Oslo Card** offers unlimited travel on all public transport in greater Oslo as well as free admission to museums, sightseeing attractions, and the race track, as well as discounts at various stores and cinemas (May–July). A one-day Oslo Card costs NKr 150, a two-day card NKr 220, and a three-day card NKr 250. Children's cards cost NKr 50, NKr 60, and NKr 70, and a family card costs NKr 350. It can be purchased at tourist information offices, hotels, and central post offices. The Oslo Package, available through the same office, combines a four-day Oslo Card with a discount on local accommodations (☞ Lodging, *above*).

By Bus
About 20 bus lines, including six night buses on weekends, serve the city. Most stop at Jernbanetorget opposite Oslo S Station. Tickets can be purchased from the driver.

By Car
If you plan to do any amount of driving in Oslo, buy a copy of the *Stor Oslo* map, available at bookstores and gasoline stations. It may be a small city, but one-way streets and few exit ramps on the expressway make it very easy to get lost.

Oslo Card holders can park for free in city-run street spots or at reduced rates in lots run by the city (P-lots), but pay careful attention to time limits and be sure to ask at the information office exactly where the card is valid. Parking is very difficult in the city—many places have one-hour limits and can cost up to NKr 25 per hour. Instead of individual parking meters in P-lots, you'll find one machine that dispenses validated parking tickets to display in your car windshield. Travelers with disabilities with valid parking permits from their home country are allowed to park free and with no time limit in spaces reserved for those with disabilities.

By Ferry
A ferry to Hovedøya and other islands in the harbor basin leaves from Vippetangen, behind Akershus Castle (take Bus 29 from Jernbanetorget or walk along the harbor from Aker Brygge). These are great spots for picnics and short hikes. From April through September, ferries run between Rådhusbrygge 3, in front of City Hall, and Bygdøy, the western peninsula, where many of Oslo's major museums are located. There is also ferry service from Aker Brygge to popular summer beach towns along the fjord's coast, including Drøbak (☞ East of the Oslo Fjord *in* Chapter 3).

By Streetcar/Trikk
Eight trikk (tram) lines serve the city. All stop at Jernbanetorget opposite Oslo S Station. Tickets can be purchased from the driver.

By Subway/T-bane
Oslo has seven T-bane lines, which converge at Stortinget station. The four eastern lines all stop at Tøyen before branching off, whereas the four western lines run through Majorstuen before emerging above-

ground for the rest of their routes to the northwestern suburbs. Tickets can be purchased at the stations. Get a free map, "Sporveiens hovedkart," of Oslo's extensive public transportation system at post offices, Trafikanten, and most centrally located stations. It is undoubtedly the best public transport map of Oslo for tourists.

By Taxi

All city taxis are connected with the central dispatching office (☎ 22/38–80–90), which can take up to 30 minutes to send one during peak hours. Cabs can be ordered from 20 minutes to 24 hours in advance. (If you leave a cab waiting after you've sent for one, there is an additional fee added to your fare.) Special transport, including vans and cabs equipped for people with disabilities, can be ordered (☎ 22/38–80–90; then dial 1 for direct reservations, 2 for advance reservations, 3 for information, and 4 if you have special needs). Taxi stands are located all over town, usually alongside Narvesen kiosks, and are listed in the telephone directory under "Taxi" or "Drosjer."

It is possible to hail a cab on the street, but cabs are not allowed to pick up passengers within 100 yards of a stand. It is not unheard of to wait for more than an hour at a taxi stand in the wee hours of the morning, after everyone has left the bars. A cab with its roof light on is available. Rates start at NKr 18 for hailed or rank cabs, NKr 55 for ordered taxis, depending on the time of day.

Contacts and Resources

Currency Exchange

After normal banking hours, money can be changed at a few places. The bank at **Oslo S Station** is open June–September, daily 8 AM–11 PM; October–May, weekdays 8–7:30, Saturday 10–5. **Oslo Gardermoen Airport** has automatic currency-exchange machines open 24 hours. All post offices exchange money. **Oslo Central Post Office** (⊠ Dronningensgt. 15) is open weekdays 8–6, Saturday 9–3.

Doctors and Dentists

Doctors: Norway's largest private clinic, **Volvat Medisinske Senter** (⊠ Borgenvn. 2A, ☎ 22/95–75–00) is near the Borgen or Majorstuen T-bane stations, not far from Frogner Park. It is open weekdays 8 AM–10 PM, weekends 10–10. **Oslo Akutten** (⊠ N. Vollgt. 8, ☎ 22/00–81–60) is an emergency clinic downtown, near Stortinget. **Centrum Legesenter** (⊠ Fritjof Nansens Pl., ☎ 22/41–41–20) is a small, friendly clinic across from City Hall.

Dentists: For emergencies only, **Oslo Kommunale Tannlegevakt** (⊠ Kolstadgt. 18, ☎ 22/67–30–00) at Tøyen Senter is open evenings and weekends. **Oslo Private Tannlegevakt** (⊠ Hansteens Gt. 3, ☎ 22/44–46–36), near the American Embassy, is a private clinic open seven days a week.

Embassies

U.S. (⊠ Drammensvn. 18, ☎ 22/44–85–50). **Canada** (⊠ Oscars Gt. 20, ☎ 22/99–53–00). **U.K.** (⊠ Thomas Heftyes Gt. 8, ☎ 22/55–24–00).

Emergencies

Police: ☎ 112 or 22/66–90–50. **Fire:** ☎ 110 or 22/11–44–55. **Ambulance:** ☎ 113 or 22/11–70–80. **Car Rescue:** ☎ 22/23–20–85. **Emergency Rooms: Oslo Legevakt** (⊠ Storgt. 40, ☎ 22/11–70–70), the city's public and thus less expensive, but slower, hospital, is near the Oslo S Station and is open 24 hours. **Volvat Medisinske Senter** (⊠ Borgenvn. 2A,

☎ 22/95–75–00) operates an emergency clinic 8 AM–10 PM weekdays, 10–10 weekends.

Guided Tours

Tickets for all tours are available from Tourist Information at Vestbanen (☞ Visitor Information, *below*) and at the Oslo S Station. Tickets for bus tours can be purchased on the buses. All tours, except HMK's Oslo Highlights tour (☞ *below*), operate during summer only.

Dogsled Tours: For a fast and exciting experience, tour the marka by dogsled. Both lunch and evening tours are available. Contact **Norske Sledehundturer** (✉ Einar Kristen Aas, 1514 Moss, ☎ 69/27–56–40, FAX 69/27–37–86).

Forest Tours: Tourist Information at Vestbanen can arrange four- to eight-hour motor safaris through the forests surrounding Oslo (☎ 22/83–00–50).

Orientation: HMK Sightseeing (✉ Hegdehaugsvn. 4, ☎ 22/20–82–06) offers several bus tours in and around Oslo. Tours leave from the Norway Information Center at Vestbanen; combination boat-bus tours depart from Rådhusbrygge 3, the wharf in front of City Hall. **Båtservice Sightseeing** (✉ Rådhusbryggen 3, ☎ 22/20–07–15) has a bus tour, five cruises, and one combination tour.

Personal Guides: Tourist Information at Vestbanen can provide an authorized city guide for your own private tour. **OsloTaxi** (✉ Trondheimsvn. 100, ☎ 22/38–80–70) also gives private tours.

Sailing: Norway Yacht Charter (✉ H. Heyerdahls Gt. 1, ☎ 22/42–64–98) arranges sailing or yacht tours and dinner cruises for groups of five people to 600.

Sleigh Rides: Vangen Skistue (✉ Laila and Jon Hamre, Fjell, 1404 Siggerud, ☎ 64/86–54–81) will arrange an old-fashioned sleigh ride through Oslomarka, the wooded area surrounding the city. In summertime, they switch from sleighs to carriages.

Street Train: Starting at noon and continuing at 45-minute intervals until 10 PM, the Oslo Train, which looks like a chain of dune buggies, leaves Aker Brygge for a 30-minute ride around the town center. The train runs daily in summer. Ask at the Norway Information Center (☞ Visitor Information, *below*) for departure times.

Walking: Organized walking tours are listed in *What's on in Oslo*, available from Tourist Information and at most hotels.

Late-Night Pharmacies

Jernbanetorgets Apotek (✉ Jernbanetorget 4B, ☎ 22/41–24–82), across from Oslo S Station, is open 24 hours. **Sfinxen Apotek** (✉ Bogstadvn. 51, ☎ 22/46–34–44), near Frogner Park, is open weekdays from 8:30 AM to 9 PM, Saturdays from 8:30 AM to 8 PM, and Sundays from 5 PM to 8 PM.

Travel Agencies

Winge Reisebureau (✉ Karl Johans Gt. 33/35, ☎ 22/00–45–90) is the agent for American Express—here you can cash traveler's checks. An **American Express** office is near the Rådhuset (✉ Fritjof Nansens pl. 6, ☎ 22/98–37–35). **Bennett Reisebureau** (✉ Linstowsgt. 6, ☎ 22/59–78–00) is a business travel agency. **Kilroy Travels Norway** (✉ Universitetssenteret, Blindern, ☎ 22/85–32–40; or Nedre Slottsgt. 23, ☎ 22/42–01–20) distributes ISIC cards for students and GO cards for people younger than 25.

Visitor Information

The main tourist office, the **Norway Information Center** (☎ 22/83–00–50 from outside Norway; or the local number, ☎ 82/06–01–00, which is a toll call), is in the old Vestbanen railway station. The hours are as follows: spring and fall 9–6; summer 9–8; winter 9–4. The office at the main railway station, **Sentralstasjonen** (✉ Jernbanetorget, no phone) is open daily 8 AM–11 PM; during winter the office takes a break from 3 PM to 4:30 PM. Look for the big, round blue-and-green signs marked with a white I. Information about the rest of the country can be obtained from **NORTRA** (✉ Nortravel Marketing, Postboks 2893, Solli, 0230 Oslo, ☎ 22/92–52–00, FAX 22/56–05–05).

3 SIDE TRIPS FROM OSLO

If you've got a weakness for the water and things maritime, getting out of Oslo to the windswept fjord beaches might be a good idea. The area northwest of Oslo draws many visitors to its green, hilly countryside. No matter which way you head, you'll find plenty to do.

Henie-Onstad Kunstsenter and Bærums Verk

❶ The **Henie-Onstad Kunstsenter** (Henie-Onstad Art Center) is just outside of Oslo, about 12 km (7 mi) southwest on E18. This modern art center resulted from a union between Norway's famous skater Sonja Henie and Norwegian shipping magnate Niels Onstad. Henie had a shrewd head for money and marriage—her third was to Onstad. They put together a fine collection of early 20th-century art, with important works by Lèger, Munch, Picasso, Bonnard, and Matisse. Henie died in 1969, but she still skates her way through many a late-night movie. The three-time Olympic gold-medal winner was the first to realize the potential of the ice show, and her technical assistant, Frank Zamboni, has been immortalized by the ice-finishing machine he developed just for her, the Zamboni. Buses 151, 152, and 251 from Oslo S Station stop near the grounds. ⊠ *1311 Høvikodden,* ☎ *67/80–48–80.* 🎟 *NKr 50.* ☉ *Tues.–Thurs. 10–9, Fri.–Mon. 11–6.*

One of Oslo's fashionable suburbs, Bærum is about 20 minutes from the city. The area is mostly residential, but along the banks of the Lomma River you'll find charming **Bærums Verk.** In the 1960s, the owners of the Bærums Verk iron foundry fixed up their old industrial town and made it into a historical site. Created in the 17th century after iron ore was discovered in the region, the ironworks of Bærum quickly became the country's primary iron source. Anna Krefting, a woman who ran the works during the 18th century, believed that workers who spent their days and nights in the foundry should live there as well and be protected by it. The ironworks of Bærum thus became a village in its own right.

❷ As you explore the beautifully restored village, you'll first notice the cramped wooden cottages lining **Verksgata** where the workers once lived. Notice that the doors are in the back of the buildings; this was in case a fire from the works spread through the main street. Crafts makers now lease space in the former living quarters. Here you can purchase wares from a doll maker, a glass blower, a carpenter, a chocolatier, and an embroiderer.

Cross the Lomma River to the entrance of the **Ovnmuseet** (Stove Museum), which displays centuries-old cast-iron stoves in the basement of the iron foundry's enormous smelter. Bærums Verk stoves were exported for centuries and still serve as antique fireplaces in many Oslo homes and service establishments. From Oslo, follow E16 in the direction of Hønefoss. Veer north on Route 168, following signs to Bærums Verk Senteret until you reach the tourist information office. ⊠ *Verksgt. 8B, Boks 39, 1353 Bærum,* ☎ *67/13–00–18 (information office).* ☉ *Verksgata weekdays 10–6, Sat. 10–3; some shops open Sun. Stove Museum weekends noon–3. Other times on request.*

NEED A BREAK?	Stop in at **Pannekake Huset** (The Pancake House, ⊠ Verksgt. 9, ☎ 67/15–07–02) for sweet or salty Dutch-style crepes and a cherry beer or hot chocolate. It's open Sunday–Monday noon–8 and Saturday noon–7.

Dining

$$$ **✕ Værtshuset Bærums Verk.** Norway's oldest standing restaurant, **★** this spot is a must on any itinerary that includes the neighboring iron works. The inn opened in 1640 and was a frequented stop on the "King's" road from Oslo to Bergen. Restored in 1987, it is now one of Norway's finest restaurants. Low ceilings, pastel-painted wooden floors, shiny pewter tableware, and the tick-tock of a grandfather clock in the dining room all create the impression that you are walking into 19th-century Scandinavia. Each room has a charm of its own,

Oslo Fjord

from the quiet, oblong Doctor's Room to the rustic kitchen with a blazing fire. Perhaps the most innovative menu of the year, which lasts only three days in March, is one modeled after the famous meal served in the film *Babette's Feast,* complete with a faux turtle soup (it is illegal to hunt turtles in Norway), blinis, and quail. ⊠ *Vertshusvn. 10, Brums Verk,* ☎ *67/80–02–0. AE, DC, MC, V. No lunch.*

East of the Oslo Fjord

The eastern side of the Oslo Fjord is summer-vacation country for many Norwegians, who retreat to cabins on the water during July. The towns have developed facilities to cater to them and brag that they inhabit the "sunny" side of the fjord.

Many towns along the fjord offer history and culture as well as a place to bathe. Viking ruins and inscriptions, fortified towns, and bohemian 19th-century artists' colonies provide just a glimpse into the region's rich past.

Some of the towns mentioned can easily be visited as day trips from Oslo. Roads can be winding, though, so you might want to devote several days to exploring the area. Note that ferries shuttle cars and people back and forth between the archipelago islands and either side of the fjord, so it is possible to combine this tour with the West of the Oslo Fjord (☞ *below*) and make a complete circle without backtracking.

Drøbak

3 *35 km (21 mi) south of Oslo.*

Mention the summer resort town of Drøbak to many Norwegians, and strangely enough, they'll start talking about Father Christmas. Although there is some question as to where the *Julenisse* (literally,

"Christmas elf") came from, Norwegians claim—at least his adopted home—is here in Drøbak.

Norwegian legend says that Julenisse is one of many elves who live in the woods and have magical powers. This Julenisse, who has established his own post office, **Julenissens Posthuset** in Drøbak, responds to nearly 30,000 letters a year from children all over the world, the majority of which come from Japan. ⊠ *Julenissen, 1440 Drøbak.*

The inviting **Tregaardens Julehus** (Christmas House) dominates the town's central square. Just around the corner from the post office, this 1876 house was once a mission for seafarers unable to reach Oslo because the fjord was frozen over. Now it sells Christmas wares and gifts such as wooden dolls and mice made of cloth—all handmade by Eva Johansen, the store's creator and owner. Spin-offs of this ever-so-authentic Christmas shop include Drøbak's gift of a fir tree to the cities of Berlin and Osaka. ⊠ *1440 Drøbak,* ☎ *64/93–41–78.*

NEED A BREAK?	Back on the main square, stop in **Det Gamle Bageri Ost & Vinstue** (The Old Bakery Wine and Cheese Room, ☎ 64/93–21–05) for hearty fare including salmon in a mouthwatering sweet mustard sauce. The timber interior is around 250 years old and the wine list is extensive.

LODGING

$$ 🏨 **Reenskaug Hotel.** The 100-year-old hotel's whitewashed exterior complements the quaintness of the town's main road. ⊠ *Storgt. 32, 1440 Drøbak,* ☎ *64/93–33–60,* FAX *64/93–36–66. 27 rooms. Restaurant, bar, nightclub, meeting rooms. AE, MC, V.*

Son

4 *25 km (15 mi) south of Drøbak.*

You can swim, sail, or sun on the banks of Son (pronounced *soon*), just south of Drøbak. An old fishing and boating village, this resort town has traditionally attracted artists and writers. Artists still flock here, as do city folk in summer. With them comes a rash of activity, which sunbathers on the immense boulders by the water can hear in the distance.

In the summer season, you can count on **Klubben Soon** (☎ 64/95–70–42) for a good mix of disco, jazz, concerts, and stand-up comedy.

Moss

5 *10 km (6 mi) south of Son.*

Although the area has been inhabited since Viking times, Moss gained borough status in the 18th century and is one of the area's main commercial and shipping centers.

OFF THE BEATEN PATH	**GALLERI F15 –** A 5-km (3-mi) ride outside Moss, on the island of Jeløy, is an art center set in an old farm. Exhibits displayed here range from photography to Scandinavian crafts. ⊠ *Alby Gård,* ☎ *69/27–10–33.* 🎟 *NKr 30.* ☉ *June–Sept., Tues.–Sun. 11–7; Oct.–May, Tues.–Sun. 11–5.*

DINING AND LODGING

$$$ ✕🏨 **Refsnes Gods.** Refsnes has one of Norway's best kitchens and a
★ fine wine cellar. Chef Katrine Bjørnstad adds a French touch to traditional Norwegian seafood. The main building dates from 1767, when it was a family estate, but it did not become a hotel until 1971. In the back is a long, tree-lined promenade extending to the shores of the Oslo Fjord. The blue-and-beige rooms are airy and pretty. ⊠ *Godset 5, 1502 Moss,* ☎ *69/*

27–83–00, ⓕⓐⓧ 69/27–83–01. *61 rooms. Restaurant, pool, solarium, fitness room, beach, boating, meeting rooms. AE, DC, MC, V.*

Fredrikstad

❻ *34 km (20 mi) south of Moss.*

Norway's oldest fortified city, Fredrikstad lies peacefully at the mouth of the Glomma, the country's longest river. Its bastions and moat date from the 1600s. The **Gamlebyen** (Old Town) has been preserved and has museums, art galleries, cafés, artisans' workshops, antiques shops, and old bookstores.

The **Fredrikstad Museum** documents the town's history. ☎ 69/30–68– 75. ▩ *NKr 30.* ☽ *May–Sept., daily noon–5.*

Smack in the center of town center lies **Fredrikstad Domskirke** (Fredrikstad Cathedral). Built in 1860 in flamboyant neo-Gothic style, it contains interior decorations by leading Norwegian artists of the time. ☎ 69/30–02–80. ▩ *Free.* ☽ *Tues.–Fri. noon–3.*

Halden

❼ *30 km (18 mi) south of Fredrikstad.*

Halden is practically at the Swedish border, a good enough reason to fortify the town. Norwegians and Swedes had ongoing border disputes, and the most famous skirmish at Fredriksten fortress resulted in the death of King Karl XII in 1718. Few people realize that slavery existed in Scandinavia, but until 1845 there were up to 200 slaves at Fredriksten, mostly workers incarcerated and sentenced to a lifetime of hard labor for trivial offenses.

Fredriksten Festning (✉ Fredriksten Fort, ☎ 69/09–09–80), built on a French star-shaped plan in the late 17th century, is perched on the city's highest point. Inside the fort itself is **Fredriksten Kro**, a good, old-fashioned pub with outdoor seating. ☎ 69/17–52–32. ▩ *NKr 40.* ☽ *Mid-May–Aug., daily 10–9.*

East of the Oslo Fjord A to Z

ARRIVING AND DEPARTING

By Boat: A ferry links Drøbak, on the east side of the fjord, with Hurum, on the west side just north of Horten. Contact Drøbak Turistinformasjon (☞ *below*) for schedule information.

By Bus: Bus 541 from outside Oslo S Station to Drøbak affords great glimpses of the fjord (and its bathers). The trip takes an hour, and buses depart hourly at ten minutes past the hour during the week, with reduced service weekends. Bus 100 (E6 Ekspress) departs every three hours during the day, stopping at Svindsen where you can catch a local bus to Halden. Contact **Nor-Way Bussekspress** (☎ 22/33–01–90 or 815/ 44–444 (works only inside Norway)) for schedules.

By Car: Follow Route E18 southeast from Oslo to Route E6. Follow signs to Drøbak and Son. Continue through Moss, following signs to Halden, farther south on E6. The route then takes you north to Sarpsborg, where you can turn left to Fredrikstad.

By Train: Trains for Halden leave from Oslo S Station and take two hours to make the 136-km (85-mi) trip, with stops in Moss, Fredrikstad, and Sarpsborg.

CONTACTS AND RESOURCES

Visitor Information: Drøbak (Drøbak Turistinformasjon, ☎ 64/93– 50–87). **Fredrikstad** (Fredrikstad Turistkontor, ✉ Turistsentret vøstre Brohode and ✉ 1632 Gamle Fredrikstad, ☎ 69/32–03–30 or 69/32– 10–60). **Halden** (Halden Turist Kontor, ✉ Storgt. 6, Box 167, 1751

Halden, ☎ 69/19–09–80). **Moss** (Moss Turistkontor, ⊠ Fleischersgt. 17, 1531 Moss, ☎ 69/25–32–95). **Son** (Son Kystkultursenter, ⊠ 1555 Son, ☎ 64/95–89–20).

West of the Oslo Fjord

Towns lining the western side of the fjord are more industrial on the whole than their neighbors on the eastern side. Still, the western towns have traditionally been some of Norway's oldest and wealthiest, their fortunes derived from whaling and lumbering. Although these activities no longer dominate, their influence is seen in the monuments and in the wood architecture. The area northwest of Oslo draws many visitors to its green, hilly countryside. These once industrial towns are now catering more and more to tourists..

Jevnaker
Follow E16 toward Hønefoss, then follow Rte. 241 to Jevnaker, which is about 70 km (42 mi) northwest of Oslo; it's about a 2-hr drive.

❽ A day trip to Jevnaker combines a drive along the Tyrifjord, where you can see some of the best fjord views in eastern Norway, with a visit to a glass factory that has been in operation since 1762. At **Hadeland Glassverk** you can watch artisans blowing glass, or, if you get there early enough, you can blow your own. Both practical table crystal and one-of-a-kind art glass are produced here, and you can buy (first quality and seconds) at the gift shop, which remains open an hour after the factory closes. The museum and gallery have a collection of 15,000 items, with about 800 on display. Bus 171, marked "Hønefoss," leaves from the university on Karl Johans Gate at seven minutes after the hour. Change in Hønefoss for the Jevnaker bus (it has no number). ⊠ *Rte. 241, Postboks 85, 5320 Jevnaker,* ☎ *61/31–05–55.* ☉ *June–Aug., Mon.–Sat. 9–5, Sun. 11–6; Sept.–May, weekdays 9–3, Sat. 10–3, Sun. noon–5.*

Åmot i Modum
❾ *Take Rte. 35 south, along the Tyrifjord. If you are coming from the E18, take Rte. 11 west to Hokksund, and Rte. 35 to Åmot. Then turn onto Rte. 287 to Sigdal. 70 km (45 mi) from Oslo.*

The small village of Åmot is famous for its cobalt mines. The blue mineral was used to make dyes for the world's glass and porcelain indus-☞ **❿** tries. The **Blaafarveværket** (Cobalt Works) was founded in 1773 to extract cobalt from the Modum mines. Today the complex is a museum and a national park. A permanent collection displays old cobalt-blue glass and porcelain. For children there's a petting farm, and there's a restaurant that serves Norwegian country fare. Up the hill from the art complex is Haugfossen, the highest waterfall in eastern Norway. Outdoor concerts are held on the grounds throughout the summer. The bus to Modum leaves from the university on Karl Johans Gate at 9:45 AM on Tuesday, Thursday, and Saturday. ⊠ *Rte. 507, 3370 Morud,* ☎ *32/78–49–00.* ☜ *Special exhibitions NKr 50; cobalt works free. Guided tours in English.* ☉ *Late May–Sept., daily 10–6.*

Drammen
⓫ *40 km (25 mi) from Oslo; 45 km (27 mi) south of Åmot i Modum.*

Drammen, a timber town and port for 500 years, is an industrial city of 50,000 on the Simoa River at its outlet to a fjord. It was the main harbor for silver exported from the Kongsberg mines. Today cars are imported into Norway through Drammen.

The **Spiralen** (Spiral), Drammen's main attraction, is a corkscrew road tunnel that makes six complete turns before emerging about 600 ft above, on Skansen Ridge. The entrance is behind the hospital by way of a well-marked road. ☒ *NKr 10 parking fee.*

Drammens Museum, a small county museum, is on the grounds of Marienlyst Manor, which dates from 1750. Glass from the Nøstetan-gen factory, which was in operation between 1741 and 1777, and a collection of rustic painted pieces are on display here. Its newer addition looks like a small temple set in the manor garden. ☒ *Konnerudgt. 7,* ☎ *32/20–09–30.* ☒ *NKr 30.* ☉ *May–Oct., Tues.–Sat. 11–3, Sun. 11–5; Nov.–Apr., Tues.–Sun. 11–3.*

DINING AND LODGING

$$ ✕ **Spiraltoppen Café.** At the top of Bragernes Hill, this café offers excellent views and generous portions of Norwegian food. Try the meatballs with stewed cabbage or the open-face sandwiches. ☒ *Bragernesåsen, Drammen,* ☎ *32/83–78–15. Reservations not accepted. AE, DC, MC, V.*

$$ ☖ **Rica Park.** As with all Rica hotels, the atmosphere is relaxed and the rooms are comfortable. The nightclub at this hotel is popular with the over-30 crowd. ☒ *Gamle Kirkepl. 3, 3019 Drammen,* ☎ *32/83–82–80,* FAX *32/89–32–07. 98 rooms. 2 restaurants, 2 bars, nightclub. AE, DC, MC, V.*

Horten

⑫ *30 km (17 mi) south of Drammen.*

Off the main route south, the coastal village of Horten has some distinctive museums. The town was once an important naval station and still retains the officers' candidates school.

The **Marinemuseet** (Royal Norwegian Navy Museum), built in 1853 as a munitions warehouse, displays relics from the nation's naval history. Outside is the world's first torpedo boat, from 1872, plus some one-person submarines from World War II. ☒ *Karl Johans Vern,* ☎ *33/03–33–97.* ☒ *Free.* ☉ *May–Oct., weekdays 10–4, weekends noon–4; Nov.–Apr., weekdays 10–3, Sun. noon–4.*

The **Redningsselskapets Museum** (Museum of the Sea Rescue Association) traces the history of ship-rescue operations. The organization has rescued more than 320,000 people since it was founded more than 100 years ago. ☒ *Strandpromenaden 8, near Horten Tourist Office,* ☎ *33/04–70–66.* ☒ *NKr 10.* ☉ *Guided tours by appointment.*

The **Preus Fotomuseum** houses one of the world's largest photographic collections. Exhibits include a turn-of-the-century photographer's studio and a tiny camera that was strapped to a pigeon for early aerial photography. ☒ *Langgt. 82,* ☎ *33/04–27–37.* ☒ *NKr 30.* ☉ *May–Aug., daily 10–4; Sept.–Apr., daily 10:30–2.*

Just beyond Horten, between the road and the sea, lies a Viking grave site, **Borrehaugene,** with five earth and two stone mounds and the 12th-century Borre church.

Åsgårdstrand

⑬ *10 km (6 mi) south of Horten.*

The coastal town of Åsgårdstrand was known as an artists' colony for outdoor painting at the turn of the century. Edvard Munch painted *Girls on the Bridge* here and earned a reputation as a ladies' man. Munch spent seven summers at **Munchs lille hus** (little house), now a museum. ☒ *Munchsgt.,* ☎ *33/08–21–31 (Horten Tourist Office).* ☒ *NKr 10.* ☉ *May, Sept., weekends 1–7; Jun.–Aug., Tues.–Sun. 11–7.*

En Route Travel south from Åsgårdstrand toward Tønsberg and you'll pass **Slagen,** the site where the Oseberg Viking ship, dating from around AD 800, was found. (It's now on display at Vikingskiphuset in Oslo.) Look for the mound where it was buried as you pass Slagen's church.

Tønsberg
⑭ *11 km (6½ mi) south of Åsgårdstrand.*

According to the sagas, Tønsberg is Norway's oldest settlement, founded in 871. The town's fortunes took a turn for the worse after the Reformation, and the city did not recover until shipping and whaling brought it into prominence in the 18th century. Little remains of Tønsberg's early structures, although the ruins at **Slottsfjellet** (Castle Hill), by the train station, include parts of the city wall, the remains of a church from around 1150, and a 13th-century brick citadel, the **Tønsberghus.** Other medieval remains are below the cathedral and near Storgata 17.

The **Vestfold Fylkesmuseum** (County Museum), north of the railroad station, houses a small Viking ship, several whale skeletons, and some inventions. There's an open-air section, too. ⊠ *Farmannsvn. 30,* ☎ *33/31–24–18.* ⊡ *NKr 20.* ☉ *Mid-May–mid-Sept., Mon.–Sat. 10–5, Sun. noon–5; mid-Sept.–mid-May, weekdays 10–2.*

Sandefjord
⑮ *125 km (78 mi) south of Oslo; 25 km (15 mi) south of Tønsberg.*

Once the whaling capital of the world and possibly Norway's wealthiest city at the turn of the century, Sandefjord celebrated its 150th birthday in 1995. Now the whales are gone and all that remains of that trade is a monument to it. Thanks to shipping and other industries, however, the city is still rich and draws many illustrious Norwegians to its beaches, such as film actress Liv Ullmann, who has a cottage here.

Kommandør Christensens Hvalfangstmuseum (Commander Christensen's Whaling Museum) traces the development of the industry from small primitive boats to huge floating factories. An especially arresting display chronicles whaling in the Antarctic. ⊠ *Museumsgt. 39,* ☎ *33/48–46–50.* ⊡ *NKr 20.* ☉ *May–Sept., daily 11–5; Oct.–Apr., daily 11–3.*

DINING AND LODGING

$$–$$$ ✕ **Ludl's Gourmet Odd Ivar Solvold.** The Austrian chef, Ludl, shows
★   Norwegians that there's more in the sea than cod and salmon. Ludl is a champion of the local cuisine, and specials may include ocean catfish, stuffed sole, a fish roulade, and lobster. Ludl's desserts are equally good, especially the cloudberry marzipan basket. ⊠ *Rådhusgt. 7, Sandefjord,* ☎ *33/46–27–41. AE, DC, MC, V.*

$$–$$$$ ▦ **Rica Park Hotel.** It *looks* formal for a hotel built right on the water in a resort town, but there's no dress code. The decor is 1960s style, but surprisingly, it doesn't seem passé. Ask for one of the newer rooms. ⊠ *Strandpromenaden 9, 3200 Sandefjord,* ☎ *33/46–55–50,* ℻ *33/46–79–00. 174 rooms, 8 suites. 2 restaurants, bar, indoor pool, health club, nightclub, convention center. AE, DC, MC, V.*

$–$$$ ▦ **Comfort Home Hotel Atlantic.** The Atlantic Home was built in 1914, when Sandefjord was a whaling center. The history of whaling is traced in exhibits in glass cases and in pictures throughout the hotel. There's no restaurant, but the hotel provides *aftens,* a supper consisting of bread and cold cuts, plus hot soup and light beer, as part of the room rate. A coffeemaker and waffle iron are at your disposal at all times. ⊠ *Jernbanealleen 33, 3201 Sandefjord,* ☎ *33/46–80–00,* ℻ *33/42–80–00. 72 rooms. Lobby lounge, sauna. AE, DC, MC, V.*

West of the Oslo Fjord A to Z

ARRIVING AND DEPARTING

By Boat: The most luxurious and scenic way to see the region is by boat: there are guest marinas at just about every port.

By Bus: Because train service to towns south of Drammen is infrequent, bus travel is the best alternative to cars. Check with **Nor-Way Bussekspress** (☎ 22/17–52–90) for schedules.

By Car: Route E18 south from Oslo follows the coast to the towns of this region.

By Train: Take a suburban train from Nationaltheatret or trains from Oslo S Station to reach Horten, Tønsberg, and Sandefjord.

CONTACTS AND RESOURCES

Visitor Information: Blaafarveværket (☎ 32/78–49–00). **Drammen** (Drammen Kommunale Turistinformasjonskontor, ✉ Bragernes Torg 6, 3008 Drammen, ☎ 32/80–62–10). **Hadeland** (☎ 61/31–10–00). **Horten and Åsgårdstrand** (Horten Turist Kontor, ✉ Tollbugt. 1a, 3187 Horten, ☎ 33/03–17–08). **Sandefjord** (Sandefjord Reiselivsforening, ✉ Torvet, 3201 Sandfjord, ☎ 33/46–05–90). **Tønsberg** (Tønsberg og Omland Reiselivslag, ✉ Nedre Langgt. 36 B, 3110 Tønsberg, ☎ 33/31–02–20).

4 TELEMARK AND THE SETESDAL VALLEY

The interior region of southern Norway, Telemark and the Setesdal Valley, lies in the shadow of the famed beaches and fjords of the coast, but certainly doesn't lack majestic scenery—forested hills meet deeply etched valleys, and lakes stretch across the serene countryside.

ALAND OF WIDE-OPEN VISTAS and deep forests, the Telemark region is veined with swift-flowing streams and scattered with peaceful lakes—a natural setting so powerful and silent that a few generations ago, trolls were the only reasonable explanation for what lurked in, or for that matter plodded through, the shadows. These legendary creatures, serious Norwegians explain, boast several heads and a couple of noses (used to stir their porridge, of course) and can grow to the size of a village. Fortunately for humans, however, they turn to stone in sunlight.

Telemark was the birthplace of downhill skiing as well as the birthplace of many ancestors to Norwegian-Americans, for the poor farmers of the region were among the first to emigrate to the United States during the 19th century.

The quiet Setesdal Valley stretches north–south next to Telemark and sits atop rich mineral resources. The region is rich with history and is well known for its colorful traditional costume (bunard) and the intricate silver jewelry that decorates it.

Kongsberg

16 *84 km (52 mi) southwest of Oslo.*

Kongsberg, with 20,000 people today, was Norway's silver town for more than 300 years. It was here that silver was discovered in its purest form. King Christian IV saw the town's natural potential when he noticed that a cow's horn had rubbed moss off a stone to expose silver. Thereupon, the Danish builder-king began construction of the town. Thus, Norway's first industrial town rose to prominence. The mines are now closed, but the Royal Mint is still going strong.

The **Norsk Bergverksmuseum** (Norwegian Mining Museum), in the old smelting works, documents the development of silver mining and exhibits pure silver, gold, emeralds, and rubies from other Norwegian mines. The **Royal Mint Museum,** in the same building, is a treasure trove for coin collectors, with a nearly complete assemblage of Norwegian coins. Children can pan for silver during summer. The **Kongsberg Ski Museum,** also part of the mining complex, houses exhibits of ancient skis and 23 Olympic and World Championship medals won by Kongsberg skiers. ⊠ *Hyttegt. 3,* ☎ *32/73–32–00.* ☒ *NKr 40.* ☉ *Mid-May–late May and mid-Aug.–late Aug., daily 10–4; June–mid-Aug., weekdays 10–6, weekends 10–4; Sept., daily noon–4; Oct.–mid-May, Sun. noon–4. Otherwise, by appointment.*

OFF THE
BEATEN PATH
SØLVGRUVENE – In Saggrenda, about 8 km (5 mi) outside Kongsberg toward Notodden, you can visit silver mines. Guided mine tours include a 2½-km (1½-mi) ride on the mine train into Kongensgruve (the King's mine) and a ride on the first personnel elevator. The temperature in the mine is about 6°C (43°F) and the tour takes about one hour and 20 minutes, so dress accordingly. ☎ *32/76–53–39.* ☒ *NKr 55.* ☉ *Tours mid-May–June and mid-Aug.–late Aug., daily at 11, 12:30, 2; July–mid-Aug., daily at 11, 12:30, 2, 3:30; Sept.–mid-May, Sun. at 2.*

Kongsberg Kirke (Kongsberg Church), finished in 1761, was built during the heyday of the silver mines, with an impressive gilded Baroque altar, organ, and pulpit all on one wall. It seats 3,000. The royal box and the galleries separated the gentry and mine owners from the workers. Organ concerts are given Wednesdays at 6 in summer. ☎ *32/73–*

19–02. ✉ *Adults NKr 30., Children NKr20.* ⊙ *Mid-May–Aug., week-days 10–5; Sept.–mid-May, Tues.–Fri. 10–2. Sun. services at 11. Additional tours by appointment.*

The Arts

In the last week of June jazz fans descend on Kongsberg for its annual **jazz festival.** Contact the tourist office (☞ *below*) for information.

Dining and Lodging

$$ ✕ **Gamle Kongsberg Kro.** This café next to the waterfall at Nybrofossen offers hearty Norwegian dishes at moderate prices. There's a miniature golf course nearby. ✉ *Thornesvn. 4,* ☎ *32/73–16–33,* ✉ *32/73–26–03. DC, MC, V.*

$–$$ 🏨 **Quality Grand Hotel.** A statue of Kongsberg's favorite son, Olympic ski jumper Birger Ruud, stands in the park in front of this modern, centrally located hotel. ✉ *Kristian Augustsgt. 2, 3600,* ☎ *32/73–20–29,* ✉ *32/73–41–29. 97 rooms, 2 suites. 2 restaurants, 2 bars, indoor pool, exercise room, nightclub, meeting rooms. AE, DC, MC, V.*

Skien

⑰ *88 km (55 mi) south of Kongsberg on Rtes. 32 and 36.*

Best known as the birthplace of playwright Henrik Ibsen, Skien, with a population of 50,000, is the capital of the Telemark region. Ibsen's hometown celebrates its favorite son every August with the **Ibsen-Kultur-festival** (✉ Skien Tourist Office, Box 192, 3701 Skien, ☎ 35/58–19–10), which includes concerts as well as drama.

The **Fylkesmuseet** (County Museum), a manor house from 1780, has a collection of Ibsen memorabilia, including his study and bedroom and the "blue salon" from his Oslo flat (other interiors are at the Norsk Folkemuseum in Oslo). Also on display is Telemark-style folk art, including rosemaling   arving. ⌧ *Øvregt. 41,* ☎ *35/52–35–94.* ⌧ *NKr 40,* ⊙ *Gar   ay–Aug., daily 10–10; museum mid-   –Aug., daily 10–6; Se␣   10–6.*

Ven␣␣ ␣st as it did whe␣   ␣bsen family lived here from 1835 to 1843. ␣␣   ␣the inspiratio␣ *The Wild Duck.* This house, part of Skien's Cou␣␣ ␣␣um, is 5 km ␣i) northwest of the city. ☎ *35/52–35–94.* ⌧ *NK␣   ⊙ Mid-May–   daily 10–6; Sept., Sun. 10–6.*

Dining and Lodging

$$ ✕ **Boden Spiseri.** Boden serves exce␣   ␣-influenced Norwegian-style food, such as medallions of reind␣   ␣ssert, *Gjoegler Boden*—ice cream with rum, raisins, and a to␣   ␣ginger—is a delight. ⌧ *Landbrygga 5,* ☎ *35/52–61–70. AE, D␣ ␣. V. No lunch.*

$–$$ ⊞ **Rainbow Høyers Hotell.** The old-fashioned quality of the exterior, with cornices and pedimented windows, is reflected in the Høyers's lobby, which is an incongruous mixture of old and new. The rooms are modern and light, thanks to the big windows. ⌧ *Kongensgt. 6, 3700,* ☎ *35/52–05–40,* FAX *35/52–26–08. 69 rooms, 1 suite. Restaurant, bar, meeting rooms. AE, DC, MC, V.*

Notodden

⑱ *68 km (42 mi) northwest of Skien and 35 km (20 mi) west of Kongsberg.*

Notodden today is not much more than a small industrial town (although it's well known for its blues fest). It is believed that the area must have been a prosperous one in the Middle Ages, though, because of the size of the town's stavkirke—85 ft high and 65 ft long.

Heddal Stave Church is Norway's largest. The church dates from the middle of the 12th century and has exceptional stylized animal ornamentation, along with grotesque human heads, on the portals. ☎ *35/02–08–40.* ⌧ *NKr 25.* ⊙ *Mid-May–June and late Aug.–mid-Sept., Mon.–Sat. 10–5; late June–late Aug., Mon.–Sat. 9–7; mid-May–mid-Sept. Sun. 11–7.*

Notodden is famous for its **summer blues festival** in August, which lasts four days and brings in Norwegian and American acts such as the Robert Cray Band. Some acts require reserved tickets, which can be done in advance at any post office in Norway (or call ☎ *75/15–75–16* from outside Norway). For more information contact Notodden tourist information (☞ Telemark and the Setesdal Valley A to Z, *below*).

En Route   Route 37 northwest from Notodden to Rjukan passes the 6,200-ft **Gaustatoppen,** a looming, snow-streaked table of rock popular with hikers.

Rjukan

⑲ *96 km (59 mi) northwest of Notodden.*

The town of Rjukan may not ring a bell, but mention "heavy water," and anyone who lived through World War II or saw the film *The Heroes of Telemark* with Kirk Douglas knows about the sabotage of the heavy water factory there, which thwarted German efforts to develop an atomic bomb. Rjukan's history actually began in the decade between 1907 and 1916, when the population grew from a few hundred to 10,000 because of a different kind of water, hydroelectric power. Norsk Hydro, one of Norway's largest industries, which uses hydroelectric power to manufacture chemicals and fertilizer, was started here.

Heavy water (used in nuclear reactors as a moderator) was produced as a by-product in the manufacture of fertilizer at Vemork, 6 km (4 mi) west of Rjukan along Route 37, where a museum, **Industriarbei-**

dermuseet Vemork, has been built. Exhibits document both the development of hydroelectric power and the World War II events. Every year on the first Saturday in July, the work of the saboteurs is commemorated, but their 8-km (5-mi) path, starting at Rjukan Fjellstue (mountain lodge) and finishing at the museum, is marked and can be followed at any time. ☎ *35/09–51–53.* ✉ *NKr 50.* ☉ *May–mid-Aug., daily 10–6; mid-Aug.–Sept., weekdays 10–4, weekends 11–6; Oct. and March–Apr., Sat. 11–4.*

Rjukan is the site of northern Europe's first cable car, **Krossobanen,** built in 1928 by Hydro to transport people to the top of the mountain. ✉ *NKr20.* ☉ *Mid-Apr.–mid-Sept. Times vary; call Rjukan tourist information for details,* ☎ *35/09–12–90.*

Lodging

$$ 🏨 **Euro Park Hotell.** This small hotel with a traditional family atmosphere is in the center of town. The rooms are decorated in light colors. The restaurant, with the curious name Ammonia, offers a wide selection. ✉ *Sam Eydes Gt. 67, 3660,* ☎ *35/09–02–88,* FAX *35/09–05–05. 39 rooms. Restaurant, bar, pub, nightclub. AE, DC, MC, V.*

$$ 🏨 **Gaustablikk Høyfjellshotell.** Built at the foot of Gaustatoppen near Rjukan, this modern timber hotel is a popular ski resort, with nine downhill slopes and 80 km (50 mi) of cross-country trails. In summer, these marked trails are perfect for walks and hikes. ✉ *3660,* ☎ *35/09–14–22,* FAX *35/09–19–75. 83 rooms, 14 suites. Restaurant, bar, indoor pool, sauna, exercise room. AE, DC, MC, V.*

Morgedal

⓴ *77 km (46 mi) southwest of Rjukan via Åmot.*

In the heart of Telemark is Morgedal, the birthplace of modern skiing, thanks to a persistent Sondre Nordheim, who in the 19th century perfected his skis and bindings and practiced jumping from his roof. His innovations included bindings that close behind the heel and skis that narrow in the middle to facilitate turning. In 1868, after revamping his skis and bindings, he took off for a 185-km (115-mi) trek to Oslo just to prove it could be done. A hundred years ago, skiers used one long pole, held diagonally, much like high-wire artists. Eventually the use of two short poles became widespread, although purists feel that the one-pole version is the "authentic" way to ski. Nordheim's traditional Telemark skiing is now the rage in Norway, though the revival was begun in the United States.

☾ The **Norsk Skieventyr** (Norwegian Skiing Adventure) in Morgedal guides you through the history of the winter sport with life-size exhibits of typical ski cottages and authentic skis and costumes. Displays include the inside of Norway's original and last ski-wax factory where specialists melted a variety of secret ingredients, including cheese, to make uphill and downhill slides smoother. The sport of yore meets its match on the last leg of the exhibit where a multiscreen-panoramic video shows modern-day footage of the don't-try-this-at-home sort. Teenagers in techno-gear and professional ski-trekkers in Telemark-style sweaters zoom around the snow to traditional fiddle music. ✉ *On Rte. 11 between Brunkeberg and Høydalsmo,* ☎ *35/05–42–50.* ✉ *NKr 50.* ☉ *May–mid-June and mid-Aug.–mid-Sept., daily 11–5; mid-June–mid-Aug., daily 9–7; late Sept.–Apr., weekends 11–5.*

Dalen

The Dalen area is the place to hike, bike, and be outdoors. From Skien you can take boat tours on the Telemark waterways, a combination of canals and natural lakes between Skien and either Dalen or Notodden (☞ Notodden, *above*). The trip to Dalen takes you through Ulefoss, where you can leave the boat and visit the neoclassical **Ulefoss Manor** (⊠ Hovedgård, ☏ 35/94–48–36), which dates from 1807. It's open weekdays June through September from 2 PM to 4 PM and Sunday from noon to 3. The historic **Dalen Hotel** (☞ *below*) is worth a peek, whether or not you stay there. A number of royal families have stayed there, and locals are said to think ghosts haunt its creaky wooden walls. *For trips to Dalen, call Telemarkreiser, ☏ 35/90–00–20; for Notodden, contact Telemarksbåtene, ⊠ 3812 Akkerhaugen, ☏ 35/95–82–11, FAX 35/95–82–96.*

Dining and Lodging

$$$ ✕🖬 **Viking Dalen Hotel.** At the end of the Telemark Canals stands this opulent, Victorian "Swiss-style" hotel, complete with dragonhead carvings, stained-glass windows, and a balcony overlooking the stunning entrance hall. ⊠ *3880 Dalen,* ☏ *35/07–70–00,* FAX *35/07–70–11. 38 rooms. Breakfast room, lobby lounges, meeting rooms. AE, V. Closed Christmas–Easter.*

$–$$ 🖬 **Telemarkstunet Natadal Uppigård.** This cluster of 18th-century farmhouses with grass roofs provides an authentic alternative to a hotel stay. Set on a steep mountainside about an hour's drive from Dalen, the cabins could be on display in Oslo's Folkemuseum. Activities here are plentiful, including horseback riding, pond swimming, and strawberry picking—all the Norwegian favorites. A stay in these rustic accommodations is comparable to camping: breakfast, linens, and housekeeping cost extra. The cabins come with kitchenettes but not always individual bathrooms. ⊠ *3841 Flatdal,* ☏ *35/05–23–00,* FAX *35/05–20–30. 3 cabins with room for 21 people; four individual rooms in main house. No credit cards.*

Valle

The Setesdal road, Rte. 39, follows the Otra River downstream and then runs alongside the Byglandsfjord; Valle is 56 km (35 mi) southeast of Dalen.

Near Valle sits **Sylvartun,** a clump of grass-roofed cottages that house a local silversmith's workshop, a jewelry shop, and an art gallery. It's also a cultural center that hosts concerts, displays local crafts, and holds summertime "Setesdal Evenings" at which professional musicians and folk dancers perform while a traditional Norwegian dinner is served. ⊠ *Rte. 39, Nomeland (near Valle),* ☏ *37/93–63–06.* ☉ *Silversmith's shop: May–Oct., Mon.–Sat. 10–6, Sun. 11–6. Folk dances: summer only. Call for opening hours and program schedules.*

OFF THE **SETESDAL MINERAL PARK** – About 97 km (57 mi) south of Valle, just south
BEATEN PATH of Evje on Route 39, in Hornnes is an interesting park where rock formations from Norway and elsewhere are displayed inside a dark mountain. ⊠ 4660 Evje, ☏ 37/93–13–10. 🖭 NKr 60. ☉ Late June–late Aug., daily 10–6.

Telemark and the Setesdal Valley A to Z

Arriving and Departing

BY BUS

The many bus lines that serve the region are coordinated through **NorWay Bussekspress** in Oslo (⊠ Bussterminalen, Galleri Oslo, ☏ 815/44–444, FAX 22/17–59–22).

BY CAR

On Route E18 from Oslo, the drive southwest to Kongsberg takes a little more than an hour. If you arrive by way of the Kristiansand ferry, the drive up Route 37 to Evje will take about an hour as well.

BY TRAIN

The train from Oslo S Station to Kongsberg takes 1 hour and 25 minutes; bus connections to Telemark are available.

Getting Around

BY BUS

Buses in the region rarely run more than twice a day, so get a comprehensive schedule from the tourist office or Nor-Way Bussekspress (☞ *above*) and plan ahead.

BY CAR

Roads in the southern part of the interior region are open and flat, but others are still curvy and mountainous. Route 11 passes through Heddal and Morgedal, and connects with 37, which goes north to Rjukan and south toward Dalen. Route 11 also connects with 37, the main Setesdal road, which goes through Evje and Valle all the way to Kristiansand.

BY TRAIN

The only train service in the southern part of the region is the Oslo–Stavanger line (via Kristiansand).

Contacts and Resources

VISITOR INFORMATION

Kongsberg (✉ Storgt. 35, ☎ 32/73–50–00). **Notodden** (✉ Storgt. 39, ☎ 35/01–20–22). **Rjukan** (✉ Torget 2, ☎ 31/29–60–00). **Skien** (✉ Reiselivets Hus, N. Hjellegt. 18, ☎ 35/95–00–61). **Setesdal** (4660 Evje, ☎ 37/93–14–00).

5 SØRLANDET: ALONG THE COAST

In summer, Oslo's residents migrate to the southern coast to soak up some sunshine. Southern Norway is an outdoor paradise, with a mild summer climate and terrain varying from coastal flatland to inland mountains and forests.

SØRLANDET, OR SOUTHERN NORWAY, is a land of wide beaches toasted by the greatest number of sunny days in Norway, waters warmed by the Gulf Stream, and long, fertile tracts of flatland. Not a people to pass up a minute of sunshine, the Norwegians have sprinkled the south with their hytter and made it their number one domestic holiday spot. Nonetheless, even at the height of summer, you can sail to a quiet skerry or take a solitary walk through the forest.

There's plenty of fish in the rivers and lakes, as well as along the coast. The region is particularly well suited to canoeing, kayaking, rafting, and hiking. Beavers, deer, foxes, and forest birds inhabit the area, so bring binoculars if you'd like to see them more closely.

The coast bordering the Skagerak, the arm of the North Sea separating Norway and Denmark, is lined with small communities stretching from Oslo as far as Lindesnes, which is at the southernmost tip. Sørlandet towns are often called "pearls on a string," and in the dusk of a summer evening, reflections of the white-painted houses on the water have a silvery translucence.

The two chief cities of Norway's south, Kristiansand on the east coast and Stavanger on the west coast, differ sharply. Kristiansand is a resort town, scenic and relaxed, whereas Stavanger, once a fishing center, is now the hub of the oil industry and Norway's most cosmopolitan city. Stavanger has many more good restaurants than other cities of comparable size, thanks to the influx of both foreigners and money. More than 100 restaurants, bars, and cafés offer everything from Thai, Chinese, and Indian to Italian, French, and, of course, Norwegian cooking. Try the restored warehouse area in the harbor for some of the best restaurants.

Between Kristiansand and Stavanger is the coastal plain of Jæren, dotted with prehistoric burial sites and the setting for the works of some of the country's foremost painters.

Numbers in the margin correspond to points of interest on the Telemark and Sørlandet map in chapter 4.

Larvik

㉑ *128 km (79 mi) from Oslo, 19 km (12 mi) south of Sandefjord.*

Larvik is the last of the big whaling towns. It's still a port, but now the traffic is made up of passengers to Fredrikshavn, Denmark.

Kong Haakons Kilde (King Haakon's Spring), also called Farris Kilde (Farris Spring), is Norway's only natural source of mineral water. A spa was built here in 1880, but people now drink the water rather than bathe in it. The spring is near the ferry quays. ⊠ *Fjellvn, 3256,* ☎ *33/12–20–00.* ⊠ *Free.* ◷ *Late June–Aug., weekdays 10–4.*

The noble Gyldenløve family once owned the large estate, **Herregården,** which dates back to 1677. Inside, the furnishings are masterful examples of trompe l'oeil: Scandinavian nobility had to make do with furniture painted to look like marble rather than the real thing. ⊠ *Herregaardssletta 1, 3257,* ☎ *33/13–04–04.* ⊠ *NKr 25.* ◷ *Late May–late Aug., daily noon–5; Sept., Sun. noon–5.*

The **Maritime Museum** is in Larvik's former customs house and chronicles the town's seafaring history. There's heavy coverage of Thor Heyerdahl's voyages, with models of *Kon-Tiki* and *Ra II.* ⊠ *Kirkestredet*

5, ☎ 33/13–04–04. ✉ NKr 25. ☉ *Late June–mid-Aug., daily noon–5; May and Sept., Sun. noon–5.*

<table>
<tr><td>OFF THE
BEATEN PATH</td><td>PORSGRUNN PORSELÆNFABRIK ASA – About 27 km (17 mi) west of Larvik in Porsgrunn is a porcelain factory where you can take a tour and purchase factory seconds. ✉ Porselensgt. 12, ☎ 35/55–00–40. ✉ NKr 20. ☉ Tours weekdays at 10, 11, and 1.</td></tr>
</table>

Dining and Lodging

$$ ✕🏨 **Grand.** The rooms are spotless and the service attentive in this large hotel overlooking the fjord. The restaurant is a good spot to sample the local fish soup and smoked-meat platters—especially at lunch. ✉ *Storgt. 38–40, 3256,* ☎ *33/18–78–00,* 🗚 *33/18–70–45. 88 rooms. Restaurant, bar, pub, dance club, nightclub. AE, DC, MC, V.*

Stavern

㉒ *8 km (5 mi) south of Larvik.*

A popular sailing center today, Stavern was Norway's main naval station between 1750 and 1850, then called Fredriksvern, named for King Fredrik V.

A fine example of Scandinavian Rococo architecture, **Stavern Church** was built in 1756. Its pews were designed so their backs could be folded down to make beds in case the church had to be used as a field hospital in time of war. ✉ *On the water east of town,* ☎ *33/19–99–75.* ☉ *Guided tours by appointment.*

En Route From Stavern to Lyngør, you'll pass through **Kragerø,** a picturesque town with its own small archipelago. Theodor Kittelsen (1857–1914), famous for his drawings of trolls and illustrations of Norwegian fairy tales, lived in Kragerø, and his birthplace is now a museum. The next pearl on the string after Kragerø is Risør, which is just off E18 on the coast. On the first weekend in August the town holds a festival that fills the harbor with beautiful antique boats.

Lyngør

㉓ *18 km (11 mi) south of Risør. To get to Lyngør, follow E18 to the sign for Sørlandsporten (Gateway to the South). Turn off just after the sign and drive 26 km (16 mi) to Lyngørfjorden Marina (☎ 37/16–68–00), where you can take a five-minute water taxi ride for NKr 80.*

Hardly changed since the days of sailing ships, **Lyngør** is idyllic and carless, lined with rows of white-painted houses bearing window boxes filled with pink and red flowers. This island community, on four tiny rocky islands off the coast, is considered by some to be Europe's best-preserved village.

There are no hotels or accommodations on Lyngør itself; however, opposite the island on the mainland is a new resort complex, **Lyngør Porten** (✉ 4912 Gjeving, ☎ 37/18–80–00, 🗚 37/18–80–81), which has both apartment-style units and cottages.

<table>
<tr><td>NEED A
BREAK?</td><td>In a historic late-19th-century white house with blue trim, Den Blå Lanterne (☎ 37/16–64–80) is Lyngør's only restaurant. Although it's pricey, you can eat as much of the famous fish soup as you like at this well-regarded restaurant—and there's often live music. It's open May through September.</td></tr>
</table>

Arendal

㉔ *33 km (20½ mi) from Lyngør on E18.*

Picturesque Arendal has more of the tidy white houses that are common to the area. In Tyholmen, the old town, you'll see many of these, as well as some brightly colored well-preserved wooden houses. A popular speed-boat race attracts international competitors each summer. This is a good town for strolling around. For a more formal tour, ask about the summer walking tours at the tourist office.

OFF THE   **MERDØGAARD MUSEUM –** On the island of Merdøy, a 30-minute boat
BEATEN PATH   ride from Arendal's Langbrygga (long wharf), is an early 18th-century
sea captain's home, now a museum. ☎ 37/08–52–43. 🎫 NKr 20. ⊙
Late June–mid-Aug., daily 11–5. Guided tours on the hr until 4.

Dining and Lodging

$$ ✕ **Madam Reiersen.** This bewitching restaurant on the waterfront
serves good food in an informal atmosphere. ⊠ *Nedre Tyholmsvn. 3,
4800,* ☎ *37/02–19–00. AE, DC, MC, V.*

$$ 🛏 **Clarion Tyholmen Hotel.** This maritime hotel, built in 1988, is in Tyholmen, with the sea at close quarters and a magnificent view of the fjord. The open-air restaurant is great in summer. ⊠ *Teaterpl. 2, 4800*
☎ *37/02–68–00,* 🖷 *37/02–68–01. 60 rooms. 2 restaurants, bar, sauna.
AE, DC, MC, V.*

Grimstad

㉕ *15 km (9.2 mi) south of Arendal.*

Grimstad's glory was in the days of sailing ships—about the same time the 15-year-old Henrik Ibsen worked as an apprentice at the local apothecary shop. Grimstad Apotek is now a part of **Ibsenhuset** (the Ibsen House) and has been preserved with its 1837 interior intact. Ibsen wrote his first play, *Catlina,* here. ⊠ *Henrik Ibsensgt. 14, 4890,* ☎ *37/04–46–53.* 🎫 *NKr 25.* ⊙ *Mid-May–mid-Sept., Mon.–Sat. 11–5, Sun. 1–5.*

Kristiansand

㉖ *55 km (34 mi) south of Grimstad on E18.*

Kristiansand, with 68,000 inhabitants, is one of Sørlandet's most prosperous cities and the domestic summer-vacation capital of Norway. According to legend, in 1641 King Christian IV marked the four corners of Kristiansand with his walking stick, and within that framework the grid of wide streets was drawn. The center of town, called the **Kvadrat,** still retains the grid, even after numerous fires.

Kristiansand's **Fisketorvet** (fish market) is near the south corner of the town's grid, right on the sea. **Christiansholm Festning** (fortress) is on a promontory opposite Festningsgata. Completed in 1672, the circular building with 15-ft-thick walls has played more a decorative than a defensive role; it was used once, in 1807, to defend the city against British invasion. Now it contains art exhibits.

The Gothic Revival **cathedral** from 1885 is the third-largest church in Norway. It often hosts summertime concerts in addition to an annual weeklong International Church Music Festival in mid-May (☎ 38/02–13–11 for information) that includes organ, chamber, and gospel music. ⊠ *Kirkegt., 4610,* ☎ *38/02–11–88.* 🎫 *Free.* ⊙ *June–Aug., daily 9–2.*

A wealthy merchant-shipowner built **Gimle Gård** (Gimle Manor) around 1800 in the Empire style. It displays furnishings from that pe-

riod, paintings, silver, and hand-blocked wallpaper. To get there from
the city center, head north across the Otra River on Bus 22 or drive to
Route E18 and cross the bridge over the Otra to Parkveien. Turn left
onto Ryttergangen and drive to Gimleveien, where you'll turn right.
⊠ *Gimlevn. 23, 4630,* ☎ *38/09–21–32.* ⊠ *NKr 30.* ☉ *July–Aug., Tues.–
Sat. noon–4, Sun. noon–6.*

The runestone in the cemetery of **Oddernes Kirke** (Oddernes Church)
tells that Øyvind, godson of Saint Olav, built this church in 1040 on
property he inherited from his father. One of the oldest churches in
Norway, it is dedicated to Saint Olav. ⊠ *Oddernesvn, 6430,* ☎ *38/
09–01–87 or 38/09–03–60.* ⊠ *Free.* ☉ *May–Aug., Sun.–Fri. 9–2.*

At **Kristiansand Kanonmuseum** (Cannon Museum) you can see the cannon that the German occupying force rigged during World War II. With
a 38-centimeter caliber, the cannon was said to be capable of shooting a projectile halfway to Denmark. ⊠ *Møvik,* ☎ *38/08–50–90.* ⊠
NKr 40. ☉ *May–mid-June and Sept., Thurs.–Sun. 11–6; late-June–Aug.,
daily 11–6.*

You'll see dwellings and workshops on a reconstructed city street at
Vest-Agder Fylkesmuseum (County Museum). Here you can visit two
tun—farm buildings traditionally set in clusters around a common area,
which suited the extended families. The museum is 4 km (3 mi) east
of Kristiansand on Route E18. ⊠ *Kongsgård, 4631,* ☎ *38/09–02–28.*
⊠ *NKr 30.* ☉ *Mid-June–mid-Aug., Mon.–Sat. 10–6; late May–mid-
June and mid-Aug.–mid-Sept., Sun. noon–6; mid-Sept.–mid-May, Sun.
noon–5; or by appointment.*

A favorite with hikers and strolling nannies, **Ravnedalen** (Raven Valley) is a lush park that's filled with flowers in springtime. Wear comfortable shoes and you can hike the narrow, winding paths up the hills
and climb 200 steps up to a 304-ft lookout. ⊠ *Northwest of town.*

☾ One of Norway's most popular attractions, **Kristiansand Dyrepark** is
actually five separate parks, including a water park (bring bathing suits
and towels), a forested park, an entertainment park, a fairy-tale park,
and a zoo, which contains an enclosure for Scandinavian animals such
as wolves and elk, plus Europe's (possibly the world's) largest breed-
ing ground for Bactrian camels. The fairy-tale park, **Kardemomme By**
(Cardamom Town), is named for a book by Norwegian illustrator and
writer Thorbjørn Egner. His story comes alive here in a precisely repli-
cated village, with actors playing townsfolk, shopkeepers, pirates, and
a delightful trio of robbers. Families who are hooked can even stay
overnight in one of the village's cozy apartments or nearby cottages
(reserve at least a year in advance). The park is 11 km (6 mi) east of
town. ⊠ *Kristiansand Dyrepark, 4609 Kardemomme By,* ☎ *38/04–
97–00.* ⊠ *NKr 185 includes admission to all parks and rides.* ☉ *Mid-
May–mid-June, weekdays 9–4, weekends 10–6; late June–mid-Aug.,
daily 10–6; late Aug.–mid-Sept., weekdays 10–4, weekends 10–6; late
Sept.–early May, weekdays 10–3, weekends 10–4.*

Dining and Lodging

$$–$$$ ✕ **Sjøhuset.** Built in 1892 as a salt warehouse, this white-trimmed red
building has since become a restaurant. The specialty is seafood, ap-
propriately, and the monkfish with Newburg sauce on green fettuccine
is colorful and delicious. ⊠ *Østre Strandgt. 12, 4610,* ☎ *38/02–62–
60. AE, DC, MC, V.*

$$ ✕ **Restaurant Bakgården.** At this small and intimate restaurant the menu
varies from day to day, but the seafood platter and lamb tenderloin
are standard. The staff is especially attentive. ⊠ *Tollbodgt. 5, 4611,*
☎ *38/02–79–55. AE, DC, MC, V. No lunch.*

$ ✕ **Mållaget Kafeteria.** At this cafeteria everything is homemade (except for the gelatin dessert). That includes such dishes as meatballs, brisket of beef with onion sauce, and trout in sour-cream sauce. It's the best deal in town, but it closes right around 6 PM, the time most people think about eating dinner. ⊠ *Gyldenløves Gt. 11, 4611,* ☎ *38/ 02–22–93. No credit cards.*

$$–$$$ 🏨 **Clarion Ernst Park Hotel.** The rooms are decorated with chintz bedspreads and drapes and practical furniture. The corner rooms have a tower nook at one end. On Saturday the atrium restaurant is the local spot for a civilized tea and lovely cakes. ⊠ *Rådhusgt. 2, 4611,* ☎ *38/ 12–86–00,* FAX *38/02–03–07. 112 rooms, 4 suites. Restaurant, 3 bars, nightclub, meeting rooms. AE, DC, MC, V.*

$$ 🏨 **Rainbow Hotel Norge.** This quiet, family hotel in the heart of town has an entrance more modern than that of the Ernst Park, but upstairs the difference is negligible. Here the rooms are furnished in bright colors and dark woods. Get up for breakfast to taste the homemade breads and rolls. ⊠ *Dronningens Gt. 5, 4610,* ☎ *38/02–00–00,* FAX *38/02–35–30. 114 rooms. Restaurant, library, meeting rooms. AE, DC, MC, V.*

Outdoor Activities and Sports

BIKING

Kristiansand has 70 km (43 mi) of bike trails around the city. The tourist office (☞ Visitor Information *in* Sørlandet A to Z, *below*) can recommend routes and rentals.

FISHING

Just north of Kristiansand there is excellent trout, perch, and eel fishing at Lillesand's **Vestre Grimevann** lake. You can get a permit at any sports store or at the tourist office (☞ Visitor Information *in* Sørlandet A to Z, *below*).

HIKING

In addition to the gardens and steep hills of **Ravnedalen** (☞ *above*), the **Baneheia Forest,** just a 15-minute walk north from the city center, is full of evergreens, small lakes, and paths that are ideal for a lazy walk or a challenging run.

WATER SPORTS

Kuholmen Marina (⊠ Roligheden Camping, ☎ 38/09–67–22) rents boats, water skis, and water scooters. **Anker Dykkersenter** (⊠ Randesundsgt. 2, Kuholmen, ☎ 38/09–79–09) rents scuba equipment. **Kristiansand Diving Club** (⊠ Myrbakken 3, ☎ 38/01–03–32 between 6 PM and 9 PM) has information on local diving.

Combining history and sailing, the magnificent full-rig, square-sail school ship *Sørlandet* (⊠ Gravene 2, 4610 Kristiansand, ☎ 38/02–98–90), built in 1927, takes on passengers for two weeks, usually stopping for several days in a northern European port. The price is about NKr 7,000.

Grovane i Vennesla

㉗ *20 km (13 mi) north of Kristiansand. Follow Rte. 39 from Kristiansand to Mosby, veer right onto 405, and continue to Grovane.*

At Grovane i Vennesla you will find the **Setesdalsbanen** (Setesdal Railway), a 4¾-km-long (3-mi-long) stretch of narrow-gauge track on which a steam locomotive from 1894 and carriages from the early 1900s run. ⊠ *Vennesla Stasjon, 4700,* ☎ *38/15–55–08.* 🎫 *NKr 50.* ☉ *Mid-June–late June and Aug., Sun. at 11:30; July, Tue.–Fri. at 6 and weekends at 11:30 and 2.*

Mandal

28 *42 km (28 mi) southwest from Kristiansand and 82 km (51 mi) from Evje.*

Mandal is Norway's southernmost town, famous for its historic core of well-preserved wooden houses and its beautiful long beach, Sjøsanden.

Mandal Kirke, built in 1821, is Norway's largest Empire-style wooden church. ☎ *38/26–35–77.* ⊙ *Tues.–Thur. 11–2.*

Lindesnes Fyr, Norway's oldest lighthouse, was built on the southern-most point of the country. The old coal-fired light dates from 1822. ☎ *38/25–88–51.* ⊙ *Mid-May–mid-Sept., 8 AM–10 PM; rest of yr, open during daylight hours.*

En Route The road from Mandal climbs and weaves its way through steep, wooded valleys and then descends toward the sea. Here you'll find the small town of Flekkefjord, which is known for its **Hollenderbyen** (Dutch Town), a historic district with small, white-painted houses lin-ing narrow, winding streets. From Flekkefjord you can take Route E18, which heads inland here, to Stavanger. It is more rewarding, however, to go on the coast road—Route 44. Follow the coast road 40 km (25 mi) past the fishing port of Egersund to Ogna.

Ogna

29 *93 km (57 mi) from Flekkefjord on Rte. 42.*

Ogna is known for the stretch of sandy beach that inspired so many Norwegian artists, among them Kitty Kjelland.

Hå Gamle Prestegaard (Old Parsonage), built in the 1780s, is now a cul-tural center for the area. ☒ *NKr 20.* ⊙ *May–mid-Sept., weekdays 11–7, Sat. noon–5, Sun. noon–7; late Sept.–Apr., Sat. noon–5, Sun. noon–7.*

Whichever road you choose to continue on out of Ogna, they both head northward along the rich agricultural coastal plain of the **Jæren dis-trict.** Flat and stony, it is the largest expanse of level terrain in this moun-tainous country. The mild climate and the absence of good harbors mean that the population here turned to agriculture, and the miles of stone walls are a testament to their labor.

Ancient monuments in Jæren are still visible, notably the **Hå gravesite** below the Hå parsonage near the Obrestad light. It consists of about 60 mounds, including two star-shaped and one boat-shaped, dating from around AD 500, all marked with stones. Take coastal Route 44.

Outdoor Activities and Sports

BIRD-WATCHING

The **Jærstrendene** in Jæren, from Randabergvika in the north to Ogna in the south, is a protected national park—and a good area for spot-ting puffins, cormorants, and black guillemots, as well as such waders as dunlins, little stints, and ringed plovers. Some areas of the park are closed to visitors, and it is forbidden to pick flowers or, for that mat-ter, to disturb anything.

FISHING

Three of the 10 best fishing rivers in Norway, the **Ognaelva, Håelva,** and **Figgjo,** are in Jæren, just south of Stavanger. Fishing licenses, sold in grocery stores and gas stations, are required at all of them.

Orre

③⓪ *26 km (16 mi) north of Ogna on Rte. 507.*

Orre is the site of a **medieval stone church.** It also has one of the few preserved Viking graveyards, dating from the Bronze Age and Iron Age. Near Orre pond, slightly inland, is a bird-watching station.

Dining

$$ ✕ **Time Station.** This eatery (in fact the only one in Bryne) is next to the town's train station. Bryne is just up the road from Orre off Route 507 and about a 40-minute train ride from Stavanger. Though the meat dishes are tasty, the house specialty is the seafood platter, with salmon, monkfish, ocean catfish, mussels, and ocean crayfish in a beurre blanc sauce. For dessert, try the *krumkake*, a cookie baked on an iron, wafer thin, shaped into a cone, and filled with blackberry cream. ✉ *Storgt. 346, 4340 Bryne,* ☎ *51/48–22–56. Reservations essential. AE, DC, MC, V. Closed Sun. No lunch weekdays.*

Sandnes

③① *25 km (16 mi) south of Stavanger, 52 km (32 mi) north of Orre.*

☾ In Sandnes is **Havana Badeland,** Norway's largest indoor aquapark for kids and adults, complete with a 300-ft water slide, whirlpool baths, saunas, a Turkish steambath, and massage parlors. ✉ *Hanaveien 17, 4300 Sandnes,* ☎ *51/62–92–00.* ▣ *NKr 110.* ☽ *Mid-June–mid-Aug., daily 10–8; late Aug.–early June, Tues., Thurs. 1–8, Wed., Fri.–Sat. 10–9.*

Ullandhaug

③② *15 km (9 mi) west of Sandnes.*

Take your imagination farther back in time at Ullandhaug, a reconstruction of an **Iron Age farm.** Three houses have been built around a central garden, and guides wearing period clothing demonstrate the daily activities of 1,500 years ago. ✉ *Grannesvn.,* ☎ *51/55–76–56.* ▣ *NKr 20.* ☽ *Mid-June–Aug., daily noon–5; early May–mid-June and early Sept., Sun. noon–4.*

You can see the place where what we know as Norway was founded by traveling 1½ km (1 mi) east on Grannesveien Ullandhaug to the **Harfsfjord.** In 872, in the Battle of Harfsfjord, Harald Hårfagre (Harald the Fair-Haired), the warrior king from the eastern country of Vestfold, finally succeeded in quelling the resistance of local chieftains in Rogaland and was promptly declared king of all Norway. A memorial in the shape of three giant swords plunged halfway into the earth marks the spot.

OFF THE **UTSTEIN KLOSTER** – Originally the palace of Norway's first king, Harald
BEATEN PATH Hårfagre, and later the residence of King Magnus VI, Utstein was used as a monastery from 1265 to 1537, when it reverted to the royal family. One of the best-preserved medieval monuments in Norway, the monastery opened to the public in 1965 and is today used to host classical and jazz concerts on Sunday afternoons during the summer.

After the concert, try the *Får i kål* (mutton, potatoes, and cabbage boiled in a peppery juice) at **Utstein Kloster Vertshus,** approximately 2 km (1 mi) from the monastery along the water's edge. To get to Utstein: buses depart from Stavanger at 12:15, returning from the monastery at 4:05, weekdays. It's about a half-hour drive from Stavanger. By car, travel north on coastal highway 1, through the world's second-longest undersea car tunnel. There is a toll of NKr 75 for the tunnel passage. ✉ *4156 Mosterøy,* ☎ *51/72–01–00.* 🎟 *NKr 25.* ☉ *May–mid-Sept., Tues.–Sat. 1–4, Sun. noon–5.*

Stavanger

㉝ *5 km (3 mi) east of Ullandhaug, 198 km (123 mi) from Kristiansand, 6 hrs from Bergen by car and ferry, 7 to 8 hrs from Oslo.*

Stavanger has always prospered from the riches of the sea. During the 19th century, huge harvests of brisling and herring established it as the sardine capital of the world. A resident is still called a Siddis, from S(ta-vanger) plus *iddis,* which means "sardine label," and the city's symbol, fittingly enough, is the key of a sardine can.

During the past two and a half decades, a different product from the sea has been Stavanger's lifeblood—oil. Since its discovery in the late 1960s, North Sea oil has transformed both the economy and the lifestyle of the city. In the early days of drilling, expertise was imported from abroad, chiefly from the United States. Although Norwegians have now taken over most of the projects, foreigners constitute almost a tenth of the inhabitants, making Stavanger the country's most international city. Though the population hovers around 142,000, the city has all the agreeable bustle of one many times its size. However, the city's charm still remains—in the heart of **Old Stavanger** you can wind down narrow cobblestone streets past small, white houses and craft shops with many-paned windows and terra-cotta roof tiles.

Stavanger Domkirke (cathedral), a large, well-preserved medieval church, is in the city center next to Breiavatnet, a small pond. Construction was begun in 1125 by Bishop Reinald of Winchester, who was probably assisted by English craftsmen. Largely destroyed by fire in 1272, the church was rebuilt to include a Gothic chancel. The result: its once elegant lines are now festooned with macabre death symbols and airborne putti. Next to the cathedral is **Kongsgård,** formerly a residence of bishops and kings but now a school and not open to visitors. 🎟 *Free.* ☉ *Mid-May–mid-Sept., Mon.–Sat. 9–6; mid-Sept.–mid-May, Mon.–Sat. 9–2, Sun. 1–6.*

Breidablikk manor house has been perfectly preserved since the '60s and feels as if the owner has only momentarily slipped away. An outstanding example of what the Norwegians call "Swiss-style" architecture, this house was built by a Norwegian shipping magnate. In spite of its foreign label, the house is uniquely Norwegian, inspired by national romanticism. ✉ *Eiganesvn. 40A, 4009,* ☎ *51/52–60–35.* 🎟 *NKr 20; or Nkr 30 for combined admission to Ledaal, Norsk Hermetikkmuseum, and Sjøfartsmuseet.* ☉ *Mid-June–mid-Aug., daily 11–4; mid-Aug.–mid-June, Sun. 11–4.*

Ledaal, the royal family's Stavanger residence, is a stately house built by the Kielland family in 1799. The second-floor library is dedicated to the writer Alexander Kielland, a social critic and satirist. ✉ *Eiganesvn. 45, 4009,* ☎ *51/52–06–18.* 🎟 *NKr 30. Also includes admission to Breidablikk, Norsk Hermetikkmuseum, and Sjøfartsmuseet.* ☉ *Mid-June–mid-Aug., daily 11–4; mid-Aug.–mid-June, Sun. 11–4.*

☾ This fascinating, albeit obscure, museum, the **Norsk Hermetikkmuseum** (Canning Museum), is housed in a former canning factory. Exhibits document the processing of brisling and sardines—the city's most important industry for nearly 100 years, thanks greatly to savvy turn-of-the-century packaging (naturally, the inventor of the sardine-can key was from Stavanger). ✉ *Øvre Strandgt. 88A, 4005,* ☎ *51/53–49–89.*

☒ *NKr 30. Also includes admission to Ledaal, Breidablikk, and Sjø-fartsmuseet.* ☉ *Mid-June–mid-Aug., daily 11–4; early June and late Aug., Tues.–Fri. 11–3, Sun. 11–4; Sept.–May, Sun. 11–4.*

Along Strandkaien, warehouses face the wharf; the shops, offices, and apartments face the street on the other side. Housed in the only two shipping merchants' houses that remain completely intact is the **Sjøfartsmuseet** (Maritime Museum). Inside, the house is just as it was a century ago, complete with office furniture, files, and posters, while the apartments show the standard of living for the mercantile class at that time. Although signs are only in Norwegian, an English-language guidebook and guided tours outside normal opening hours are available. ☒ *Nedre Strandgt. 17–19, 4005,* ☎ *51/52–59–11.* ☒ *NKr 30. Also includes admission to Ledaal, Breidablikk, and Norsk Hermetikkmuseum.* ☉ *Mid-June–mid-Aug., daily 11–4; early June and late Aug., Sun. 11–4.*

You can easily spot the spiky **Valbergtårnet** (☒ Valberget 4, ☎ 51/89–55–01) from any spot on the quay. Built on the highest point of the old city, this tower was a firewatch. Today it is a crafts center, which may not interest you, but it's still worth a visit for the view.

If you are of Norwegian stock you can trace your roots at **Det Norske Utvandresenteret** (Norwegian Emigration Center). Bring along any information you have, especially where your ancestors came from in Norway and when they left the country. The center is on the fourth floor of the brick *Ligningskontoret* (Tax Office) building a few minutes' walk from the harbor. You can make arrangements via fax to have the center do research for you, but the wait for this service is long. If you're in the area in early summer, call for information on the "emigration festival" that the center organizes each June. ☒ *Bergjelandsgt. 30, 4012 Stavanger,* ☎ *51/50–12–74,* 🖷 *51/50–12–90.* ☒ *Free, but each written request costs NKr180.* ☉ *Weekdays 9–3, Sat. 9–1.*

Rogaland Kunstmuseum houses the country's largest collection of works by Lars Hertervig, a Romantic painter who is considered one of the country's greatest artists. Other exhibits include Norwegian art from the early 19th century to the present. The museum is near Mosvannet (Moss Lake), which is just off highway E18 at the northern end of downtown. ☒ *Tjensvoll 6, 4021 Mosvannsparken,* ☎ *51/53–09–00.* ☒ *NKr 50.* ☉ *Tues.–Fri. 10–2, Sat. 11–2, Sun. 11–5.*

☾ **Kongeparken Amusement Park** has a 281-ft-long figure of Gulliver and a lifelike dinosaur exhibit as its main attractions, and plenty of rides. ☒ *4330 Ålgård,* ☎ *51/61–71–11.* ☒ *NKr 125.* ☉ *Mid-May–mid-June, weekends 10–6; mid-June–mid-Aug., daily 10–7; mid-Aug.–Sept., weekends 10–7.*

OFF THE
BEATEN PATH

PREKESTOLEN – Pulpit Rock, a huge cube with a vertical drop of 2,000 ft, is not a good destination if you suffer from vertigo but is great for a heart-stopping view. The clifflike rock sits on the banks of the finger-shaped Lysefjord. You can join a tour to get there (☞ Guided Tours, *below*), or you can do it on your own from June 16 to August 25 by taking the ferry from Fiskepiren across Hildefjorden to Tau. (It takes about 40 minutes from Stavanger.) In summer, a bus runs regularly from the ferry to the parking lot at the Pulpit Rock Lodge. It takes 1½ to 2 hours to walk from the lodge to the rock—the well-marked trail crosses some uneven terrain, so good walking shoes or boots are vital. Food and lodging are near the trail.

LYSEFJORDSENTERET – Lysefjord Center, whose shape mimics the mountains, takes visitors through a multimedia simulation of how a trickling brook created this sliver of a fjord. A ferry to the bottom of Pulpit Rock will drop off passengers midway (for more information, call **Rogaland Traffik,** ☎ 918/62–414, or **Clipper Fjord Sightseeing,** ☎ 51/89–52–70). The center is free but the multimedia simulation costs NKr 20. ⊠ *Oanes, 4110, Forsand,* ☎ *51/70–31–23.* ⊙ *May–Aug., weekdays noon–6, Sat. noon–7, Sun. noon–8.*

Dining and Lodging

$$$$ ✕ **Jans Mat & Vinhus.** The cellar setting is rustic, with old stone walls
★ and robust sideboards providing a nice counterpoint to the refined menu. Saddle of Rogaland county lamb is boned and rolled around a thyme-flavored stuffing, and the fillet is topped with a crunchy mustard crust. For dessert, try the nougat parfait dusted with cocoa. ⊠ *Breitorget 4, 4006,* ☎ *51/85–45–85. Reservations essential. Jacket and tie. AE, DC, MC, V. No lunch. Closed Sun.*

$$$ ✕ **Sjøhuset Skagen.** Just a few doors down from N.B. Sørensen's (☞ *below*), this spot is similar in decor, but with a greater variety of food. Try the crepes stuffed with roe of chapelin, onion, and sour cream, and the marinated salmon—Norwegian-style—with potatoes in a dill-and-cream sauce. The Brie served with cloudberries marinated in whiskey is excellent. ⊠ *Skagen 16, 4006,* ☎ *51/89–51–80. AE, DC, MC, V.*

$$$ ✕ **Straen Fiskerestaurant.** Right on the quay with two old-fashioned dining rooms, Straen is considered by many the city's best fish restaurant. The three-course meal of the day is always the best value. On the ground floor underneath Straen, you'll find **Timbuktu** (☎ 51/84–38–00), a new restaurant with a gallery bar and hip minimalistic interior—specialties include sushi and bouillabaisse. ⊠ *Nedre Strandgt. 15, 4005,* ☎ *51/84–37–00 or 51/52–61–00. AE, DC, MC, V. No lunch. Closed Sun.*

$$ ✕ **City Bistro.** Choose from reindeer medallions with rowanberry jelly, deer fillet with lingonberries and pears, fried monkfish, or oven-baked dried codfish at this bistro, where you'll dine at massive oak tables in a turn-of-the-century house. ⊠ *Madlavn. 18–20, 4008,* ☎ *51/53–95–70. Reservations essential. AE, DC, MC, V. No lunch.*

$$ ✕ **Harry Pepper.** This trendy Mexican restaurant has a popular bar. The color schemes are fun, bright, and gaudy, as are the displays of tacky souvenirs. ⊠ *Øvre Holmegt. 15, 4006,* ☎ *51/89–39–93. AE, DC, V.*

$–$$ ✕ **N.B. Sørensen's Dampskibsexpedition.** In a restored warehouse
★ decorated with nautical ropes, rustic barrels, and gaslights, this bar and restaurant is right on the quay. The food is nouvelle Norwegian. Try the marinated shrimp appetizer and the baked monkfish. The dish of the day, as well as the red house wine, which is always waiting for customers in an N.B. Sørensen's bottle on each table, is one of the better deals in Stavanger. ⊠ *Skagen 26, 4006,* ☎ *51/89–12–70. AE, DC, MC, V.*

$ ✕ **Café Sting.** Right at the foot of the Valbergtårnet, it's a restaurant–gallery–concert hall–meeting place day and night. All food from this international menu is made in-house and is better than most other inexpensive fare in Norway. Try local mussels in white wine, garlic scampi, or coconut chicken with jasmine rice. ⊠ *Valberget. 3, 4006,* ☎ *51/89–38–78. AE, DC, MC, V.*

$$$–$$$$ ⊞ **Radisson Atlantic Hotel.** The largest hotel in Stavanger, the Atlantic overlooks Breiavatnet pond in the heart of downtown. The feel is that of an international luxury hotel with several restaurants and the most popular nightclubs in town, but with little local flair. Rooms, which come in four different standards, are immaculate with heavy quilts, thick carpets, and cushy stuffed chairs; a number of newly renovated rooms

overlook the sea or the lake. ⊠ *Olav V's Gt. 3, 4005 Stavanger,* ☎ *51/52–75–20,* FAX *51/53–48–69. 351 rooms, 5 suites. Restaurant, bar, café, pub, dance club, nightclub, meeting rooms. AE, DC, MC, V.*

$$–$$$ 🏨 **Skagen Brygge.** Housed in three rehabilitated old sea houses, almost all rooms are different here, from modern to old-fashioned maritime, with exposed beams and brick and wood walls; many have harbor views. The hotel has an arrangement with 14 restaurants in the area—they make the reservations and the tab ends up on your hotel bill. ⊠ *Skagenkaien 30, 4006,* ☎ *51/85–00–00,* FAX *51/89–58–83. 106 rooms. Bar, sauna, Turkish bath, health club, convention center. AE, DC, MC, V.*

$–$$$ 🏨 **Victoria Hotel.** Stavanger's oldest hotel was built at the turn of the century and still retains a clubby, Victorian style, with elegant carved beds and leather sofas. Rooms on the front overlook the harbor. Ask about a discount at the Trimoteket health club, just behind the hotel. ⊠ *Skansegt. 1, 4006 Stavanger,* ☎ *51/86–70–00,* FAX *51/89–54–10. 107 rooms, 3 suites. Restaurant, bar, breakfast room, meeting room. AE, DC, MC, V.*

$–$$ 🏨 **Grand Hotel.** This place on the edge of the town center doesn't aim to be fancy; rooms are comfortable and bright, done in light pastels and white. In summer the rates drop significantly. ⊠ *Klubbgt. 3, Boks 80, 4012,* ☎ *51/89–58–00,* FAX *51/56–19–42. 92 rooms. Bar, breakfast room. AE, DC, MC, V.*

Nightlife and the Arts

NIGHTLIFE

In summer people are out at all hours, and sidewalk restaurants stay open until the sun comes up. Start a sunny evening at **Hansen Hjørnet**'s outdoor restaurant and bar (⊠ Skagenkn. 18, ☎ 51/89–52–80). Walk along **Skagenkaien** and **Strandkaien** for a choice of pubs and nightclubs. Among media junkies the place for a beer and a bit of CNN is the **Newsman** (⊠ Skagen 14, ☎ 51/53–57–09). **Taket Nattklubb** (⊠ Nedre Strandgt. 15, ☎ 51/84–37–00) is for the mid-20s and above crowd, whereas **Berlin** (⊠ Lars Hertervigs Gt. 5, ☎ 51/52–40–40) brings in youngish martini drinkers.

THE ARTS

Stavanger Konserthus (⊠ Concert Hall, Bjergsted, ☎ 51/56–17–16) features local artists and hosts free summertime foyer concerts. Built on an island in the archipelago in the Middle Ages, today **Utstein Kloster** (☞ *above*) is used for its superior acoustics and hosts classical and jazz concerts from June to August.

Outdoor Activities and Sports

BIKING

If you want to cycle around town, you can rent a bike at **Sykkelhuset** (⊠ Løkkevn. 33, ☎ 51/53–99–10). From Stavanger you can take your bike onto the ferry that departs for Finnøy. Spend the day or longer: weeklong cottage rentals are available from **Finnøy Fjordsenter** (⊠ 4160, Judaberg, ☎ 51/71–26–46, FAX 51/54–17–62). For more information about cottages in the archipelago and maps, contact the Stavanger Tourist Board (☞ Visitor Information *in* Sørlandet A to Z, *below*). The Ministry of the Environment can also provide information; call its **Bike Project** (⊠ Sandnes Turistinformasjon, Langgt. 8, 4300 Sandnes, ☎ 51/60–55–55).

FISHING

North of Stavanger is the longest salmon river in western Norway, the **Suldalslågen,** made popular 100 years ago by a Scottish aristocrat who built a fishing lodge there. **Lindum** still has cabins and camping facilities, as well as a dining room. Contact the **Lakseslottet Lindum** (⊠ N–

4240 Suldalsosen, ☎ 52/79–91–61). The main salmon season is July through September. On the island of **Kvitsøy,** in the archipelago just west of Stavanger, you can rent an apartment, complete with fish-smoking and -freezing facilities, and arrange to use a small sail- or motorboat. Contact **Kvitsøy Maritime Senter** (⊠ Box 35, 4090 Kvitsøy, ☎ 51/73–51–88).

GOLF
The **Stavanger Golfklubb** (⊠ Longebakken 45, 4042 Hafrsfjord, ☎ 51/55–54–31) offers a lush, 18-hole, international-championship course and equipment rental.

HIKING
Stavanger Turistforening (⊠ Postboks 239, 4001 Stavanger, ☎ 51/84–02–00) can plan a hike through the area, particularly in the rolling **Setesdalsheiene** and the thousands of islands and skerries of the **Ryfylke Archipelago.** The tourist board oversees 33 cabins for members (you can join on the spot) for overnighting along the way. Also in the Ryfylke area is a hike up **Kjerag,** a sheet of granite mountain that soars 3,555 ft, at the Lysefjord, near Forsand—ideal for thrill seekers.

SKIING
Skiing in **Sirdal,** 2½ hours from Stavanger, is good from January to April. Special ski buses leave Stavanger on the weekends at 8:30 AM during the season. Especially recommended is **Sinnes** for its non–hair-raising cross-country terrain. Downhill skiing is available at **Alsheia** on the same bus route. Contact **SOT Reiser** (⊠ Treskeveien 5, 4040 Hafrsfjord, Stavanger, ☎ 51/59–90–66) for transportation information.

WATER SPORTS
Diving is excellent all along the coast—although Norwegian law requires all foreigners to dive with a Norwegian as a way of ensuring that wrecks are left undisturbed.

Shopping
Figgjo Ceramics (⊠ Rte. E18, 4333 Figgjo, ☎ 51/68–35–00; 51/68–35–70 after 3:30) is outside town; the factory's beginnings in World War II are documented in an adjoining museum. A seconds shop has discounts of about 50%. **Skjæveland Strikkevarefabrikk** (⊠ 4330 Ålgård, ☎ 51/61–85–06) has a huge selection of sweaters at discount prices.

Sørlandet A to Z

Arriving and Departing

BY BOAT
Color Line (⊠ Strandkaien, Stavanger, ☎ 51/53–84–44) has four ships weekly on the Stavanger–Newcastle route. High-speed boats to Bergen are operated by **Flaggruten** (☎ 51/86–87–80). There is also a car ferry from Hirtshals, in northern Denmark, that takes about four hours to make the crossing. Another connects Larvik to Frederikshavn, on Denmark's west coast. In Denmark contact **DSB** (☎ 33/14–17–01); in Norway contact **Color Line** (☎ 51/53–84–44 or 38/07–88–88 in Kristiansand) or **DFDS Seaways** (☎ 22/41–90–90).

BY BUS
Aust-Agder Trafikkselskap (☎ 37/02–65–00), based in Arendal, has one departure daily in each direction for the 5½- to six-hour journey between Oslo and Kristiansand.

Sørlandsruta (☎ 38/26–84–70), based in Mandal, has two departures in each direction for the 4½-hour trip from Kristiansand (Strandgt. 33) to Stavanger.

For information about both long-distance and local bus and train services in **Stavanger,** call ☎ 51/52–26–00; the bus terminal is outside the train station. In **Kristiansand,** call ☎ 38/26–84–70.

BY CAR

From Oslo, it is 329 km (203 mi) to Kristiansand and 574 km (352 mi) to Stavanger. Route E18 parallels the coastline but stays slightly inland on the eastern side of the country and farther inland in the western part. Although seldom wider than two lanes, it is easy driving because it is so flat.

BY PLANE

Kristiansand: **Kjevik Airport,** 16 km (10 mi) outside town, is served by **Braathens SAFE** (☎ 38/00–80–00), with nonstop flights from Oslo, Bergen, and Stavanger, and **SAS** (☎ 81/00–33–00), with nonstop flights to Copenhagen. **MUK Air** serves Aalborg, Denmark; **Agder Fly** serves Göteborg, Sweden, and Billund, Denmark. Tickets on the last two can be booked with Braathens or SAS.

The **airport bus** departs from the Braathens SAFE office (✉ Vestre Strandgate ☎ 38/00–80–00) approximately one hour before every departure and proceeds, via downtown hotels, directly to Kjevik. Tickets cost NKr 40.

Stavanger: **Sola Airport** is 14 km (9 mi) from downtown. **Braathens SAFE** (☎ 51/51–10–00) has nonstop flights from Oslo, Kristiansand, Bergen, Trondheim, and Newcastle. **SAS** (☎ 81/00–33–00) has nonstop flights from Bergen, Oslo, Copenhagen, Aberdeen, Göteborg, London, and Newcastle. **KLM** (☎ 51/64–81–20) and **British Airways** (☎ 80/03–31–42) have nonstop flights to Stavanger from Billund and London, respectively.

The **Flybussen** (airport bus) leaves the airport every 15 minutes. It stops at hotels and outside the railroad station in Stavanger. Tickets cost NKr 35.

BY TRAIN

The **Sørlandsbanen** leaves Oslo S Station four times daily for the approximately five-hour journey to Kristiansand and three times daily for the 8½- to 9-hour journey to Stavanger. Two more trains travel the 3½-hour Kristiansand–Stavanger route. Kristiansand's train station is at Vestre Strandgata (☎ 38/07–75–30). For information on trains from Stavanger, call ☎ 51/56–96–00.

Getting Around

BY BUS

Bus connections in Sørlandet are infrequent; the tourist office can provide a comprehensive schedule. Tickets on Stavanger's excellent bus network cost NKr 14.

BY CAR

Sørlandet is flat, so it's easy driving throughout. The area around the Kulturhus in the Stavanger city center is closed to car traffic, and one-way traffic is the norm in the rest of the downtown area.

BY TAXI

All **Kristiansand** taxis are connected with a central dispatching office (☎ 38/03–27–00), as are **Stavanger** taxis (☎ 51/88–41–00). Journeys within Stavanger are charged by the taxi meter, otherwise by the kilometer. The initial charge is NKr 24 (NKr 36 at night), with NKr 13 per km during the day and NKr 15 at night.

Contacts and Resources

DOCTORS AND DENTISTS

Doctors: In Kristiansand, **Kvadraturen Legesenter** (⊠ Vestre Strandgt. 32, 4611, ☎ 38/02–66–11) is open 8–4.

Dentists: In Kristiansand, **Skoletannklinikken** (⊠ Festningsgt. 40, ☎ 38/02–19–71) is open 7–3.

EMERGENCIES

Police: ☎ 112. **Fire:** ☎ 111. **Ambulance:** ☎ 113. **Car Rescue:** in Kristiansand, ☎ 38/12–47–00; in Stavanger, ☎ 51/58–29–00.

Hospital Emergency Rooms: In Kristiansand, Røde Kors (Red Cross) **Legevakt** (Egsvei, ☎ 38/02–64–30) is open weekdays 4 PM–8 AM and weekends 24 hours. In Stavanger, call **Rogaland Sentralsykehus** (☎ 51/51–80–00).

GUIDED TOURS

Kristiansand: Tours of Kristiansand run summer only. The **City Train** (⊠ Rådhusgt. 11, 4611, ☎ 38/03–05–24) is a 15-minute tour of the center. The M/S **Maarten** (⊠ Pier 6 by Fiskebrygga, ☎ 38/12–13–14 or 942/93–617) offers two-hour tours of the eastern archipelago and a three-hour tour of the western archipelago daily 10 AM, early June–August 8.

Stavanger: A two-hour bus tour leaves from the marina at **Vågen** daily at 1 between June and August. **Rødne Clipperkontoret** (⊠ Skagenkaien 18, 4006, ☎ 51/89–52–70) offers three different tours. **Rogaland Trafikkselskap** (☎ 51/56–71–71 or 51/52–26–00) does the same, in either high-speed boats or ferries.

LATE-NIGHT PHARMACIES

Elefantapoteket (⊠ Gyldenløvesgt. 13, 4611, Kristiansand, ☎ 38/02–20–12) is open weekdays 8:30–8, Saturday 8:30–6, Sunday 3–6. **Løveapoteket** (⊠ Olav V's Gt. 11, 4005, Stavanger, ☎ 51/52–06–07) is open daily 8 AM–11 PM.

VISITOR INFORMATION

Arendal (SørlandsInfo, ⊠ Arendal Næringsråd, Friholmsgt. 1, 4800, ☎ 37/00–55–44). **Kristiansand** (⊠ Dronningensgt. 2, Box 592, 4601, ☎ 38/12–13–14, FAX 38/02–52–55). **Larvik** (⊠ Storgt. 48, 3250, ☎ 33/13–91–00). **Mandal** (Mandal og Lindesnes Turistkontor, ⊠ Bryggegt., 4500, ☎ 38/27–83–00). **Stavanger** (Stavanger Kulturhus, ⊠ Sølvberget, ☎ 51/85–92–00).

6   BERGEN

Bergen is the gateway to Norway's fjord country, and though it's Norway's second largest city, it's managed to maintain an intimate, small-town feeling.

PEOPLE FROM BERGEN like to say they do not come from Norway but from Bergen. Enfolded at the crook of seven mountains and fish-boned by seven fjords, Bergen does seem far from the rest of Norway.

Hanseatic merchants from northern Germany settled in Bergen during the 14th century and made it one of their four major overseas trading centers. The surviving Hanseatic buildings on Bryggen (the quay) are neatly topped with triangular cookie-cutter roofs and scrupulously painted red, blue, yellow, and green. A monument in themselves (they are on the UNESCO World Heritage List), they now house boutiques, restaurants, and museums. In the evening, when the harborside is illuminated, these modest buildings, together with the stocky Rosenkrantz Tower and the yachts lining the pier, are reflected in the water—and provide one of the loveliest cityscapes in northern Europe.

During the Hanseatic period, this active port was Norway's capital and largest city. Boats from northern Norway brought dried fish to Bergen to be shipped abroad by the Dutch, English, Scottish, and German merchants who had settled here. By the time the Hansa lost power, the city had an ample supply of wealthy local merchants and shipowners to replace them. For years Bergen was the capital of shipping, and until well into the 19th century, it remained the country's major city.

Culturally Bergen has also had its luminaries, including dramatist Ludvig Holberg, Scandinavia's answer to Molière—whom the Danes claim as their own. Bergensers know better. Norway's musical geniuses Ole Bull and Edvard Grieg also came from the city of the seven hills. Once you've visited Troldhaugen, Grieg's "Hill of Trolls," you'll understand his inspiration. In fact, the city of Bergen has been picked as the European Union's "European Center of Culture" for the year 2000.

About 219,000 people live in the greater metropolitan area now, compared with nearly 500,000 in Oslo. Even though the balance of power has shifted to the capital, Bergen remains a strong commercial force, thanks to shipping and oil, and is a cultural center, with an international music and arts festival every spring. Although it's true that an umbrella and slicker are necessary in this town, the raindrops—actually 219 days per year of them—never obstruct the lovely views.

EXPLORING BERGEN

The heartbeat of Bergen is at Torgalmenningen, the main pedestrian street that runs from the city's central square to the Fisketorget, which sits on the harbor and faces *Bryggen* (the wharf). From here, the rest of the city spreads up the sides of the seven mountains that surround Bergen, with some sights concentrated near the university or a small lake called Lille Lungegårdsvann. Fløyen, the mountain to the east of the harbor, is the most accessible for day-trippers. Before you begin your walking tour, you can take the funicular up to the top of it for a particularly fabulous overview of the city. Bergen is a very walkable city—especially when the sun's shining. If the weather's nice, you may want to take a couple of hours and just wander the streets, exploring the narrow cobblestone alleyways, charming wood houses, and quaint cafés.

Numbers in the text correspond to numbers in the margin and on the Bergen map.

Historic Bergen: Bryggen to Fløyen

A Good Walk

Start your tour in the center of town at Torget, also called **Fisketorget** ㉞ or the Fish Market, where fishermen and farmers deal their goods. Next, walk over to **Bryggen** ㉟, the wharf on the northeast side of Bergen's harbor. The gabled wood warehouses lining the docks mark the site of the city's original settlement. Take time to walk the narrow passageways between buildings; shops and galleries are hidden among the wooden facades. Follow the pier to the **Hanseatisk Museum** ㊱ at Finnegården and have a look inside. Afterward, continue your walk down the wharf, past the historic buildings to the end of the Holmen promontory and to **Bergenhus Festning** ㊲ (Bergenhus Fort), which dates from the 13th century; the nearby **Rosenkrantztårnet** is a 16th-century tower residence. After you've spent some time out here, retrace your steps back to the Radisson SAS Hotel. Beside the hotel is **Bryggens Museum** ㊳, which houses some magnificent archaeological finds. Just behind the museum is the 12th-century church called **Mariakirken** ㊴. Around the back of the church up the small hill is Øvregaten, a street that's the back boundary of Bryggen. Walk down Øvregaten four blocks to **Fløybanen** ㊵, the funicular that runs up and down Fløyen, one of the city's most popular hiking mountains. Don't miss a trip to the top, whether you hike or take the funicular—the view is like no other. At the base of the funicular is Lille Øvregaten. On this street, and in the area of crooked streets and hodgepodge architecture nearby, you'll find most of Bergen's antiques shops. On your left, at the intersection with Kong Oscars Gate is **Bergen Domkirke** ㊶ (Bergen Cathedral). Last, head back to Torgalmenningen in the center of town for a late afternoon snack at one of the square's cafés.

TIMING

This tour will take a good portion of a day. Be sure to get to the Fisketorget early in the morning, as many days it may close as early as 1 or 2. Also, try to plan your trip up Fløyen for a sunny day. Although it may be tough, as Bergen is renowned for rain, you may want to wait a day or two to see if the skies clear up.

Sights to See

OFF THE BEATEN PATH

AKVARIET – Penguins—several kinds, one of which has a platinum feather "hairdo," strangely appropriate in this land of blonds—seem to be the main attraction at the aquarium. There are also several seals and 50 tanks with a wide variety of fish. Try to catch the movie on Bergen, which is presented on a 360° "supervideograph" screen; it's directed by one of Norway's most beloved animators, Ivo Caprino. The aquarium is on Nordnes Peninsula, a 15-minute walk from the fish market, or take Bus 4. ⊠ *Nordnesparken,* ☎ *55/55–71–71.* ☜ *NKr 75.* ☉ *May–Sept., daily 9–8; Oct.–Apr., daily 10–6. Feeding times: 11, 2, and 6 in summer; noon and 4 in winter.*

㊶ **Bergen Domkirke** (Bergen Cathedral). This building is constructed in a profusion of styles. The oldest parts, the choir and lower portion of the tower, date from the 13th century. ⊠ *Kong Oscars Gt. and Domkirkegt.,* ☎ *55/31–04–70.* ☉ *Weekdays 11–2 in summer only.*

㊲ **Bergenhus Festning** (Bergenhus Fortress). The buildings here date from the mid-13th century. **Håkonshallen,** a royal ceremonial hall erected during the reign of Håkon Håkonsson between 1247 and 1261, was badly damaged by the explosion of a German ammunition ship in 1944 but was restored by 1961. The nearby **Rosenkrantztårnet** (Rosenkrantz Tower), also damaged in the same explosion, has been extensively re-

Bergen

Akvariet

Nordnes-
parken

Hurtigruten
Pier

Sjøgaten

Bergenhus **37**

Rosenkrantz **tårnet**

Bryggen **38** **39**

35

TO STAVANGER

Iepps gt.

36

34 **40** Fløybanen

Vetrlidsalm

Rosenkrantzgt.

Korskirke alm

Lille Øvregt.

Domkirke **41**

42

Domkirkegt.

43

Lille
Lungegårdsvann **44**

45

Lungegårdsgt.

Fløybanen
(Funicular)

Strømgaten

J.Reins gt.

H.Tanks gt.

KEY
— Rail Lines
- Funicular
Ferry

0   250 yards

0   250 meters

Nygårdsparken

46 **49**

TO OSLO

TO OSLO

Fløyen

Bergen Domkirke, **41**
Bergenhus
Festning, **37**
Bryggen, **35**
Bryggens
Museum, **38**
Fantoft Stavkirke, **48**
Fisketorget, **34**
Fløybanen, **40**
Grieghallen, **45**
Hanseatisk Museum, **36**
Lysøen, **47**
Mariakirken, **39**

Rasmus Meyers
Samlinger, **44**
Stenersens
Samling, **43**
Troldhaugen, **46**
Ulriken
Mountain, **49**
Vestlandske
Kunstindustri-
museum, **42**

stored as well. The Danish governor of Bergenhus, Erik Rosenkrantz, built this tower in the 1560s as an official residence and fortification. It is furnished in a formal, austere style. ⊠ *Bergenhus,* ☎ *55/31–60–67.* ☒ *NKr 15.* ⊙ *Mid-May–mid-Sept., daily 10–4; mid-Sept.–mid-May, daily noon–3 (until 6 on Thurs.). Guided tours every hr. Closed during Bergen International Music Festival.*

㉟ **Bryggen** (The Docks, Wharf, or Quays). A trip to Bergen is not complete until you visit Bryggen. One of the most charming walkways in Europe (especially on a sunny day—this town is known for rain, just ask any Bergenser), this row of 14th-century painted wooden buildings facing the harbor was built by Hansa merchants. The buildings, which are on the UNESCO World Heritage List, are mostly reconstructions, with the oldest dating from 1702. Several fires, the latest in 1955, destroyed the original structures.

㊳ **Bryggens Museum.** Artifacts found during excavations on Bryggen, including 12th-century buildings constructed on site from the original foundations, are on display here. The collection provides a good picture of daily life before and during the heyday of the Hansa, down to a two-seater outhouse. ⊠ *Dregsalmenningen 3, 5000,* ☎ *55/58–80–10.* ☒ *NKr 20.* ⊙ *May–Aug., daily 10–5; Sept.–Apr., weekdays 11–3, Sat. noon–3, Sun. noon–4.*

㉞ **Fisketorget** (Fish Market). At the turn of the century, views of this active and pungent square, with fishermen in Wellington boots and mackintoshes and women in long aprons, were popular postcard subjects. Times haven't changed; the marketplace remains just as picturesque—bring your camera. ⊙ *Mon.–Wed. and Fri. 7–4, Thurs. 7–7, Sat. 7–3.*

NEED A
BREAK?
For an inexpensive snack, try one of the open-face salmon sandwiches sold at the Fish Market. In summer, an array of beautiful, juicy berries is usually available at the adjacent fruit stands. The Norwegian *jordbær* (strawberries) are sure to be some of the best you'll ever have—smaller, but much more flavorful than most American varieties.

㊽ **Fløybanen** (Fløyen Funicular). The most astonishing view of Bergen is from the top of **Fløyen**, the most popular of the city's seven mountains. A funicular (a cable car that runs on tracks on the ground) takes you to a lookout point 1,050 ft above the sea. Several marked trails lead from Fløyen into the surrounding wooded area, or you can walk back to town on Fjellveien, which is a common Sunday activity for many locals. ☒ *NKr 30; one-way tickets are half-price.* ⊙ *Rides every half hour 7:30 AM–11 PM, Sat. from 8 AM, Sun. from 9 AM. It runs until midnight May–Sept.*

㊱ **Hanseatisk Museum** (Hanseatic Museum). One of the best-preserved buildings in Bergen, it was the office and home of an affluent German merchant. The apprentices lived upstairs, in boxed-in beds with windows cut into the wall so the tiny cells could be made up from the hall. Although claustrophobic, they retained body heat, practical in these unheated buildings. The 16th-century interior here will give you a feel for the life of a Hanseatic merchant. ⊠ *Bryggen, 5000,* ☎ *55/31–41–89.* ☒ *NKr 35; off-season NKr 20.* ⊙ *June–Aug., daily 9–5; Sept.–May, daily 11–2. Ticket is also valid for entrance to Schøtstuene, Hanseatic Assembly Rooms.*

㊴ **Mariakirken** (St. Mary's Church). It began as a Romanesque church in the 12th century but gained a Gothic choir, richly decorated portals, and a splendid Baroque pulpit, much of it added by the Hanseatic merchants who owned it during the 15th and 16th centuries. Organ recitals are held Tuesday and Thursday mid-June through late August and during the International Music Festival in late May. ⊠ *Dreggen, 5000,* ☎ *55/31–59–60.* ⊡ *NKr 10 in summer.* ☉ *Mid-May–early Sept., weekdays 11–4; early Sept.–mid-May, Tues.–Fri. noon–1:30.*

Rasmus Meyers Allé and Grieghallen

A Good Walk

From Torgalmenningen, walk to Nordahl Bruns Gate and turn left for the **Vestlandske Kunstindustrimuseum** ㊷, the West Norway Museum of Applied Art. After viewing some of the museum's elaborately crafted works, exit the museum and head for Christies Gate. Follow it along the park and turn left on Rasmus Meyers Allé, which runs along the small lake, Lille Lungegårdsvann, to reach **Stenersens Samling** ㊸, an art museum that has some very impressive holdings, with works by Kandinsky and Klee. Just beyond Stenersens is **Rasmus Meyers Samlinger** ㊹, another museum with equally exciting works, including a large Munch collection. Behind these museums on Lars Hills Gate is **Grieghallen** ㊺, Bergen's famous music hall. Although the building's architecture is interesting from street level, try to get a peek of it from the top of Fløyen, where the shape may remind you of a grand piano.

TIMING

All of the museums on this tour are quite small and very near to each other, so you probably won't need more than half a day to complete this tour.

Sights to See

㊺ Grieghallen. Home of the Bergen Philharmonic Orchestra and stage for the annual International Music Festival, this music hall is a conspicuous slab of glass and concrete, but the acoustics are marvelous. Built in 1978, the hall was named for the city's famous son, composer Edvard Grieg (1843–1907). The season runs only in summer. ⊠ *Lars Hills Gt. 3A,* ☎ *55/21–61–50.*

㊹ Rasmus Meyers Samlinger. Meyer, a businessman who lived from 1858 to 1916, assembled a superb art collection, with many names that are famous today but were unknown when he acquired them. Here you'll see the best Munch paintings outside Oslo, as well as major works by Scandinavian impressionists. The gallery hosts summertime Grieg concerts. ⊠ *Rasmus Meyers Allé 7,* ☎ *55/56–80–00.* ⊡ *NKr 35(includes entry to Stenersens Samling and Vestlandske museum).* ☉ *Mid-May–mid-Sept., daily noon–5; late Sept.–early May, Tues.–Sun. noon–5.*

㊸ Stenersens Samling. This is an extremely impressive collection of modern art for a town the size of Bergen. Modern artists represented at this museum include Max Ernst, Paul Klee, Vassily Kandinsky, Pablo Picasso, and Joan Miró, as well as—guess who—Edvard Munch. There is also a large focus here on Norwegian art since the mid-18th century. ⊠ *Rasmus Meyers Allé 3,* ☎ *55/56–80–00.* ⊡ *NKr 35.* ☉ *Mid-May–mid-Sept., daily noon–5; mid-Sept.–mid-May, Tues.–Sun. noon–5.*

㊷ Vestlandske Kunstindustrimuseum (West Norway Museum of Applied Art). Seventeenth- and 18th-century Bergen silversmiths were renowned throughout Scandinavia for their heavy, elaborate Baroque designs. Tankards embossed with flower motifs or inlaid with coins form a rich display. ⊠ *Permanenten, Nordahl Bruns Gt. 9,* ☎ *55/32–51–08.* ⊡ *NKr 35.* ☉ *Mid-May–mid-Sept., daily noon–5; mid-Sept.–mid-May, Tues.–Sun. noon–5.*

Troldhaugen, Fantoft, Lysøen, and Ulriken

A Good Drive

If you get your fill of Bergen's city life, you can head out to the countryside to four of the area's interesting, but low-key attractions. Follow Route 1 (Nesttun/Voss) out of town about 5 km (3 mi) to **Troldhaugen** ㊸, the villa where Edvard Grieg spent 22 years of his life. After you've spent some time wandering the grounds of Troldhaugen, head for **Lysøen** ㊼, the Victorian dream castle of Norwegian violinist Ole Bull. Getting here is a 30-minute trek by car and ferry, but it's well worth the effort. From Troldhaugen, get back on Route 1 or Route 586 to Fana, over Fanafjell to Sørestraumen. Follow signs to Buena Kai. From here, take the ferry over to Lysøen. After visiting Lysøen, on your way back to Bergen, you can see the **Fantoft Stavkirke** ㊽, which unfortunately was badly damaged in a fire in 1992 but has been completely rebuilt. Lastly, end your day with a hike up **Ulriken Mountain** ㊾, the tallest of Bergen's seven mountains. If you're too worn out from your day of sightseeing, but still want to take in the view from the top, you can always take the Ulriken cable car.

TIMING

Driving time (or bus time) will consume much of your day on this tour. However, the landscape is beautiful, so visiting these sights is a pleasant way to explore Bergen's environs with some direction. You can enjoy the day at a leisurely pace, but note closing times below. Try to end your day with a "Music on the Mountain" concert at Ulriken.

Sights to See

★ ㊽ **Fantoft Stavkirke** (Fantoft Stave Church). Originally built in the early 12th century in Sognefjord, this ancient wooden stave church was later moved to its present site. Stave churches are unique to Norway, representing a sort of first step, spiritually and architecturally, into Christianity, without complete relinquishment of pagan beliefs. They also parallel Viking ships, as they are built of strips of wood laid edge to edge rather than in log-cabin style. (The church was badly damaged by an arsonous fire in 1992 but has been completey rebuilt.) From *sentral bystasjonen* (the main bus station next to the railway station), take any bus leaving from Platform 19, 20, or 21. ✉ *Paradis,* ☎ *55/28–07–10.* 💷 *NKr 30.* ☉ *Mid-May–mid-Sept., daily 10:30–6; or by appointment.*

㊼ **Lysøen.** Ole Bull, not as well known as some of Norway's other cultural luminaries, was a virtuoso violinist and patron of visionary dimension. In 1850, after failing to establish a "New Norwegian Theater" in America, he founded the National Theater in Norway. He then chose the young, unknown playwright Henrik Ibsen to write full-time for the theater and later encouraged and promoted another neophyte—15-year-old Edvard Grieg.

Built in 1873, this villa, complete with an onion dome, gingerbread gables, curved staircase, and cutwork trim just about everywhere, has to be seen to be believed. Inside, the music room is a frenzy of filigree carving, fretwork, braided and twisted columns, and gables with intricate openwork in the supports, all done in knotty pine. Bull's descendants donated the house to the national preservation trust in 1973. The entrance fee includes a guided tour of the villa held at 12:15, 1:15, 2:15, and 3:15.

The ferry, *Ole Bull,* leaves from Buena Kai on the hour Monday–Saturday noon–3 and Sunday 11–4; the last ferry leaves Lysøen Monday–Saturday at 4, Sunday at 5; return fare is NKr 30. By bus, take the "Lysefjordruta" bus from Gate 19 or 20 at the main bus station to Buena

Kai (there are no buses on Sunday). From here take the *Ole Bull* ferry. Return bus fare is NKr 68. ☎ *56/30–90–77.* ☑ *NKr 25.* ⊗ *Mid-May–late Aug., Mon.–Sat. noon–4, Sun. 11–5; Sept., Sun. noon–4.*

46 **Troldhaugen** (Troll Hill). Composer Edvard Grieg began his musical career under the tutelage of his mother, then went on to study music in Leipzig and Denmark, where he met his future wife, Nina, a Danish soprano. Even in his early compositions, his own unusual chord progressions fused with elements of Norwegian folk music. Norway and its landscape were always an inspiration to Grieg, and nowhere is this more in evidence than at his villa by Nordåsvannet, where he and his wife, Nina, lived for 22 years beginning in about 1885. An enchanting white clapboard house with restrained green gingerbread trim, it served as a salon and gathering place for many Scandinavian artists and it's brimming with paintings, prints, and other memorabilia. On Grieg's desk you'll see a small red troll—which, it is said, he religiously bade good night before he went to sleep. The house also contains his Steinway piano, which is still used for special concerts. Behind the grounds, at the edge of the fjord, you'll find a sheer rock face that was blasted open to provide a burial place for the couple. **Troldsalen** (Troll Hall), with seating for 200 people, is used for concerts. Catch a bus from Platform 19, 20, or 21 at the bus station, and get off at Hopsbroen, turn right, walk 200 yards, turn left on Troldhaugsveien, and follow the signs for 20 minutes. ☎ *55/91–17–91.* ☑ *NKr 40.* ⊗ *Mid-Apr.–Sept., daily 9–6; Oct.–Nov. and Apr., weekdays, 10–2, Sat. noon–4, Sun. 10–4; Feb.–Mar., weekdays 10–2, Sun. 10–4.*

49 **Ulriken Mountain.** Admire summer sunsets from the highest of the seven Bergen mountains—Ulriken—while enjoying free "Music on the Mountain" concerts most nights from 7, May through September. The Ulriken cable car will transport you up the mountain. You can catch the cable car near Haukeland hospital. It's best reached near the Montana Youth Hostel (Buses 2 or 4). ✉ *Ulriken 1, 5009 Bergen,* ☎ *55/29–31–60.* ☑ *NKr 60.* ⊗ *The cable car runs every 7 minutes and operates 9–9 in summer, 9–sunset in winter.*

DINING

Among the most characteristic of Bergen dishes is a fresh, perfectly poached whole salmon, served with new potatoes and parsley-butter sauce. To try another typical Bergen repast, without the typical bill, stroll among the stalls at Fisketorvet, where you can munch bagfuls of pink shrimp, heart-shaped fish cakes, and round buns topped with salmon. Top it off with another local specialty, a *skillingsbolle,* a big cinnamon roll, sometimes with a custard center but most authentic without.

$$$$ ✕ **Kafé Kristall.** This small, intimate restaurant is one of the most
★ fashionable in town. The chef here combines his own eclectic contemporary style with traditional Norwegian ingredients. ✉ *Kong Oscars Gt. 16,* ☎ *55/32–10–84. AE, DC, MC, V. Closed Sun. No lunch.*

$$$$ ✕ **Lucullus.** Although the decor seems a bit out of kilter—modern art matched with lace doilies and boardroom chairs—the food in this restaurant is always good. This is a good place to splurge on the four-course meal that's offered. ✉ *Hotel Neptun, Walckendorfsgt. 8,* ☎ *55/90–10–00. Jacket and tie. DC, MC, V Closed Sun. No lunch.*

$$$–$$$$ ✕ **Finnegaardstuene.** This classic Norwegian restaurant near Bryggen
★ has four small rooms that make for a snug, intimate atmosphere. Some of the timber interior dates from the 18th century. The seven-course menu emphasizes seafood, although the venison and reindeer are excellent. Traditional Norwegian desserts such as cloudberries and cream

are irresistible. ⊠ *Rosenkrantzgt. 6,* ☎ *55/55–03–00. AE, DC, MC, V. Closed Sun.*

$$$ ✕ **To Kokker.** The name means "two cooks," and that's what there are.
★ Ranked among Bergen's best restaurants by many, this spot is on Bryggen, in a 300-year-old building complete with crooked floors and slanted moldings. Try the roasted reindeer or the marinated salmon. Desserts use local fruit. ⊠ *Enhjørningsgården,* ☎ *55/32–28–16. Reservations essential. AE, DC, MC, V. Closed Sun. No lunch.*

$$ ✕ **Bryggeloftet & Stuene.** It's always full, upstairs and down. The menu's the same in both places, but only the first floor is authentically old. Poached halibut served with boiled potatoes and cucumber salad, a traditional favorite, is the specialty, but there's also sautéed ocean catfish with mushrooms and shrimp, and grilled lamb fillet. ⊠ *Bryggen 11,* ☎ *55/31–06–30. AE, DC, MC, V.*

$$ ✕ **Munkestuen.** With its five tables and red-and-white-check tablecloths,
★ this mom-and-pop place looks more Italian than Norwegian, but locals regard it as a hometown legend—make reservations as soon as you get into town, if not before (they can be booked up to four weeks in advance). Try the monkfish with hollandaise sauce or the fillet of roe deer with morels. ⊠ *Klostergt. 12,* ☎ *55/90–21–49. Reservations essential. AE, DC, MC, V. Closed weekends and 3 wks in July. No lunch.*

$ ✕ **Baker Brun.** This Bergen institution, now in several locations, is great
★ for a quick bite. Try skillingsbolle or *skolebrød,* a sweet roll with custard and coconut icing—both are scrumptious. For something less sweet, this bakery serves fresh-baked wheat rolls with Norwegian *hvit ost* (white cheese) and cucumber. ⊠ *Zachariasbryggen,* ☎ *55/34–96–00; Søstergården, Bryggen,* ☎ *53/34–96–40. No credit cards.*

$ ✕ **Børs Café.** What began as a beer hall in 1894 is now more of a pub, with hearty homemade food at reasonable prices. The salted mutton with mashed potato and turnips has been served for more than a century; fried halibut cooked in cream or butter sauce, dried codfish, and the usual open-face sandwiches are always on the menu. ⊠ *Strandkaien 12,* ☎ *55/32–47–19. No credit cards.*

$ ✕ **Kjøbmandsstuen** and **Augustus.** You can't beat these two cafeterias under the same management for lunch or for cake and coffee in the afternoon. Vegetarians will be impressed by the number of salads and quiches, in addition to pâté and open-faced sandwiches. ⊠ *Kjømandsstuen: C. Sundtsgt. 24,* ☎ *55/30–40–00. Augustus: Galleriet,* ☎ *55/32–35–25. AE, DC, MC, V.*

$ ✕ **Pasta Sentralen.** If you're looking for good cheap eats, this place will give you bang for your buck. You can't beat the NKr 54 daily special, which includes a generous main course, bread, and soda. More than 40 types of delicious homemade pasta are served here, as are pizzas and other Italian dishes. ⊠ *Vestre Strømkaien 6 (near Lars Hilles Gate),* ☎ *55/96–00–37. No credit cards.*

LODGING

From June 20 through August 10, special summer double-room rates are available in 21 Bergen hotels; rooms can be reserved only 48 hours in advance. In the winter, weekend specials are often a fraction of the weekday rates, which are geared toward business travelers. The tourist office (☎ 55/32–14–80) will assist in finding accommodations in hotels, guest houses, or private houses.

$$–$$$ ▥ **Clarion Admiral Hotel.** This dockside warehouse from 1906, right
★ on the water across Vågen from Bryggen, was converted into a hotel in 1987. The building is geometric Art Nouveau, and although the small

rooms are ordinary, the larger rooms overlooking the harbor have some of the best nighttime views in town. The harborside restaurant, Emily, has a small but good buffet table. ⊠ *C. Sundts Gt. 9–13, 5001,* ☎ *55/23–64–00,* ℻ *55/23–64–64. 210 rooms, 3 suites. Restaurant, bar, meeting rooms. AE, DC, MC, V.*

$$–$$$ 🏨 **Radisson SAS Hotel Norge.** Other hotels come and go, but the Norge stays. It's an established luxury hotel in the center of town, right by the park. The architecture is standard modern, with large rooms that blend contemporary Scandinavian comfort with traditional warmth. The warm, thick *dyner* (featherbedlike comforters) are so comfy, it's hard to get out of bed in the mornings. ⊠ *Ole Bull Pl. 4, 5012,* ☎ *55/57–30–00,* ℻ *55/57–30–01. 347 rooms, 12 suites. 2 restaurants, 2 bars, indoor pool, health club, nightclub, meeting rooms. AE, DC, MC, V.*

$$–$$$ 🏨 **Radisson SAS Royal Hotel.** This popular Bergen hotel opened in 1982 behind the famous buildings at Bryggen on the site of old warehouses. Ravaged by nine fires since 1170, the warehouses have been rebuilt each time in the same style, which SAS has incorporated into the architecture of the hotel. The rooms are small but pleasant. ⊠ *Bryggen, 5003,* ☎ *55/54–30–00,* ℻ *55/32–48–08. 273 rooms, 10 suites. 3 restaurants, bar, pub, nightclub, indoor pool, sauna, health club, dance club, convention center. AE, DC, MC, V.*

$–$$ 🏨 **Augustin Hotel.** The oldest family-run hotel in Bergen in the center of town has been restored to its original late–Art Nouveau character. ⊠ *C. Sundts Gt. 22–24, 5004,* ☎ *55/30–40–00,* ℻ *55/30–40–10. 83 rooms. Meeting rooms. AE, DC, MC, V.*

$–$$ 🏨 **Romantik Hotel Park Pension.** Near the university, this small family-run hotel is in a well-kept Victorian building. Both the public rooms and the guest rooms are furnished with antiques. It's a 10-minute walk from downtown. Don't oversleep and miss the simple and delicious Norwegian breakfast—fresh bread, jams, cheeses, and cereal—included in the price. ⊠ *Harald Hårfagres Gt. 35, 5007,* ☎ *55/32–09–60,* ℻ *55/31–03–34. 21 rooms. Breakfast room. AE, DC, MC, V.*

$–$$ 🏨 **Tulip Inn Bryggen Orion.** Facing the harbor in the center of town, the Orion is within walking distance of many of Bergen's most famous sights, including Bryggen and Rosenkrantztårnet. The rooms are decorated in warm, sunny colors. The open fireplace at the bar is cozy in the winter. ⊠ *Bradbenken 3, 5003,* ☎ *55/31–80–80,* ℻ *55/32–94–14. 229 rooms. Restaurant, bar, nightclub. AE, DC, MC, V.*

$ 🏨 **Fantoft Sommerhotell.** This student dorm, 6 km (3½ mi) from downtown, becomes a hotel from May 20 to August 20. Family rooms are available. Accommodation is simple but adequate. Take Bus 18, 19, or 20 to Fantoft. ⊠ *5036 Fantoft,* ☎ *55/27–60–00,* ℻ *55/27–60–30. 72 rooms. Restaurant. AE, DC, MC, V.*

NIGHTLIFE AND THE ARTS

Nightlife

Bars and Clubs

Most nightlife centers on the harbor area. **Zachariasbryggen** is a restaurant and entertainment complex right on the water. **Engelen** (the Angel) at the SAS Royal Hotel attracts a mixed weekend crowd when it blasts hip-hop, funk, and rock. The **Hotel Norge** piano bar and disco are more low-key, with an older crowd. **Dickens** (⊠ 8–10 Ole Bull Pl., ☎ 55/90–07–60), across from the Hotel Norge, is a relaxed meeting place for an afternoon or evening drink. Right next to Dickens is **Losjehagen** (☎ 55/90–08–20), an outdoor patio especially popular in summer. **Wesselstuen,** also on Ole Bull Plads (☎ 55/90–08–20) is a cozy place where you'll find students and the local intelligentsia. **Café**

Opera (⊠ 24 Engen, ☎ 55/23–03–15) is a sumptuous place to go for a drink or a coffee. It's great for people-watching and whiling away the time. **Banco Rotto** (⊠ Vågsalmenningen 16, ☎ 55/32–75–20), in a 19th-century bank building, is one of Bergen's most popular watering holes, for young and old alike. The café here—one of the fanciest in town—serves delicious desserts. The three-story **Rick's Café & Salonger** (⊠ Veiten 3, ☎ 55/23–03–11) has a disco, an Irish pub, and Bergen's longest bar; the decor is straight out of the film *Casablanca*.

Bergen has an active gay community with clubs and planned events. Call **Landsforeningen for Lesbisk og Homofil Frigjøring** (National Association for Lesbian and Gay Liberation, ⊠ Nygårdsgt. 2A, ☎ 820/ 00–977) Wednesday 7–9 to ask about events in the city. In the same building is a popular gay hangout, **Café Finken,** which is open daily until 1 AM.

Live Music

Bergensers love jazz, and the **Bergen Jazz Festival** (⊠ Georgernes Verft 3, 5011 Bergen, ☎ 55/32–09–76) is held here during the third week of August. **Bergen Jazz Forum** (same address) is *the* place, both in winter and summer, when there are nightly jazz concerts. For rock, **Hulen** (the Cave) (⊠ Olav Ryesvei 47, ☎ 55/32–32–87) has live music on weekends.

The Arts

Bergen is known for its **Festspillene** (International Music Festival), held each year during the last week of May and the beginning of June. It features famous names in classical music, jazz, ballet, the arts, and theater. Tickets are available from the Festival Office at **Grieghallen** (⊠ Lars Hilles Gt. 3, 5015, ☎ 55/21–61–00).

During the summer, twice a week, the **Bergen Folklore Dance Group** performs a one-hour program of traditional dances and music from rural Norway at Bryggens Museum. Tickets are sold at the tourist office and at the door. ⊠ *Bryggen,* ☎ *55/32–14–80.* ☜ *NKr 95.* ☉ *Performances June–Aug., Tues. and Thurs. at 9.*

A more extensive program, **Fana Folklore** is an evening of folklore— with traditional wedding food, dances, and folk music, plus a concert— at the 800-year-old Fana Church. The event has been going on for more than 40 years. ⊠ *A/S Kunst (Art Association) Torgalmenning 9,* ☎ *55/ 91–52–40;* ⊠ *Fana Folklore, 5047 Fana,* ☎ *55/91–52–40.* ☜ *NKr 230 (includes dinner and return bus transportation).* ☉ *June–Aug., Mon., Tues., Thurs., and Fri. at 7 PM. Catch the bus from the center of Bergen and return by 10:30 PM.*

Concerts are held at **Troldhaugen,** home of composer Edvard Grieg (☞ Exploring, *above*), all summer. Tickets are sold at the tourist office or at the door. Performances are given late June–August, Wednesday and Sunday at 7:30, Saturday at 2, and September–October, Sunday at 2.

OUTDOOR ACTIVITIES AND SPORTS

Below is a sampling of activities for the Bergen area, but outdoors lovers should be aware that the city is within easy reach of the Hardangervidda, the country's great plateau, which offers limitless outdoor possibilities (☞ Hardangervidda *in* Central Norway, Chapter 7).

Fishing

The **Bergen Angling Association** (⊠ Fosswinckelsgt. 37, ☎ 55/32–11– 64) provides information on permits; it's closed in July. Among the many charters in the area, the **Rifylke Fjord Tour** (☎ 911/59–048 or 946/09–548) offers two-hour journeys from Bergen twice daily along the coast. Anglers can catch coal fish, cod, mackerel, and haddock.

Hiking

Take the funicular up **Fløyen** (☞ Exploring, *above*), and minutes later you'll be in the midst of a forest. For a simple map of the mountain, ask at the tourist office for the cartoon "Gledeskartet" map, which outlines 1½- to 5-km (1- to 3-mi) hikes. **Ulriken Mountain** (☞ Exploring, *above*) is popular with walkers. Maps of the many walking tours around Bergen are available from bookstores and from **Bergens Turlag** (touring club, ✉ Tverrgata 2–4, 5017 Bergen, ☎ 55/32–22–30), which arranges hikes and maintains cabins for hikers.

In the archipelago west of Bergen, there are many hiking options, ranging from the simple path between Morland and Fjell to the more rugged mountain climb at Haganes. For details, contact the **Bergen Tourist Office** (☎ 55/32–14–80).

Yachting

The 100-year-old Hardanger yacht **Mathilde** (✉ Stiftinga Hardangerjakt, 5600 Kaldestad, ☎ 56/55–22–77), with the world's largest authentic yacht rigging, does both one- and several-day trips, as well as coastal safaris.

SHOPPING

Shopping Centers

Sundt City (✉ Torgalmenningen 14, ☎ 55/31–80–20) is the closest you'll get to a traditional department store in Norway, with everything from fashion to interior furnishings. However, you'll find better value for your kroner if you shop around for souvenirs and sweaters. **Kløverhuset** (✉ Strandkaien 10, ☎ 55/31–37–90), between Strandgaten and the fish market, has 40 shops under one roof. You'll find outlets for the ever-so-popular Dale knitwear, souvenirs, leathers, and fur. **Galleriet**, on Torgalmenningen, is the best of the downtown shopping malls. Here you will find **Christiana Glasmagasin** and more exclusive small shops along with all the chains, like **Hennes & Mauritz** and **Lindex**. **Bystasjonen**, by the bus terminal, is a small shopping center conveniently located for last-minute items.

Specialty Stores

Antiques
There are many antiques shops on **Øvregaten,** especially around Fløybanen. **Cecilie Antikk** (✉ Kong Oscarsgt. 32, ☎ 55/96–17–53) deals primarily in antique Norwegian glass, ceramics, and old and rare books.

Glass, Ceramics, Pewter
Viking Design (✉ Torgalmenning 1, ☎ 55/31–05–20) specializes in pewter—you'll find that some pieces can be picked up quite reasonably. **Tilbords, Bergens Glasmagasin** (✉ Olav Kyrresgt. 9, ☎ 55/31–69–67) claims to have the town's largest selection of glass and china, both Scandinavian and European designs. **Prydkunst-Hjertholm** (✉ Olav Kyrresgt. 7, ☎ 55/31–70–27) is the ideal shop for gifts; most everything is of Scandinavian design. You'll find pottery and glassware of the highest quality—much of it from local artisans.

Handicrafts

Husfliden (⊠ Vågsalmenning 3, ☎ 55/31–78–70) caters to all your handicrafts needs, including a department for Norwegian national costumes. This is one of the best places to pick up handmade Norwegian goods, especially handwoven textiles and hand-carved wood items. **Berle** (⊠ Bryggen 5, ☎ 55/31–73–00) has a huge selection of traditional knitwear and other souvenir items—don't miss the troll cave. Downstairs is an interior design shop with Scandinavian furniture. There's also an automatic foreign-money exchange machine.

Jewelry

Theodor Olsens Eftf (⊠ Ole Bull Pl. 7, ☎ 55/55–14–80) stocks silver jewelry of distinctive Norwegian and Scandinavian design.

BERGEN A TO Z

Arriving and Departing

By Boat

Boats have always been Bergen's lifeline to the world. **Color Line** (⊠ Skuteviksboder 1–2, 5023, ☎ 55/54–86–60) ferries serve Newcastle. Others connect with the Shetland and Faroe islands, Denmark, Scotland, and Iceland. All dock at Skoltegrunnskaien.

Express boats between Bergen and Stavanger run three times daily on weekdays, twice daily on weekends, for the four-hour trip. All arrive and depart from Strandkai Terminalen (☎ 55/23–87–80).

The *Hurtigruten* (⊠ Coastal Express, Veiten 2B, 5012, ☎ 55/23–07–90) departs daily from Frielenes Quay, Dock H, for the 11-day round-trip to Kirkenes in the far north.

By Bus

The summer-only bus from Oslo to Bergen, **Geiteryggekspressen** (literally, "Goat-Back Express," referring to the tunnel through Geiteryggen Mountain, which looks like a goat's back, between Hol and Aurland) leaves the Nor-Way bus terminal (⊠ Galleri Oslo, ☎ 815/44–444) at 8 AM and arrives in Bergen 12½ hours later. Buses also connect Bergen with Trondheim and Ålesund. Western Norway is served by several bus companies, which use the station at Strømgaten 8 (☎ 177).

By Car

Bergen is 485 km (300 mi) from Oslo. Route 7 is good almost as far as Eidfjord at the eastern edge of the Hardangerfjord, but then it deteriorates considerably. The ferry along the way, crossing the Hardanger Fjord from Brimnes to Bruravik, runs continually 5 AM to midnight and takes 10 minutes. At Granvin, 12 km (7 mi) farther north, Route 7 joins Route E68, which is an alternative route from Oslo, crossing the Sognefjorden from Refsnes to Gudvangen. From Granvin to Bergen, Route E68 hugs the fjord part of the way, making for spectacular scenery.

Driving from Stavanger to Bergen involves from two to four ferries and a long journey packed with stunning scenery. The Stavanger tourist information office can help plan the trip and reserve ferry space.

By Plane

Flesland Airport is 20 km (12 mi) south of Bergen. **SAS** (☎ 81/00–33–00) and **Braathens SAFE** (☎ 55/23–55–23) are the main domestic carriers. **British Airways** (serviced by Braathens SAFE) and **Lufthansa** (☎ 800/33–142) also serve Flesland.

Between the Airport and Downtown: Flesland is a 30-minute bus ride from the center of Bergen at off-peak hours. The **Flybussen** (Airport

Bus) departs three times per hour (less frequently on weekends) from the SAS Royal Hotel via Braathens SAFE's office at the Hotel Norge and from the bus station. Tickets cost NKr 35.

Driving from Flesland to Bergen is simple, and the road is well marked. Bergen has an electronic toll ring surrounding it, so any vehicle entering the city weekdays between 6 AM and 10 PM has to pay NKr 5. There is no toll in the other direction.

A taxi stand is outside the Arrivals exit. The trip into the city costs about NKr 250.

By Train

The Bergensbanen has five departures daily, plus an additional one on Sunday, in both directions on the Oslo–Bergen route; it is widely acknowledged as one of the most beautiful train rides in the world. Trains leave from Oslo S Station for the 7½- to 8½-hour journey. For information about trains out of Bergen, call ☎ 55/96–60–50.

Getting Around

The best way to see the small center of Bergen is on foot. Most sights are within walking distance of the marketplace.

By Bus

Tourist tickets for 48 hours of unlimited travel within the town boundaries cost NKr 90, payable on the yellow city buses. All buses serving the Bergen region depart from the central bus station at Strømgaten 8 (☎ 177). Buses between the main post office (Småstrandgt. and Olav Kyrres Gt.) and the railway station are free.

By Car

Downtown Bergen is enclosed by an inner ring road. The area within is divided into three zones, which are separated by ONE WAY and DO NOT ENTER signs. To get from one zone to another, return to the ring road and drive to an entry point into the desired zone. It's best to leave your car at a parking garage (the Birkebeiner Senter is on Rosenkrantz Gate, and there is a parking lot near the train station) and walk. You pay an NKr 5 toll every time you drive into the city—but driving out is free.

By Taxi

Taxi ranks are located in strategic places downtown. All taxis are connected to the central dispatching office (☎ 55/99–70–00) and can be booked in advance (☎ 55/99–70–10).

Sightseeing Passes

The 24-hour **Bergen Card,** which costs NKr 130 (NKr 200 for 48 hours), gives free admission to most museums and attractions, and rebates of 25% to 50% off sightseeing, rental cars, transportation to and from Bergen, and free parking (limited to marked areas). It's available at the tourist office and in most hotels.

Contacts and Resources

Dentists

The dental emergency center at Lars Hilles Gate 30 (☎ 55/32–11–20) is open daily 10–11 AM and 7–9 PM.

Emergencies

Emergency Rooms: The outpatient center at Lars Hilles Gate 30 (☎ 55/32–11–20), near Grieghallen, is open 24 hours.

Guided Tours

Bergen is the guided-tour capital of Norway because it is the starting point for most fjord tours. Tickets for all tours are available from the tourist office.

Fjord Tours: Bergen is the much-acclaimed "Gateway to the Fjords," with dozens of fjord-tour possibilities. The following is only meant as a sampling; check with the tourist office (☞ *below*) for additional recommendations. The ambitious all-day **"Norway-in-a-Nutshell"** bus-train-boat tour (you can book through the tourist office) goes through Voss, Flåm, Myrdal, and Gudvangen—truly a breathtaking trip—and is the best way to see a lot in a short amount of time.

Traveling by boat is an advantage because the contrasts between the fjords and mountains are greatest at water level, and the boats are comfortable and stable (the water is practically still), so seasickness is rare. Stops are frequent, and all sights are explained. **Fjord Sightseeing** (☎ 55/25–90–00) offers a four-hour local fjord tour. **Fylkesbaatane** (County Boats) **i Sogn og Fjordane** (☎ 55/90–70–70) has several combination tours. Tickets are sold at the tourist office (☞ *below*) and at the quay.

Orientation Tours: **Bergen Guided Tours** (☎ 55/59–32–00) offers three city tours departing from Hotel Norge, including one to Edvard Grieg's home and the Fantoft Stave Church. The **Bergen Guide Service** (☎ 55/32–77–00) offers a historic tour of the buildings at Bryggen, as well as entrance to Bryggens Museum, the Hanseatic Museum, and Schøtstuene after the tour, which is conducted by knowledgeable guides. **Bergens-Expressen** (☎ 55/53–11–50), a "train on tires," leaves from Torgalmenningen for a one-hour ride around the center of town, summer only.

Late-Night Pharmacies

Apoteket Nordstjernen (☎ 55/31–68–84), by the bus station, is open daily from 7:30 AM to midnight, Sundays from 8:30 AM.

Money and Expenses

Exchanging Money: Outside normal banking hours, the Tourist Information Office on Bryggen can change money. Post offices exchange money and are open Monday through Wednesday and Friday 8 to 5, Thursday 8 to 6, and Saturday 9 to 2.

Opening and Closing Times

Most shops are open Monday–Wednesday and Friday 9–5. On Thursday, as well as Friday for some shops, the hours are 9–7. On Saturday shops are open 9–3. The shopping centers are open weekdays 9–8 and Saturdays 9–6.

Visitor Information

The **Tourist Information Office** (☎ 55/32–14–80) at Bryggen has brochures and maps and can arrange for accommodations and sightseeing. There is also a currency exchange.

7 CENTRAL NORWAY: THE HALLINGDAL VALLEY TO HARDANGERFJORD

In summer, the rugged peaks and flat plateaus of central Norway provide a spectacular backdrop for hikers and bikers: crystal clear streams ramble down mountainsides, flocks of sheep graze in the pastures, and snowcapped summits glisten in the distance. Come winter this area—especially Geilo, Gol, and Hemsedal—teems with skiers, both cross-country and downhill.

NORWAY'S INTERIOR BETWEEN Oslo and Bergen
is a land of superlatives—the tallest peaks, the
biggest national park, and the highest mountain
plateau—in Europe. It's prime vacation land for wilderness-sports
lovers, with fishing, canoeing, rafting, hiking, and horseback riding over
the Hardangervidda plateau in the summer, and skiing, particularly on
the slopes of Geilo, in winter.

Hallingdal Valley

120 km (74½ mi) from Oslo; 92 km (57 mi) from Drammen to Nesbyen.

Route 7 from Drammen winds through the historic Hallingdal Valley,
which is lined with small farming communities and ski resorts. Hallingdal is known for its many well-preserved wooden log buildings. **Nesbyen,** a small town in the heart of the valley, has a folk museum as
well as many campsites and a youth hostel.

En Route   About 21 km (13 mi) from Nesbyen you'll come across the small community of **Gol.** This town is popular with campers in summer and skiers
in winter who throng the mountains to the north and east of Gol during ski season.

Hemsedal

50   *35 km (21½ mi) from Gol.*

Spring, summer, winter, or fall, the valley of **Hemsedal,** and its surrounding area, is a great destination. Clear streams, blue lakes, and
striking mountains provide plenty of outdoor activities. In fact, here
in Hemsedal, Norwegian World Cup skiers often practice in the top
local ski center (☞ Skiing, *below*).

Outdoor Activities and Sports
SKIING

Hemsedal Skisenter (☎ 32/05–53–00) has 34 km (21 mi) of alpine
slopes, 175 km (108 mi) of cross-country trails, and 17 ski lifts. The **Vin-
terlandkortet ski pass** is accepted at all 71 ski slopes in Geilo, Hemsedal,
Gol, Nesbyen, and Ål, and is available at ski centers and tourist offices.

Torpo

51   *52 km (32 mi) from Hemsedal.*

Driving from Gol to Geilo, you'll pass through the tiny town of Torpo,
known for its church, presumably the oldest building in Hallingdal.
Torpo stave church is believed to have been built in the late 12th century. Its colorful painted ceiling is decorated with scenes from the life
of Saint Margaret. It's open June through August, daily 9:30–5:30.

Geilo

52   *35 km (21 mi) west of Torpo; 251 km (155½ mi) from Oslo; 256 km
(159 mi) from Bergen.*

Geilo is dead-center between Bergen and Oslo. The country's most popular winter resort, it often draws more than a million visitors a year
to its alpine slopes and cross-country trails; many people ski directly
from their hotels and cabins. Recently Geilo has become a popular summer destination, with fishing, boating, hiking, and riding. Plan ahead
if you want to visit at Easter, when Norwegians flock here for a final
ski weekend.

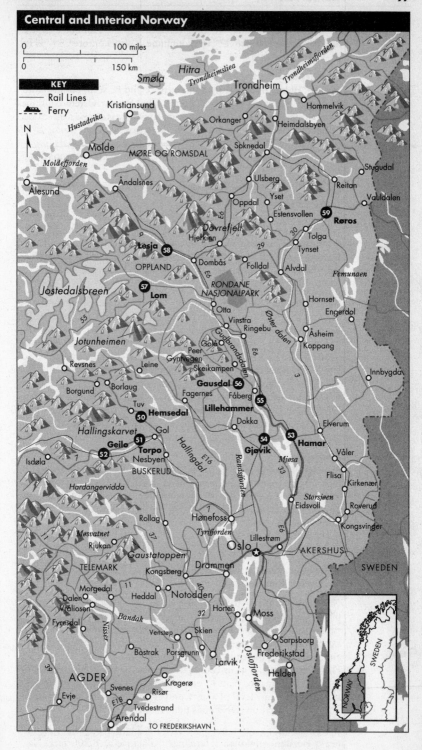

On the first Saturday in August, the **Holsdagen** festival presents folk music and a traditional wedding ceremony in the **Hol Stave Church** and **Hol Folkemuseum** (✉ Hol Kommune, Kulturkontoret, 3576 Hol, ☎ 32/08–81–40).

Dining and Lodging

$$$–$$$$ ✕🛏 **Dr. Holms Hotell.** Truly a place to see and be seen, Holms Hotell
★ is among Norway's top resort hotels. Chef Steinar Østent continues the gourmet reputation of the restaurant, and there is an excellent seafood buffet on Friday evenings during the ski season. ✉ *3580 Geilo,* ☎ *32/ 09–06–22,* FAX *32/09–16–20. 127 rooms. Restaurant, 2 bars, pub, 2 indoor pools, beauty parlor, sauna, exercise room, meeting rooms. AE, DC, MC, V.*

Outdoor Activities and Sports

RAFTING AND CANOEING

In Geilo they've combined rafting and canoeing with skiing, outfitting rubber rafts with a wood rudder, and taking off down the slopes for a bracing, if peculiar, swoosh. Contact the tourist board for details. **Norwegian Wildlife and Rafting** (☎ 61/23–87–27) and **Dagali Rafting** (☎ 32/09–38–20) organize trips in the Sjoa and Dagali areas.

SKIING

Geilo Skiheiser (☎ 32/09–59–20) has 24 km (15 mi) of alpine slopes, 130 km (81 mi) of cross-country trails, 18 lifts, and also a ski-board tunnel. Among the area's other four ski centers, **Vestlia** (☎ 32/09–01–88), west of the Ustedalsfjord, is a good choice for families; **Halstens-gård** (☎ 32/09–10–20) and **Slaatta** (☎ 32/09–03–70) have a range of alpine and cross-country trails; and **Havsdalsenteret** (☎ 32/09–17–77) attracts a young crowd to its long alpine slopes. Ski passes give access to all lifts in all five centers (a day pass costs NKr 220 and a week pass NKr 900). The **Vinterlandkortet ski pass** is accepted at all 71 ski slopes in Geilo, Hemsedal, Uvdal, and Ål and is available at ski centers and tourism offices.

Shopping

Brusletto & Co. (☎ 32/09–02–00), in central Geilo, is a purveyor of high-quality hunting knives with silver-inlaid handles made from burnished metal, walnut, and rosewood. Norwegian men wear these knives, used for hunting and hiking, on their belts—something akin to jewelry.

Hardangervidda

90 km (56 mi) from Geilo to Eidfjord; Rte. 7 is the main road that crosses Hardangervidda.

Geilo is the gateway to **Hardangervidda,** Europe's largest mountain plateau and Norway's biggest national park—10,000 square km (3,861 square mi) of unique scenery, with the largest herd of wild reindeer in Europe, lakes and streams teeming with trout and char, and many birds and animals on the endangered list. It also has rich and varied flora. Flat in the east and at its center, the plateau is more mountainous in the west. Touring the plateau, either on horseback or on foot, you can find a trail for any level of ability, and along the trails, the Norwegian Touring Association (DNT) has built cabins.

About an hour's drive north of Geilo is Hardangervidda's highest peak, **Hardangerjøkulen** (Hardanger Glacier), at 6,200 feet. Near Hardangerjøkulen you can take a guided hike to the archaeological digs of 8,000-year-old Stone Age settlements. Contact the Geilo Tourist Office (☎ 32/09–59–00).

At the base of the plateau is the innermost arm of the **Hardangerfjord.** Although it's not as dramatic as some of the other fjords, it is pastoral, with royal-blue water and lush apple orchards.

En Route The western settlement of **Finse** (on the Bergen railroad), about 34 km (21 mi) from Geilo, is one of the most frigid places in southern Norway, with snow on the ground as late as August. Here polar explorers Nansen and Scott tested their equipment, and the snow scenes in the *Star Wars* movies were filmed. It, too, is a good starting point for tours of Hardangervidda.

If you'd like to try summer skiing, contact the **Dekedalen Skisenter** (3590 Finse, ☎ 56/58–88–62).

Central Norway A to Z

Arriving and Departing

BY TRAIN

This region is served by the Oslo–Bergen line.

Contacts and Resources

VISITOR INFORMATION

The main **tourist offices** of the region are in **Geilo** (☎ 32/09–59–00); **Gol** (☎ 32/02–97–00); and **Nesbyen** (☎ 32/07–18–55).

8 INTERIOR NORWAY: LILLEHAMMER TO RØROS

Colorful farmhouses dot Norway's interior countryside, where rivers run wild through rolling valleys and mountains reach up to the sky. You'll see medieval stave churches, preserved mining towns, open-air museums, and the world's oldest paddleboat in this land with a rich heritage. Lillehammer hosted the 1994 Winter Olympics.

NORTHWARD IN NORWAY'S INNER MIDSECTION, the land turns to rolling hills and leafy forests, and the principal town, Lillehammer, attracts skiers from around the world to its slopes and trails; in 1994 it hosted the Winter Olympics. As you travel north, you'll enter Gubrandsdalen (*dal* means valley), one of the longest and most beautiful valleys in the country. Gudbrandsdalen extends from Lake Mjøsa, north of Oslo, diagonally across the country to Åndalsnes. At the base of the lake is Eidsvoll, where Norway's constitution was signed on May 17, 1814. Most visitors come to the region for the beautiful scenery and outdoor activities; tourism has increased substantially in this area since the 1994 Winter Olympics.

At the northern end of the region is the copper-mining town of Røros—which is on UNESCO's World Heritage List—a bucolic little town that's changed little for the past 100 years. The tourist board aptly calls the triangle between Oppland and Hedmark counties, south to Lillehammer, Troll Park. In a reminiscent tribute to the much celebrated 1994 games, this area is also billed as the "Olympic" part of Norway. The otherworldly quality of oblique northern light against wildflower-covered hills has inspired centuries of folk tales as well as artists from Wagner to Ibsen, who was awarded a government grant to scour the land for these very stories. Even today, locals claim he applied for the grant just to have the opportunity to hike the hills.

Numbers in the margin correspond to points of interest on the Central and Interior Norway map in Chapter 7.

Hamar

53 *134 km (83 mi) from Oslo; 66 km (41 mi) from Eidsvoll.*

During the Middle Ages, Hamar was the seat of a bishopric. Four Romanesque arches, which are part of the cathedral wall, remain the symbol of the city today. Ruins of the town's 13th-century monastery now form the backbone of a glassed-in exhibition of regional artifacts that date back to the Iron Age but also include more recent findings. Also on the grounds of the **Hedmarksmuseet and Domkirkeodden** (Hedemark Museum and Cathedral) sit 50 or so idyllic grass-roofed houses from the region, and a local favorite, the proliferating herb garden. ⊠ 2301 Hamar, ☎ 62/54–27–00. 🖼 NKr 60. ☉ Late-May–mid-June and mid-Aug.–Sept., daily 10–4; mid-June–mid-Aug., daily 10–6.

Hamar got a new lease on life in 1994 when the **Hamar Olympiahall** played host to the speed-skating and figure-skating events of the Lillehammer Winter Olympics. Now used for local exhibitions and conferences, the hall takes the shape of an upside-down Viking ship. Looking out on the town's nature reserve, the hall was built according to the highest environmental and construction standards. Its special laminated wood is so dense that no fire could burn it down. Contact Hamar Olympiahall (⊠ Åkersvika, 2300 Hamar, ☎ 62/51–75–00) for details on tours and sports facilities.

One of Europe's first railway museums, the **Jernbanemuseet** documents how Norway's railways developed, with life-sized locomotives on narrow-gauge tracks outside and train memorabilia inside. Tertittoget, NSB's last steam locomotive, gives rides from mid-May to mid-August. ⊠ Strandvn. 132, ☎ 62/51–31–60. 🖼 NKr 30. ☉ June and Aug., daily 10–4; July, daily 10–6.

The world's oldest paddleboat, the 140-year-old **D/S *Skibladner,*** also called the "White Swan of the Mjøsa," departs from Hamar, connecting the towns along the lake. The steamer stops daily at Hamar and creeps up to Lillehammer three days a week. The other days it stops at Eidsvoll. Many Norwegian emigrants to North America took the paddler's route from Lillehammer to Eidsvoll to connect with an Oslo-bound train. Be sure to ask for a schedule from the tourist information or the *Skibladner* office. A traditional dinner, consisting of poached salmon and potatoes, with strawberries and cream for dessert, is available for an extra fee. ⊠ *Parkgt. 2., 2300 Hamar,* ☎ *62/52–70–85.* ☉ *Mid-June–mid-Aug.*

NEED A BREAK?	**Sea Side Mat & Vin Hus** (☎ 62/52–62–10) sits on the dock near where the *Skibladner* calls; the brass fixtures and lakeside view will surely put you in a maritime mood. The simple fare includes sandwiches, salads, and omelets.

Gjøvik

54   *45 km (30 mi) from Hamar.*

The *Skibladner* stops several times a week at this quiet, hillside town, which claims to be home to the world's largest underground auditorium. So if you get a chance, check out the **Gjøvik Olympiske Fjellhall** (Olympic Mountain Hall), buried 400 ft below the midtown mountain. ☎ *61/13–82–00.*

OFF THE BEATEN PATH	**GILE GÅRD –** Farmhouses dot the rolling green countryside along this side of the Mjøsa. Some of them serve as lodgings, and others are just picturesque stops along the way. The Gile family has owned the Gile Farm since the 18th century, although the land has been used as farmland for some 5,000 years. In summer, a variety of uncommon flowers sprout atop the many Viking burial mounds that lie untouched around the house. Call for a schedule of events at the farmhouse. ⊠ *2850 Lena (off Rte. 33),* ☎ *61/16–03–73.* ☉ *Tues. Call for more information.*

Lillehammer

55   *40 km (25 mi) from Gjøvik, 60 km (37 mi) from Hamar.*

The winter-sports center of Lillehammer has 23,000 inhabitants. In preparation for the 1994 Winter Olympics, this small town built a ski-jumping arena, an ice-hockey hall, a cross-country skiing stadium, and a bobsled and luge track, in addition to other venues and accommodations. However, far-sighted planning kept expansion surprisingly minimal, ensuring that the town was not left in a state of Olympic obsolescence. After the games, which proved hugely successful, many of the structures built to house the foreign media were turned over to the regional college, and one-third of the athletes' quarters were transported to Tromsø to be used as housing.

Kulturhuset Banken, a magnificent, century-old bank building, is the main locale for cultural events. It is decorated with both contemporary and turn-of-the-century art. Don't miss the murals on the ceiling of the ceremonial hall. ⊠ *Kirkegt. 41,* ☎ *61/26–68–10.* ☉ *Tours for groups by appointment only.*

The **Olympiaparken** (Olympic Park) includes the Lysgårdsbakkene ski-jumping arena (🎟 Arena NKr 15. ☉ Daily 8–8), where the Winter Olympics' opening and closing ceremonies were held. From the tower you can see the entire town. Also in the park are **Håkons Hall,** used for ice hockey, and the **Birkebeineren Stadion** (ski stadium), which holds cross-country and biathlon events. ⊠ *Elvegaten 19,* ☎ *61/25–11–40.* ▨ *Free, but admission fee charged at individual facilities during athletic events.*

Norges Olympiske Museum (Olympic Museum) chronicles in an impressive exhibition hall every summer and winter Olympics since those of ancient Greece to the present day. The architects of Maihaugen's "We Won the Land" (☞ *below*) have also created the exhibits here. ⊠ *Håkons Hall, Olympic Park.* ☎ *61/25–21–00.* ▨ *NKr 50.* ☉ *June–Sept., daily 10–6; Oct.–May, Tues.–Sun. 11–4.*

The winter-sports facilities provide amusement all year-round in Lillehammer. You can try the **Downhill and Bobsled simulator** between Håkons Hall and Kristins Hall in the Olympic Park. It's a five-minute ride that replicates the sensations of being on a bobsled. ▨ *NKr 25.* ☉ *Jan.–late June and late Aug., daily 11–4; late June–mid-Aug., daily 10–7.*

Those older than the age of 12 can try the **Bobsled on Wheels**—it's the real thing with wheels instead of blades—at the Lillehammer Bobsled and Luge Stadion. Speeds of 100 km (60 mi) per hour are reached, so you'll get a distinct impression of what the sport is all about. ☎ *94/37–43–19.* ▨ *Wheeled bobsled NKr 125.* ☉ *Late May–early June and mid-Aug.–mid-Sept., daily noon–5; June–mid-Aug., daily 11–7.*

A highlight of Lillehammer's ski year is the **Birkebeineren cross-country ski race,** which commemorates the trek of two warriors whose legs were wrapped in birchbark (hence *birkebeiner*—birch legs), which was customary for people who couldn't afford wool or leather leggings. They raced across the mountains from Lillehammer to Østerdalen in 1205, carrying the 18-month-old prince Håkon Håkonsson away from his enemies. The race attracts 8,000 entrants annually. Cartoon figures of Viking children representing Håkon on skis and his aunt Kristin (on ice skates) were the official mascots for the Olympic games.

★ ☾ Lillehammer claims fame as a cultural center as well. Sigrid Undset, who won the Nobel Prize in literature in 1928, lived in the town for 30 years. It is also the site of **Maihaugen,** Norway's oldest (and, according to some, Scandinavia's largest) open-air museum, founded in 1887. The massive collection was begun by Anders Sandvik, an itinerant dentist who accepted folksy odds and ends—and eventually entire buildings—from the people of Gudbransdalen in exchange for repairing their teeth. Eventually Sandvik turned the collection over to the city of Lillehammer, which provided land for the museum.

Maihaugen's permanent indoors exhibit, **"We Won the Land,"** will leave you slack-jawed. Completed in 1993, this inventive meander chronicles Norway's history, starting in 10,000 BC when life was somewhere inside a mere drop of melting ice. After walking past life-sized, blue-hued dolls representing periods from the Black Death and 400 years of Danish rule, you will arrive in the 20th century to unsettling visions of the postwar West: a mannequin-junkie sits crumpled in a city stairwell and a lonely old lady tosses feed to the pigeons. Sound effects, period music (including the Rolling Stones), and realistic smells bring each room eerily to life. ⊠ *Maihaugvn 1,* ☎ *61/28–89–00.* ▨ *NKr 70.* ☉ *June–Aug., daily 9–6; May and Sept., daily 10–5; Oct.–Apr., Tues.–Sun. 11–4. Admission includes guided tour.*

One of the most important art collections in Norway is housed at the **Lillehammer Kunstmuseum** (Lillehammer Art Museum). In addition to Munch pieces, the gallery has one of the largest collections of works from the national romantic period. ⊠ *Stortorgt. 2,* ☎ *61/26–94–44.* ▨ *NKr 30.* ☉ *May–Sept., daily 10–5; Sept.–May, Tues.–Sun. 11–4.*

OFF THE
BEATEN PATH

HUNDERFOSSEN PARK – This amusement park takes pride in displaying the world's biggest troll, who sits atop a fairy-tale cave where carved-boulder trolls hold up the ceilings, and scenes from troll tales are depicted. There's a petting zoo for small children, rides, plus an energy center, with Epcot-like exhibits about oil and gas, and a five-screen theater. The park is 13 km (8 mi) north of Lillehammer. ⊠ *2638 Fåberg,* ☎ *61/27–72–22.* 🎟 *NKr 160.* ⊙ *Early June–mid-Aug., daily 10–8.*

Dining and Lodging

When the world came to Lillehammer in 1994, not everyone could stay in downtown hotels. A delightful alternative is a farm stay, which many VIPs took advantage of during the Olympics. Many farms lie in the vicinity around Lillehammer, with a good number on the other side of Lake Mjøsa. For more information and a photo-packed brochure, call **Country Holidays in Troll Park** (⊠ Olympia Utvikling, ☎ 61/28–99–70).

$$–$$$ ✕ **Lundegården Brasserie & Bar.** A piece of the Continent in the middle of Storgata, this restaurant is a haven where guests can enjoy a light snack in the bar area or a full meal. The menu offers such dishes as baked salmon with pepper-cream sauce and seasonal vegetables. The rattan furnishings in the bar and the starched white tablecloths in the dining room make for a pleasant interior. ⊠ *Storgt. 108A,* ☎ *61/26–90–22. Reservations essential. AE, DC, MC, V. No lunch.*

$$–$$$ ✕ **Nikkers Spiseri.** The staff is service-minded at this classic Norwegian restaurant, which serves cakes, sandwiches, and hot dishes. Lunch specials and à la carte evening meals are offered. ⊠ *Elvegt. 18,* ☎ *61/27–05–56. AE, DC, MC, V.*

$$–$$$ 🏨 **Comfort Home Hotel Hammer.** This 1990s hotel is named after the original Hammer farm, which first opened its doors to guests in 1665. The rooms are decorated in shades of green with oak furniture, both modern and rustic. Waffles, coffee, light beer, and an evening meal are included in the price. ⊠ *Storgt. 108, 2615,* ☎ *61/26–35–00,* ℻ *61/26–37–30. 67 rooms. Lobby lounge, sauna, meeting rooms. AE, DC, MC, V.*

$$–$$$ 🏨 **Mølla Hotell.** A converted mill houses one of Lillehammer's newer hotels. The intimate reception area on the ground floor gives the feeling of a private home. The top-floor bar—called Toppen—has a good view of Mjøsa, the town, and the ski-jump arena. Downstairs is a cheaper eatery called Egon. ⊠ *Elvegt. 12,* ☎ *61/26–92–94,* ℻ *61/26–92–95. 58 rooms. Bar, sauna, exercise room. AE, DC, MC, V.*

$$–$$$ 🏨 **Rica Victoria Hotel.** This classic, centrally located hotel has small, relaxing rooms, some of which look out on the main street and the outdoor café it owns, Terassen. **Victoria Stuene,** the hotel's restaurant, is among Norway's best. ⊠ *Storgt. 84b, 2600,* ☎ *61/25–00–49,* ℻ *61/25–24–74. 121 rooms. Lobby lounge, 2 restaurants, outdoor café, nightclub, meeting rooms, conference center. AE, DC, MC, V.*

$$ 🏨 **Gjestehuset Ersgaard.** Dating from the 1500s, originally called Eiriksgård (Eirik's Farm), today this white manor house has all modern facilities but retains its homey atmosphere. The surroundings are beautiful, including views of Lillehammer and Lake Mjøsa, which can be enjoyed from the large terrace. ⊠ *Nordseterv. 201 (at the Olympic Park),* ☎ *61/25–06–84,* ℻ *61/25–06–84. 30 rooms, 20 with baths. AE, DC, MC, V.*

$–$$ 🏨 **Birkebeineren Hotel, Motell & Apartments.** Rooms are functional in these central accommodations. ⊠ *Olympiaparken,* ☎ *61/26–47–00,* ℻ *61/26–47–50. 52 hotel rooms, 35 motel rooms, 40 apartments. Dining room, sauna. AE, DC, MC, V.*

$–$$ 🏨 **Breiseth Hotell.** This friendly hotel is right beside the railroad station and within walking distance of shops and businesses. The Dølaheimen Kafe serves hearty Norwegian meals. ⊠ *Jernbanegt. 1–5,* ☎

61/24–77–77, FAX *61/26–95–05. 89 rooms. Bar, brasserie, sauna. AE, DC, MC, V.*

Outdoor Activities and Sports

FISHING

Within the Troll Park, the **Gudbrandsdalåen** is touted as one of the best-stocked rivers in the country, and the size of Mjøsa trout (locals claim 25 pounds) is legendary. For seasons, permits (you'll need both a national and a local license), and tips, call local tourist boards (☞ Visitor Information *in* Interior Norway A to Z, *below*).

RAFTING AND CANOEING

The **Sjoa River,** close to Lillehammer, offers some of the most challenging rapids in the country. Contact **Heidal Rafting** (☎ 61/23–60–37).

SKIING

Lillehammer, the 1994 Winter Olympics town, is a major skiing center (20 km of alpine, 400 km of cross-country trails; 7 ski lifts). However, downtown Lillehammer is a good half-hour drive from most ski areas. If you want to ski right out the door of your hotel, call the tourist office to book a hotel by the slopes. Within the Lillehammer area, there are five ski centers: **Hafjell** (☎ 61/27–47–00), 10 km (6 mi) north, is an Olympic venue with moderately steep slopes; **Kvitfjell** (☎ 61/28–21–05), 50 km (31 mi) north, another Olympic site, has some of the most difficult slopes in the world; **Skei** and **Peer Gynt** (☞ Skiing *in* Gausdal, *below*), 30 km (19 mi) north and 80 km (50 mi) northwest, respectively; and **Galdhøpiggen Sommerskisenter** (☞ Skiing *in* Lom, *below*), 135 km (84 mi) northwest of Lillehammer. One ski-lift, one-day ticket, called a **Troll Pass** (🎫 NKr 195), is good for admission to lifts at five sites in the area (☞ Skiing *in* Lillehammer, *above*).

Gausdal

56 *18 km (11 mi) northwest of Lillehammer.*

The composer of Norway's national anthem and the 1903 Nobel Prize winner in literature, Bjørnstjerne Bjørnson lived at **Aulestad,** in Gausdal, from 1875 until he died in 1910. After his wife, Karoline, died in 1934, their house was opened as a museum. ✉ *2620 Follebu,* ☎ *61/22–41–10.* 🎫 *NKr 30.* 🕐 *Late May–Sept., daily 10–3:30.*

At Gausdal, just north of Lillehammer, you can turn onto the scenic, well-marked **Peer Gynt Vegen** (Peer Gynt Road), named for the real-life person behind Ibsen's character. A feisty fellow, given to tall tales, he is said to have spun yarns about his communing with trolls and riding reindeer backward. As you travel along the rolling hills sprinkled with old farmhouses and rich with views of the mountains of Rondane, Dovrefjell, and Jotunheimen, the road is only slightly narrower and just 3 km (2 mi) longer than the main route. It passes two major resorts, **Skeikampen/Gausdal** and **Golå/Wadahl,** before rejoining E6 at Vinstra. Between Vinstra and Harpefoss, at the Sødorp Church, you can visit Peer Gynt's stone grave and what is said to be his old farm. Although you can walk the grounds, the 15th-century farm is privately owned.

En Route The E6 highway passes through **Vinstra,** the village of Peer Gynt, where, around mid-August every year, the Peer Gynt Festival celebrates the character and his lore. The road continues along the great valley of the River Lågen, birthplace of *Gudbrandsdalsost,* a sweet brown goat cheese. From this road you'll see rolling views of red farmhouses and lush fields stretching from the valley to the mountainsides.

Dining and Lodging

$$$ ✕🍽 **Golå Høyfjellshotell og Hytter.** Tucked away in Peer Gynt terri-
★ tory north of Vinstra, this peaceful hotel is furnished in Norwegian coun-
try style. The restaurant has a simple menu of fresh local fish and game,
which is elegantly prepared. ⊠ *2646 Golå,* ☎ *61/29–81–09,* 🆁🅰🆇 *61/
29–85–40. 42 rooms. Restaurant, pool, downhill and cross-country
skiing, children's programs, meeting rooms. AE, DC, MC, V.*

Outdoor Activities and Sports

HIKING

You can pick up maps and the information-packed **"Peer Gynt"** pam-
phlet at the tourism office in Vinstra; then hike anywhere along the
50-km (31-mi) circular route, passing Peer's farm, cottages, and mon-
ument. Overnighting in cabins or hotels is particularly popular on the
Peer Gynt Trail, where you can walk to each of the **Peer Gynt hotels.**
(⊠ Box 115, 2647 Hundorp, ☎ 61/29–66–66, 🆁🅰🆇 61/29–66–88).

SKIING

Skei (☎ 61/22–85–55), near Gausdal, has both cross-country and
alpine trails. **Peer Gynt** (☎ 61/29–85–28) has respectable downhill but
is stronger as a cross-country venue. One ski-lift ticket, called a **Troll
Pass** (⊠ NKr 175), is good for admission to lifts at five sites in the
area (☞ Skiing *in* Lillehammer, *above*).

Lom

57 *At Otta, Rte. 15 turns off for the 62-km (38-mi) drive to Lom.*

Lom, in the middle of Jotunheimen national park, is a picturesque, rus-
tic town, with log-cabin architecture, a stave church from 1170, and
plenty of decorative rosemaling.

Lom Stavkirke (Lom Stave Church), a mixture of old and new con-
struction, is on the main road. The interior, including the pulpit, a large
collection of paintings, pews, windows, and the gallery, is Baroque. ☎
61/21–12–86. ⊠ *NKr 20.* ☉ *June–Aug., daily 9–9.*

Dining and Lodging

$–$$ ✕🍽 **Fossheim Turisthotell.** Arne Brimi's and successor Kristofer Hoy-
★ land's cooking has made this hotel famous. Hoyland's a self-taught cham-
pion of the local cuisine and now a household name in Norway; his
dishes are based on nature's kitchen, with liberal use of game, wild mushrooms, and berries. Built as a staging inn in 1897, the hotel has been
updated several times. However, it retains its traditional character, with
solid-timber walls and antique furnishings, conveying an intimate and
memorable ambience. ⊠ *2686,* ☎ *61/21–10–05,* 🆁🅰🆇 *61/21–15–10. 54
rooms. Restaurant, bar. AE, DC, MC, V.*

$$ 🍽 **Vågå Hotel.** About halfway between Otta and Lom on Route 15,
this homey, no-frills hotel lies in the lovely mountain village that hosts
a number of hang-gliding competitions every summer. It's a good place
to park for the night if you're skiing, hiking, or rafting the next day.
⊠ *2680 Vågåmo,* ☎ *61/23–70–71,* 🆁🅰🆇 *61/23–75–25. 60 rooms. Restau-
rant, bar, indoor pool, meeting rooms. AE, D, MC, V.*

$ 🍽 **Elveseter Hotell.** There are many reasons to overnight at this unusually
original hotel, including a swimming pool in a barn dating from 1579.
About 24 km (15 mi) from Lom in Bøverdalen, this family-owned hotel
feels like a museum: every room has a history, and doors and some walls
have been painted by local artists. The public rooms are filled with mu-
seum-quality paintings and antiques. ⊠ *2687 Bøverdalen,* ☎ *61/21–
20–00,* 🆁🅰🆇 *61/25–48–74. 100 rooms. Restaurant, bar, indoor pool, meet-
ing rooms. AE, MC, V. Closed mid-Sept.–May.*

Outdoor Activities and Sports

DOGSLEDDING

In Jotunheimen, **Magnar Aasheim and Kari Steinaug** (⊠ Sjoa Rafting, ☎ 61/23–98–50) have one of the biggest kennels in Norway, with more than 30 dogs. You can travel as a sled-bound observer or control your own team of four to six dogs, most of which are ridiculously friendly Siberian and Alaskan huskies.

HIKING

In summer you can hike single-file (for safety purposes, in case of calving or cracks) on the ice and explore ice caves on the **Galdhøpiggen** glacier. Call Lom Fjellføring (☎ 61/21–21–42) or the tourist office (☞ *below*).

For hikers with sturdy legs, there's a path along a mountain ridge overlooking Gjende lake that makes for a good day-long hike (it's a favorite with Norwegians). A boat will drop you at the path's starting point and you'll end up atop **Bessegen** in Jotunheimen. For information, call the tourist office (☞ *below*).

NATIONAL PARKS

In this region you'll find **Ormtjernkampen,** a virgin spruce forest, and **Jotunheimen,** a rougher area spiked with glaciers, as well as Norway's highest peak, the **Galdhøpiggen.**

SKIING

To the east of the Gudbrandsdalen is the **Troll-løype** (Troll Trail), 250 km of country trails that vein across a vast plateau that's bumped with mountains, including the Dovrefjells to the north. For information, contact the Otta Tourist Office (⊠ 2670 Otta, ☎ 61/23–02–44). **Beitostølen** (9 km [5 mi] of downhill slopes, 150 km [93 mi] of cross-country trails; 7 ski lifts), on the southern slopes of the Jotunheim range, has everything from torchlit night skiing to hang gliding. **Galdhøpiggen Sommerskisenter** (⊠ 2686 Bøverdalen, ☎ 61/21–21–42 or 61/21–17–50) sits on a glacier, which makes it great for summer skiing.

Lesja

58 *159 km (99 mi) from Lom.*

As you follow Route E6 toward Lesja, the broad, fertile valleys and snow-capped mountains of the Upper Gudbrandsdal provide staggering scenery for the drive. The area around Lesja is trout-fishing country; Lesjaskogvatnet, the lake, has a mouth at either end, so the current changes in the middle. The landscape becomes more dramatic with every mile as jagged rocks loom up from the river, leaving the tiny settlement of **Marstein** without sun for five months of the year.

OFF THE BEATEN PATH — **JORUNDGÅRD MIDDELALDER SENTER –** Anyone who read Sigrid Undset's 1928 Nobel prize-winning trilogy, *Kristin Lavransdatter,* will remember that the tale's heroine grew up on a medieval farm of the same name. In 1996 actress Liv Ullmann directed a film based on the book a few feet away from where the story was said to have taken place. The authentic medieval farm she built is now Jorundgård Medieval Center, a historical and cultural museum. ⊠ *Sel,* ☎ *61/23–37–00 or 61/23–02–44.* ☜ *NKr 40, guided tours every ½ hr.* ☉ *June–mid-Sept., daily 10–6.*

Outdoor Activities and Sports

GUIDED TOURS

From 1932 to 1953, musk ox were transported from Greenland to the Dovrefjell, where about 60 still roam—bring binoculars to see them.

For information on safarilike tours, call the Dombås Tourist Office (☎ 61/24–14–44).

The scrubby, flat, and wide **Rondane** to the southeast of Lesja, and **Dovre-fjell,** peaked to the north, have some of the country's steepest mountains and are home to wild musk ox, reindeer, and birds.

Røros

59   *317 km (197 mi) from Lesja; 157 km (97 mi) from Trondheim.*

At the northern end of the Østerdal, the long valley to the east of Gudbrandsdalen, lies Røros. For more than 300 years practically everyone who lived in this one-company town was connected with the copper mines. Notice there are two main axes: one leading to the church, the other to the company. Since many of the early settlers were German engineers, Røros resembles more closely a crowded German *dorf* (hamlet or village) than it does a more spread-out Norwegian farm village. The last mine in the region closed in 1986, but the town has survived thanks to other industries, including tourism, especially after it was placed on UNESCO's World Heritage List.

Røros's main attraction is the **Old Town,** with its 250-year-old workers' cottages, slag dumps, and managers' houses, one of which is now City Hall. Descendants of the man who discovered the first copper ore in Røros still live in the oldest of the nearly 100 protected buildings. The tourist office has 75-minute guided tours of this part of town, starting at the information office and ending at the church. ☜ *NKr 40.* ☉ *Tours early June and late Aug.–mid-Sept., Mon.–Sat. at 11; late June–mid-Aug., Mon.–Sat. at 10, noon, 1, 2, and 3, Sun. at 3; mid-Sept.–May, Sat. at 11.*

The **Røroskirke** (Røros Church), which rises above all the other buildings in the town, is an eight-sided stone structure from 1784 (the mines' symbol is on the tower). It can seat 1,600, quite surprising in a town with a population of only 3,500 today. The pulpit looms above the center of the altar, and seats encircle the top perimeter. Two hundred years ago wealthy locals paid for the privilege of sitting there. ☎ *72/41–00–00.* ☜ *NKr15.* ☉ *Early June and late Aug.–mid-Sept., weekdays 2–4, Sat. noon–2; mid-June–late Aug., Mon.–Sat. 10–5, Sun. 2–4; Oct.–May, Sat. noon–2.*

OFF THE
BEATEN PATH
OLAVSGRUVA – The guided tour of Olaf's Mine, a former copper mine outside town and now a museum, takes visitors into the depths of the earth, complete with sound-and-light effects. Remember to bring warm clothing and good shoes, as the temperature belowground is about 5°C (41°F) year-round. ⊠ *Rte. 31,* ☎ *72/41–44–50.* ☜ *NKr 45,* ☉ *guided tours early June and late Aug.–Sept., Mon.–Sat. at 1 and 3, Sun. at noon; late June–mid-Aug., daily at 10:30, noon, 1:30, 3, 4:30, and 6 (with entertainment program); Oct.–May, Sat. at 3.*

The **Rørosmuseet** (Røros Museum), in an old smelting plant, documents the history of the mines, with working models in one-tenth scale demonstrating the methods used in mining. ☎ *72/41–05–00.* ☜ *NKr 45.* ☉ *Late July–mid-Aug., weekdays 11:30–6, weekends 10:30–4; mid-Aug.–Late July, weekdays 11–3, weekends 11–2.*

Dining and Lodging

If you want to explore the green, pastured mountains just south of Røros, more than a dozen farmhouses take overnight visitors. Some are hytter, but others, such as the **Vingelsgaard Gjestgiveri** (☎ 62/49–45–43), have entire wings devoted to guest rooms. Call **Vingeln Turistinformasjon** (☎ 62/49–46–65) for more information.

$$–$$$ ✕▣ **Best Western Bergstadens Hotel.** The lobby here can be very inviting, especially when there's a fire in the stone fireplace. The main draw is the dining room: chef Lars Winther sticks to local traditions and products—fish from mountain streams and berries from the nearby forest. ✉ *Oslovn. 2, 7460,* ☎ *72/40–60–80,* FAX *72/41–01–55. 73 rooms, 2 suites. 2 restaurants, 2 bars, pub, pool, sauna, nightclub, meeting rooms. AE, DC, MC, V.*

Outdoor Activities and Sports

SKIING

At the northern end of the Gubransdalen region, west of Røros, is **Oppdal** (45 km of alpine pistes, 186 km of cross-country trails; 10 ski lifts), a World Cup venue. Like most other areas, it has lighted trails and snow-making equipment.

Shopping

There are so many craftsmen in downtown Røros that the tourist office will arrange a tour of their workshops for those interested. In the mountains south of Røros, Aashilde Westgaard sells a smattering of antiques and junk from her farmhouse-boutique, **Skraphandlerbua** (✉ 2542 Vingeln, ☎ 62/49–45–40). If you're planning to explore the area, ask the tourist bureau in Røros (☞ *below*) for directions to this odd and wonderful shop.

Interior Norway A to Z

Arriving and Departing

BY CAR

The wide, two-lane Route E6 north from Oslo passes through Hamar and Lillehammer. Route 3 follows Østerdalen (the eastern valley) from Oslo. Route 30 at Tynset leads to Røros and E6 on to Trondheim, 156 km (97 mi) farther north.

BY TRAIN

There are good train connections between Oslo and the major interior towns to the north. The region is served by the Oslo–Trondheim line and two other lines.

Getting Around

BY CAR

Roads in the north become increasingly hilly and twisty as the terrain roughens into the central mountains. The northern end of the region is threaded by E16, E6, and Routes 51 and 3. Don't speed: high-tech markers at the roadside, particularly prevalent in the area of Vinstra and Otta, are actually cameras. Exceed the speed limit and you'll receive a ticket in the mail.

Contacts and Resources

VISITOR INFORMATION

Gjøvik (✉ Jernbanegt. 2, ☎ 61/17–16–88). **Vinstra** (☎ 61/29–47–70). **Hamar** (✉ Vikingskipet, Olympia Hall, ☎ 62/51–02–25). **Lillehammer** (✉ Lilletorget, ☎ 61/25–92–99). **Lom** (☎ 61/21–29–90). **Øyer** (☎ 61/27–70–00). **Røros** (✉ Peder Hiortsgt. 2, ☎ 72/41–00–00). **Vågåmo** (✉ Brennvegen 1, 2680, ☎ 61/23–78–80).

9 THE WEST COAST: FJORD COUNTRY

The Norwegian fjords snake inland from the Russian border in the far north all the way to Norway's southern tip. In spectacular inlets like Sognefjord and Geirangerfjord, vertical walls shoot up out of the water, jagged snowcapped peaks blot out the sky, and water tumbles down off mountains in an endless variety of colors, from thundering turquoise to wispy white.

THIS FJORD-RIDDLED COAST, from south of Bergen to Kristiansund, is stippled with islands and grooved with deep barren valleys, with most of the fertile land edging the water. The farther north you travel, the more rugged and wild the landscape. The motionless Sognefjord is the longest inlet, snaking 190 km (110 mi) inland. It is 4,000 ft deep—a depth that often makes it appear black. Some of its sections are so narrow, with rock walls looming on either side, that they look as if they've been sliced from the mountains.

At the top of Sogn og Fjordane county is a succession of fjords referred to as Nordfjord, with Jostedalsbreen, mainland Europe's largest glacier, to the south. Sunnfjord is the coastal area between Nordfjord and Sognefjord, with Florø, the county seat, on an island close to Norway's westernmost point.

In the county of Møre og Romsdal, you'll see mountains that are treeless moonscapes of gray rock and stone cliffs that hang out over the water far below. Geirangerfjord is the most spectacular fjord.

There is more to the central region than fidgety coasts and peaks. In fact, tourists have been visiting central fjord country ever since the English "discovered" the area some 150 years ago in their search for the ultimate salmon. One of these tourists was Germany's Kaiser Wilhelm, who spent every summer except one, from 1890 to 1913, in Molde and helped rebuild Ålesund into one of the most fantastic fits of architectural invention in Scandinavia.

The best way to see the fjord country is to make an almost circular tour—from Oslo to Åndalsnes, out to the coastal towns of Ålesund, Molde, and Kristiansund, then over Trollstigveien to Geiranger, by ferry to Hellesylt, down to Stryn, around Loen and Olden and through the subglacial tunnel to Fjærland, and by ferry to Balestrand, connecting with another ferry down to Flåm, where the railroad connects with Myrdal on the Bergen line (☞ Fjord Tours *in* Bergen A to Z *in* Chapter 6). Then the trip can either continue on to Bergen or back to Oslo.

While traveling, keep in mind that outside of some roadside snack bars and simple cafeterias, restaurants are few in fjord country. The majority of visitors dine at the hotels, where food is generally abundant and simple.

Åndalsnes

Ⓜ *495 km (307 mi) from Bergen, 354 km (219 mi) from Trondheim.*

★ Åndalsnes, an industrial town of 3,000 people, has at least three things going for it: as the last stop on the railroad, it is a gateway to fjord country; Trollstigveien (Trolls' Path); and Trollveggen (Trolls' Wall).

From **Horgheimseidet,** which used to have a gingerbread hotel for elegant tourists—often European royalty—you can view **Trollveggen,** the highest sheer rock wall in Europe (3,300 ft).

Trollstigveien, one of Europe's most fantastic roads, starts in Åndalsnes. This road took 100 men 20 summers (from 1916 to 1936) to build, in a constant fight against rock and water. Trollstigveien and Ørneveien (at the Geiranger end) zigzag over the mountains separating two fjords. They're open only in summer. Halfway up, the spray from **Stigfoss** (Path Falls) blows across the bridge.

The West Coast

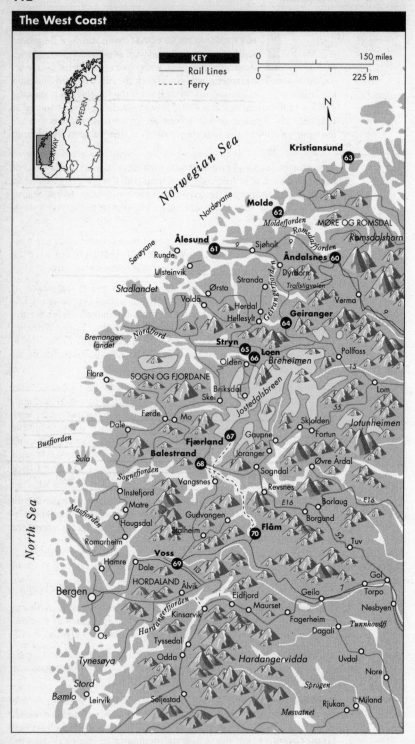

KEY
— Rail Lines
--- Ferry

0   150 miles
0   225 km

N

NORWAY
SWEDEN

Norwegian Sea

Kristiansund **63**

Nordøyane

Molde **62**
Moldefjorden
Romsdalfjorden
MØRE OG ROMSDAL
Romsdalshorn

Sørøyane
Ålesund **61**
Sjøholt
Åndalsnes **60**
Runde
Dyrdorn
Trollstigveien
Ulsteinvik
Stranda
Verma
Stadlandet
Ørsta
Herdal
Volda
Hellesylt
Geiranger **64**
Geirangerfjorden

Bremanger-
landet
Nordfjord
Stryn **65**
Loen **66**
Breheimen
Pollfoss

Florø
SOGN OG FJORDANE
Olden
15

Briksdal
Jostedalsbreen
Lom

Skei
Skjolden
Fortun
Jotunheimen
55

Dale
Førde
Mo
Fjærland **67**
Gaupne
Buefjorden
Joranger
Øvre Årdal

Sula
Balestrand **68**
Sogndal

Sognefjorden
Vangsnes
Revsnes
E16
E16
Instefjord
Borlaug

Matre
Borgund
Haugsdal
Gudvangen
Flåm **70**
Masfjorden
Stalheim
52
Tuv
Romarheim

Voss **69**
Gol
Hamre
Dale
Torpo
North Sea
HORDALAND
Ålvik
Geilo
7
Nesbyen
Bergen
Eidfjord
Maurset
Hardangerfjorden
Fagerheim
Tunnhovdfj.
Kinsarvik
Dagali
Os
Tyssedal
Uvdal
Tynesøya
Odda
Hardangervidda
Nore
Stord
Sprogen
Bømlo
Leirvik
Seljestad
Rjukan
Miland
Møsvatnet

Lodging

$$ 🏨 **Grand Hotel Bellevue.** The cheery rooms have bright carpeting and old prints of the fjord decorating the walls. ⊠ *Åndalsgt. 5, 6300,* 📞 *71/22–75–00,* 📠 *71/22–60–38. 86 rooms. Restaurant, bar, meeting rooms. AE, DC, MC, V.*

Ålesund

⬤ *240 km (150 mi) west of Åndalsnes.*

★ On three islands and between two bright blue fjords is Ålesund, home to 38,000 inhabitants and one of Norway's largest harbors for exporting dried and fresh fish. Nearly 800 buildings in the center of town were destroyed by fire in 1904. In the rush to shelter the 10,000 homeless victims, Kaiser Wilhelm II, who often vacationed here, led a mercurial rebuilding that married the German Art Nouveau with Viking flourishes. Winding streets are crammed with buildings topped with turrets, spires, gables, dragonheads, and curlicues. To get the most of what you see, try to join one of the tourism office's walking tours.

To learn more about what they call Jugendstil architecture, visit the exhaustive **Aalesunds Museum,** whose photographs, drawings, and models of the town before and after the fire will make you appreciate the disaster even more. ⊠ *R. Rønnebergsgt. 16,* 📞 *70/12–31–70.* 📠 *NKr 20.* 🕙 *Mid-June–mid-Aug., weekdays 11–4, Sat. 11–3, Sun. noon–3; mid-Aug.–mid-June, weekdays 11–3, weekends noon–3.*

You can drive or take a bus (📞 70/12–41–70) up nearby Aksla Mountain to a vantage point, **Kniven** (the knife), for a splendid view of the city—which absolutely glitters at night.

If you're traveling by car, you should consider a trip to the islands of **Giske.** A clump of round-topped, temperate islands off the Atlantic coast, they are each accessible by tunnel. If you go as far as Godøy in the summertime, stop at the **Alnes Lighthouse** (📞 70/18–50–90), where you can buy handicrafts and light refreshments.

☾ One of Ålesund's newest attractions, the **Atlantic Sea Park** sits on the ocean 3 km (2 mi) west of town. Ideal for a family outing, this dramatically situated park has fishing stands, hiking trails, and swimming sites, plus Scandinavia's largest aquarium. ⊠ *Tueneset,* 📞 *70/10–70–60.* 📠 *NKr 75.* 🕙 *June–Aug., daily 10–8; Sept.–May, Sun. 10–6.*

OFF THE
BEATEN PATH

RUNDE – Norway's southernmost major bird rock, Runde, is near Ålesund. It's one of the largest in Europe and a breeding ground for some 130 species, including puffins, gannets, and shags. The island is otherwise known for the "Runde Hoard," 1,300 kilograms (2,860 pounds) of silver and gold coins retrieved from a Dutch ship that sank in 1725. A catamaran leaves from Skateflua quay for the 25-minute trip to Hareid, where it connects with a bus for the 50-km (31-mi) trip to Runde. A path leads from the bus stop to the nature reserve. Call the Runde tourist office (☞ Visitor Information *in* The West Coast A to Z, *below*) for more information.

Dining and Lodging

$$ ✕ **Fjellstua.** This mountaintop restaurant has tremendous views over the surrounding peaks, islands, and fjords. There are several dining venues here, but the main restaurant serves a variety of dishes and homemade desserts. ⊠ *Top of Aksla mountain,* 📞 *70/12–65–82. AE, DC, MC, V. Closed mid-Dec.–Feb.*

$$ ✕ **Gullix.** The decor is over the top, but you can't fault the food, which ranges from sautéed monkfish garnished with shrimp, mussels, and crayfish to grilled, marinated filet mignon of lamb. ⊠ *Rådstugt. 5B,* ☎ *70/12–05–48. AE, DC, MC, V.*

$$ ✕ **Sjøbua.** Pick your own lobster from the large tank at one of Nor-
★ way's most renowned restaurants. The mixed fish and shellfish plat-
ter comes highly recommended. ⊠ *Brunholmgt. 1,* ☎ *70/12–71–00. AE, DC, MC, V. Closed Sun.*

$ ✕ **Brosundet Cafe.** This coffee shop in First Hotel Atlantica has its own
★ bakery, so there are always homemade bread and rolls. It serves tra-
ditional Norwegian specialties, including bløtkake and *nøttekake* (nut cake), as well as stews and fish dishes. ⊠ *R. Rønnebergsgt. 4,* ☎ *70/ 12–91–00. Reservations not accepted. AE, DC, MC, V.*

$$$ ▥ **Quality Scandinavie Hotel.** The impressive building with towers and
★ arches dates from 1905, whereas most rooms are modern and beauti-
fully decorated. ⊠ *Løvenvoldgt. 8, 6002,* ☎ *70/12–31–31,* ⅎⅫ *70/13– 23–70. 65 rooms. Restaurant, bar, pizzeria, meeting rooms. AE, DC, MC, V.*

$$–$$$ ▥ **First Hotel Atlantica.** Reproduction van Gogh prints hang on the brightly colored walls of this hotel's cheery guest rooms. ⊠ *R. Røn-nebergsgt. 4, 6004,* ☎ *70/12–91–00,* ⅎⅫ *70/12–62–52. 52 rooms. Restaurant, café. AE, DC, MC, V.*

$$ ▥ **Comfort Home Hotel Bryggen.** This hotel, with stone walls and glassed-in atria, is housed in a converted turn-of-the-century fish ware-house. Strewn with wooden oars, life vests, and fishing tools, the lobby gives a glimpse on the importance of fishing to Ålesund. A light evening buffet is included in the rates. Fishing equipment is available; although Bryggen is on the water, anglers are advised to go farther afield for a better catch. ⊠ *Apotekergt. 1–3, 6021,* ☎ *70/12–64–00,* ⅎⅫ *70/12– 11–80. 85 rooms. Sauna, Turkish bath, fishing, meeting rooms. AE, DC, MC, V.*

$$–$$$ ▥ **Scandic Hotel.** This large, postmodern building complex stands next to the Exhibition Hall. Its interior design has a maritime theme. The rooms are spacious. ⊠ *Molovn. 6, 6004,* ☎ *70/12–81–00,* ⅎⅫ *70/ 12–92–10. 117 rooms, 6 suites. Restaurant, bar, indoor pool, sauna. AE, DC, MC, V.*

Molde

🔢 *69 km (43 mi) north of Ålesund on Route 668.*

During World War II the German air force suspected that King Haakon VII was staying in a red house here and bombed every red house in town. These days, Molde is a modern town, after being almost entirely rebuilt. The best time to see Molde is during the town's annual jazz festival in late July. Big names from around the world gather for a huge jam ses-sion. Tickets for the fest can be purchased at all post offices in Norway.

If you like to walk, take the footpath that leads uphill to the charm-ing **Romsdalsmuseet** (Romsdal Open-Air Museum). The path begins on Storgata near the Alexandra Hotel at the King's Birch Tree, named after the place where the king and crown prince were sheltered during the war. On the way to the museum, stop at Reknes Park for a view of the 222 mountain peaks on the other side of the Romdalsfjord. Costumed tour guides will lead you through the open-air museum's 40 grass-roofed farmhouses and churches dating back to the 14th century. ⊠ *Museumsvn. 14,* ☎ *71/25–25–34.* ☉ *Early June and late Aug., Mon.–Sat. 10–2, Sun. noon–3; mid-June–mid-Aug., Mon.–Sat. 10–6, Sun. noon–6.*

☎ 70/26–30–90, FAX 70/26–31–77. *48 rooms, 18 cabins. Restaurant, bar, boating, fishing. MC, V.*

65 *If you continue on to Stryn from Geiranger, take the ferry across the Geiranger Fjord to Hellesylt, a 75-minute ride. It's about 50 km (30 mi) from Hellesylt to Stryn on Rte. 60.*

Stryn, Loen, and Olden, at the eastern end of Nordfjord, were among the first tourist destinations in the region more than 100 years ago. Stryn is famous for its salmon river and summer ski center—**Stryn Sommerskisenter** (⊠ 6880 Stryn, ☎ 57/87–19–95).

OFF THE BEATEN PATH
  BRIKSDALSBREEN – This is the most accessible arm of the Jostedal glacier. Drive along the mountain road or take a bus (from Olden, Loen, or Stryn) to Briksdal. From here, the glacier is a 45-minute walk from the end of the road, or you can ride there with pony and trap, as tourists did 100 years ago. Local guides lead tours (☞ Guided Tours *in* The West Coast A to Z, *below*) over the safe parts of the glacier.

Lodging

$$$ 🏨 **Kong Oscar's Hall.** Mike and Møyfrid Walston have brought back to life a derelict but magnificent hotel from the heyday of the dragon style, 1896, complete with a tower with dragonheads on the eaves. In winter, rooms are available only with advance reservations. ⊠ 6880, ☎ FAX 57/87–19–53. *5 suites. Restaurant. No credit cards.*

Shopping

Strynefjell Draktverkstad (⊠ 6890 Oppstryn, ☎ 57/87–72–20) specializes in stylish knickers, trousers, and skirts made of heavy wool. It's a 10-minute drive east of Stryn on Route 15.

Loen

66 *10 km (6 mi) southeast of Stryn.*

Loen and Olden are starting points for expeditions to branches of Europe's largest glacier, Jostedalsbreen. Hovering over the entire inner Nordfjord and Sognefjord regions, this glacier covers 800 square km (309 square mi). In geological time, this 5,000-year-old glacier is relatively young. The ice is in constant motion, crawling as much as 2 km (1¼ mi) a day in certain places.

OFF THE BEATEN PATH
  KJENNDALSBREEN FJELLSTOVE – It's possible to visit the Kjenndal arm of the glacier on the *M/B Kjendal*, which departs from Sande, near Loen. It sails down the 14-km (9-mi) arm of the lake under mountains covered by protruding glacier arms and past Ramnefjell (Ramne Mountain), scarred by rock slides, to Kjenndalsbreen Fjellstove. A bus runs between the Alexandra lodge (☞ *below*) and the glacier.

Dining and Lodging

$$–$$$ ✕🏨 **Alexandra.** Even though the original dragon-style building exists
★   only in pictures in the lobby, it is still the most luxurious hotel around. The food, prepared by chef Thomas Kampf, is particularly good. ⊠ 6789 Loen, ☎ 57/87–50–00, FAX 57/87–77–70. *193 rooms. 2 restaurants, bar, indoor pool, tennis courts, exercise room, boating, nightclub, convention center. AE, DC, MC, V.*

Dining and Lodging

$$–$$$ ✕🖿 **First Hotel Alexandra Molde.** This premier hotel
★ Britain's Princess Alexandra of Wales, who stayed here
Many of the elegant rooms overlook the water. Spisestue
rant, is worth a special trip. May Britt Reite prepares su
pepper-marinated veal fillet. ✉ *Storgt. 1–7, 6400,* ☎ 7
FAX *71/20–37–87. 150 rooms, 11 suites. 2 restaurants, ba*
door pool, exercise room, meeting rooms. AE, DC, MC,

Kristiansund

63 *68 km (42 mi) north of Molde on Route 64.*

This town was spared the destruction of its historic harbor, V
ing World War II. Many buildings in Kristiansund are well p
including **Woldbrygga,** a cooper's (barrel maker's) workshop fr
to 1965, with its original equipment still operational. ✉ *Da*
☎ *71/67–15–78.* 🚌 *NKr 20.* ☺ *Sun. 1–4.*

Housed in an 18th-century warehouse, **Milnbrygge,** the No
Klippfish Museum, pays tribute to the process and the histor
town's *klippfish* (dried-cod) industry—fishy smells and all. ✉
tiansund Harbor, ☎ *71/58–63–80 tourist information.* 🚌 *Nk*
Mid-June–mid-Aug., Mon.–Sat. noon–5, Sun. 1–4.

Dining and Lodging

$$–$$$ ✕ **Smia Fiskerestaurant.** Dishes like fishballs and whale peppe
are available here, but the decidedly Mediterranean dish—baca
is strangely part of local culture. Built inside an 18th-centur
smithy, the place is decorated with hanging fishnets, Spanish
bottles, and vintage klippfish tins. ✉ *Fosnagt. 30B,* ☎ *71/67–11*
AE, DC, MC, V.

$$–$$$ 🖿 **Comfort Hotel Fosna.** Ask for a room with a harbor view in this ch
acterful waterfront hotel. An evening meal is included. ✉ *Hauggt. 1*
6501, ☎ *71/67–40–11,* FAX *71/67–76–59. 50 rooms. Outdoor café, pian*
bar, pub, nightclub, meeting rooms. AE, DC, MC, V.

Geiranger

64 *85 km (52½ mi) southwest of Åndalsnes, 413 km (256 mi) from*
Bergen.

★ **Geiranger** is the ultimate fjord—Norway at its most dramatic. The most
scenic route to Geiranger is the two-hour drive along Route 63 over
Trollstigveien from Åndalsnes (☞ *above*). Once you are here, the Ørneveien (Eagles' Road) down to Geiranger, completed in 1952 with 11
hairpin turns, leads directly to the fjord.

The 16-km-long (10-mi-long), 960-ft-deep Geirangerfjord's best-known
attractions are its waterfalls—the Seven Sisters, the Bridal Veil, and the
Suitor—and the abandoned farms at Skageflå and Knivsflå, which are
visible (and accessible) only by boat (☞ Guided Tours *in* The West Coast
A to Z, *below*).

Lodging

$$$ 🖿 **Union Hotel.** This family-owned hotel is more than 100 years old.
It has modern and comfortable rooms, with many windows. ✉ *6216,*
☎ *70/26–30–00,* FAX *70/26–31–61. 168 rooms, 13 suites. Restaurant,*
bar, indoor and outdoor pool, minigolf, steam room, nightclub. AE,
DC, MC, V.

$$ 🖿 **Grande Fjord Hotell.** Idyllically set at the edge of the fjord, this small
hotel complex has more charm than the big hotels in the area. The rooms
are simple and some have balconies overlooking the fjord. ✉ *6216,*

Fjærland

67 *From Olden it's 62 km (37 mi) of easy, though not particularly inspiring, terrain to Skei, at the base of Lake Jølster, where the road goes under the glacier for more than 6 km (4 mi) of the journey to Fjærland.*

Fjærland, until 1986, was without road connections altogether. In 1991 the **Norsk Bremuseum** (Norwegian Glacier Museum) opened just north of Fjærland. It has a huge screen on which a film about glacier trekking plays and a fiberglass glacial maze, complete with special effects courtesy of the *Star Wars* movies' set designer. ☎ 57/69–32–88. ⊠ NKr 70. ☼ *June–Aug., daily 9–7; Apr.–May and Sept.–Oct., daily 10–4.*

OFF THE BEATEN PATH

ASTRUPTUNET – Halfway across the southern shore of Lake Jølster (about a 10-minute detour from the road to Fjærland) is Astruptunet, the farm of artist Nicolai Astrup (1880–1928). The best of his primitive, mystical paintings sell in the $500,000 range, ranking him among the most popular Norwegian artists. His home and studio are in a cluster of small turf-roofed buildings on a steep hill overlooking the lake. ☎ 57/72–67–82 or 57/72–81–05. ⊠ NKr 50. ☼ July, daily 10–6; late May–June and Aug.–early Sept., Tues.–Sun. 10–5; or by appointment.

Dining and Lodging

$$$ ✕⊞ **Hotel Mundal.** This small, old-fashioned yellow-and-white gingerbread hotel opened in 1891. The café serves wholesome, traditional Norwegian fare. ⊠ 5855, ☎ 57/69–31–01, ⊠ 57/69–31–79. 35 rooms. Café, bar, meeting rooms. DC, V. Closed mid-Sept.–mid-May.

Shopping

Audhild Vikens Vevstove (⊠ Skei, ☎ 57/72–81–25) specializes in handicrafts, particularly woven textiles.

Balestrand

68 *30 km (18½ mi) up the fjord by ferry, 204 km (126 mi) by car to Fjærland.*

Fjærland is connected to Sogndal by tunnel. Balestrand is on the southern bank of **Sognefjord,** one of the longest and deepest fjords in the world. Along its wide banks are some of Norway's best fruit farms, with fertile soil and lush vegetation (the fruit blossoms in May are spectacular). Ferries are the lifeline of the region.

Lodging

$$ ⊞ **Kvikne's Hotel.** This huge, wooden gingerbread house at the edge
★ of the Sognefjord has been a landmark since 1913. The view is the best part. This spot also has good swimming, hiking, rowing, and fishing possibilities. ⊠ 6899, ☎ 57/69–11–01, ⊠ 57/69–15–02. 190 rooms. 2 restaurants, exercise room, fishing. AE, DC, MC, V.

Voss

69 *80 km (50 mi) south of Vangsnes.*

Voss is a good place to stay the night, either in the town itself or 36 km (23 mi) away at Stalheim. The road to Stalheim, an old resort, has 13 hairpin turns in one 1½-km (1-mi) stretch of road that can be almost dizzying—it's 1,800 ft straight down—but well worth the trip for the view. Voss is connected with Oslo and Bergen by train and by roads (some sections are narrow and steep).

Lodging

$$$$ 🏨 **Fleischers Hotel.** The modern addition along the front detracts from the turreted and gabled charm of this old hotel. Inside, the old style has been well maintained, particularly in the restaurant. The rooms in the old section are pleasantly old-fashioned; in the rebuilt section (1993) they are modern and inviting. ✉ *Evangervegen 13, 5700,* ☎ *56/52–05–00,* FAX *56/52–05–01. 90 rooms, 30 apartments. Restaurant, bar, indoor pool, hot tub, sauna, tennis court, nightclub, nursery. AE, DC, MC, V.*

$$–$$$ 🏨 **Stalheim Hotel.** This grand hotel has been painted dark red and blends into the scenery perfectly. It has an extensive collection of Norwegian antiques and even its own open-air museum, with 30 houses. ✉ *5715 Voss,* ☎ *56/52–01–22,* FAX *56/52–00–56. 127 rooms, 3 suites. 2 restaurants, bar, fishing. AE, DC, MC, V.*

Outdoor Activities and Sports

HIKING

Walks and hikes are especially rewarding in this region, with spectacular mountain and water views everywhere. Be prepared for abrupt weather changes in spring and fall. Voss is a starting point for mountain hikes in Slølsheimen, Vikafjell, and the surrounding mountains. Contact the Voss Tourist Board (☞ Visitor Information, *below*) for tips.

RAFTING

For rafting in Dagali or Voss, contact **Voss Rafting Centre** (✉ ☎ *56/51–05–75*) for information on organized trips.

SKIING

Voss (40 km of alpine slopes; 1 cable car, 8 ski lifts; 8 illuminated and 2 marked cross-country trails) is an important alpine skiing center in Norway. Call the Voss Tourist Board (☞ Visitor Information, *below*) for details.

Flåm

🕖 *131 km (81 mi) from Voss.*

One of the most scenic train routes in Europe zooms from Myrdal, high into the mountains and down to the quaint town of Flåm. After the day-trippers have departed, it's a wonderful place to spend the night.

OFF THE   **MYRDAL** – Take a ferry from Balestrand to Flåm, from where you can
BEATEN PATH   make Norway's most exciting railway journey to Myrdal. Only 20 km (12 mi) long, it takes 40 minutes to travel 2,850 ft up a steep mountain gorge and 53 minutes to go down. The line includes 20 tunnels. From Flåm it is also an easy drive back to Oslo on E16 along the Lærdal River, one of Norway's most famous salmon streams and King Harald's favorite.

Lodging

$$$ 🏨 **Fretheim Hotell.** With the fjord in front and mountains in back, the setting is perfect. The inside has comfy lounges and rooms decorated in a Norwegian folk style. ✉ *5743,* ☎ *57/63–22–00,* FAX *57/63–23–03. 123 rooms. 2 restaurants, bar, fishing. AE, MC, V.*

The West Coast A to Z

Arriving and Departing

BY BOAT

The *Hurtigruten* (the coastal steamer) stops at Skansekaia in **Ålesund,** northbound at noon, departing at 3, and stops southbound at midnight, departing at 1. A catamaran runs between Ålesund and Molde at least twice daily.

BY CAR
From Oslo, it is 450 km (295 mi) on Route E6 to Dombås and then Route 9 through Åndalsnes to Ålesund. The well-maintained two-lane road runs inland to Åndalsnes and then follows the coastline out to Ålesund.

The 380-km (235-mi) drive from Bergen to Ålesund covers some of the most breathtaking scenery in the world. Roads are narrow two-lane ventures much of the time; passing is difficult, and in summer traffic can be heavy.

BY PLANE
Ålesund's **Vigra Airport** is 15 km (9 mi) from the center of town. Braathens SAFE (☎ 70/11–45–00 or 70/11–49–16, Ålesund; ☎ 70/18–32–45, Vigra) has nonstop flights from Oslo, Bergen, Trondheim, and Bodø.

Between the Airport and Downtown: It's a 25-minute ride from Vigra to town with Flybussen. Tickets cost NKr 50. Buses are scheduled according to flights—they leave the airport about 10 minutes after all arrivals and leave town about 60 or 70 minutes before each departure.

BY TRAIN
The *Dovrebanen* and *Raumabanen* between Oslo S Station and Åndalsnes via Dombås run three times daily in each direction for the 6½-hour ride. At Åndalsnes, buses wait outside the station to pick up passengers for points not served by the train. The 124-km (76-mi) trip to Ålesund takes close to two hours.

Getting Around

BY BOAT
In addition to regular ferries to nearby islands, boats connect Ålesund with other points along the coast. Excursions by boat are available through the tourist office.

BY BUS
Bus routes are extensive. The tourist office has information about do-it-yourself tours by bus to the outlying districts. Three local bus companies serve Ålesund; all buses depart from the terminal on Kaiser Wilhelms Gate.

BY CAR
Ferries are a way of life in western Norway, but they are seldom big enough or don't run often enough during the summer, causing delays. Considerable hassle can be eliminated by reserving ahead, as cars with reservations board first. Call the tourist office of the area where you will be traveling for ferry information (☞ Visitor Information, *below*).

Contacts and Resources

EMERGENCIES
Hospital Emergency Rooms/Doctors/Dentists: ☎ 70/12–33–48. **Car Rescue:** ☎ 70/14–18–33.

GUIDED TOURS
Cruises: The **M/S *Geirangerfjord*** (☎ 70/26–30–07) offers 90-minute guided minicruises on the Geirangerfjord. Tickets are sold at the dock in Geiranger. ☒ *Nkr 70.* ☉ *June–Aug. Tours at 10, 11:45, 1:30, 3:30, and 5:30; July, additional tour at 8 PM.*

Flying: **Firdafly A/S** (☎ 57/86–53–88), based in Sandane, has air tours over Jostedalsbreen. Hotel Alexandra in Loen (☞ *above*) arranges group flights.

Glacier: From Easter through September, **Jostedalen Breførlag** (⊠ 5828 Gjerde, ☎ 57/68–31–11) offers glacier tours, from an easy 1½-hour family trip on the Nigard branch (equipment is provided) to advanced glacier courses with rock and ice climbing.

Hiking: **Aak Fjellsportsenter** (☎ 71/22–71–00) in Åndalsnes specializes in walking tours of the area.

Orientation: A 1½-hour guided stroll through Ålesund, concentrating mostly on the Art Nouveau buildings, departs from the **tourist information center (Rådhuset)** Saturday, Tuesday, and Thursday at 1 PM from mid-June to mid-August. ⊠ *NKr 45.*

LATE-NIGHT PHARMACIES

Nordstjernen (⊠ Korsegt. 8, Ålesund, ☎ 70/12–59–45) is open weekdays 9–5, Saturday 9–2, and Sunday 6 PM–8 PM.

VISITOR INFORMATION

Ålesund (⊠ Rådhuset, ☎ 70/12–12–02). **Åndalsnes** (⊠ C Corner Nesgt. and Romsdalsvn., ☎ 71/22–16–22). **Balestrand** (⊠ Dockside, ☎ 57/69–12–55). **Flåm** (⊠ Railroad station, ☎ 57/63–21–06). **Geiranger** (⊠ Dockside, ☎ 70/26–30–99). **Hellesylt** (⊠ Dockside, ☎ 70/26–50–52). **Lærdal** (☎ 57/66–65–09). **Molde** (⊠ Rådhuset, ☎ 70/12–12–02). **Sogndal** (☎ 57/67–30–83). **Runde** (☎ 70/01–37–90). **Stryn** (☎ 57/87–23–33). **Ulvik** (⊠ Dockside, ☎ 56/52–63–60). **Voss** (☎ 56/52–08–00). **Fjord Norway** (☎ 55/31–26–40) in Bergen is a clearinghouse for information on all of western Norway.

10 TRONDHEIM TO THE NORTH CAPE

A narrow but immensely long strip of land stretches between Trondheim and Kirkenes in northern Norway. In this vast territory, you'll encounter dramatically different ways of life and a variety of geographical features, from the sawtooth, glacier-carved peaks of the Lofoten Islands to the world's strongest tidal current in Bodø.

THE COAST OF NORTHERN NORWAY fidgets up from Trondheim, scattering thousands of islands and skerries along the way, until it reaches the northernmost point of Europe. Then it continues even farther, straggling above Sweden and Finland to point a finger of land into Russia.

Long and thin, this area covers an astonishing variety of land- and cityscapes, from bustling Trondheim to elegant Tromsø. Some areas, especially when seen from the deck of the mail boats, seem like endless miles of wilderness marked by an occasional dot—a lonely cabin or a herd of reindeer. Views are often exquisite: glaciers, fjords, rocky coasts, and celestial displays of the midnight sun in summer and northern lights (aurora borealis) in winter.

Nordkapp (North Cape) has a character that changes with the seasons. In summer it teems with visitors and tour buses, and in winter, under several feet of snow, it is bleak, subtle, and astonishingly beautiful. It is accessible then only by squealing Sno-Cat snowmobile, a bracing and thoroughly Norwegian adventure.

Keep in mind while traveling, as in the rest of provincial Norway, that most better restaurants are in hotels. If you visit northern Norway between May and August, try the specialty of *måsegg* and *Mack-øl*, more for curiosity value than for taste. *Måsegg* (seagulls' eggs) are always served hard-boiled and halved in their shells. They're larger than chicken eggs, and they look exotic, with greenish-gray speckled shells and bright orange yolks, but they taste like standard supermarket eggs. *Mack-øl* (similar to pils) is brewed in Tromsø at the world's northernmost brewery.

Trondheim

71 *496 km (307½ mi) north of Oslo, 744 km (461 mi) from Bergen.*

Trondheim's original name, Nidaros (still the name of the cathedral), is a composite word referring to the city's location at the mouth of the Nid River. The wide streets of the city center are still lined with brightly painted wooden houses and picturesque warehouses.

The Tiffany windows are magnificent at the **Nordenfjeldske Kunstindustrimuseum** (Decorative Arts Museum), which houses one of the finest art collections in Scandinavia. ⊠ *Munkegt. 5,* ☎ *73/52–13–11.* ☞ *NKr 40.* ☉ *June–late Aug., weekdays 10–5, Sun. noon–5; late Aug.–May, weekdays 10–3 (Thurs. until 7), Sun. noon–4.*

Saint Olav formulated a Christian religious code for Norway in 1024 while he was king; he was killed in battle against local chieftains at Stiklestad. After he was buried, water sprang from his grave and people began to believe that his nails and hair continued to grow beneath the ground. It is here on his grave that **Nidaros Domkirke** (Nidaros Cathedral) was built. The town became a pilgrimage site for the Christians of northern Europe, and Olav was canonized in 1164.

Although construction was begun in 1070, the oldest existing parts of the cathedral date from around 1150. The crown jewels, which visitors can view, are still kept in the cathedral. Guided tours are offered in English mid-June to mid-September, weekdays at 11, 2, and 4. ⊠ *Kongsgårdsgt. 2,* ☎ *73/52–52–33.* ☞ *NKr 12. Ticket also permits entry to Erkebispegården (☞ below).* ☉ *Mid-June–mid-Aug., weekdays 9–6:30, weekends 9–4; May–mid-June and mid-Aug.–mid-Sept., week-*

*Norwegian
Sea*

87 **Svalbard**

*Nordkyn-
halvøya* Berlevåg Vardø

Nordkapp Båtsfjord

82 Grense
81 Jakobselv

Honningsvåg Tana bru 98 **Storskog**

Hammerfest Kåfjord E6

80 Kistrand **Kirkenes** 85 86

Rypefjord Seiland Lakselv E6 885

Sørøya E6 Øvre Pasvik RUSSIA

Øksfjordjøkulen **Alta** 79 **Karasjok**

Alteidet 84

Hjemmeluft 63

Kvænangsfjellet **FINNMARK**

Olderdalen

Tromsø 78 **Kautokeino** 83

Seljelvnes *TROMS*

Andenes *Senja* Andselv Øverbygd **FINLAND**

Vesterålen *Andøya* Setermoen

Harstad 77

Vesterålen Islands HINNØYA 76

Austvågøya Lofoten Lødigen **Narvik**
  Kabelvåg Islands
Vestvågøya Borg Svolvær
Flakstadøya Henningsvær Skutvika
  Nusfjord Stamsund
Moskenesøy Reine
Lofoten Sund
  Å
Verøy Sørland *Vestfjorden*

Røst **Bodø** 74 75 **Saltstraumen**
  Fauske
  Rognan *Arctic Circle*

Polarsirkelsenteret 73

Mo i Rana 72

Sandnessjøen Korgen

Mosjøen *SWEDEN*

*Norwegian
Sea* Hommelstø

Vegafjorden **BØRGEFJELL
NASJONALPARK**

Hortafjorden Vik Terråk Gäddede
  Salsbruket

Folla **Namsos**

NORD- Snåsa
TRØNDELAG
  Steinkjer

*Trondheims-
fjorden* E6

Hitra 71 **Trondheim**

Kristiansund

FINLAND

Gulf of Bothnia

N

KEY
- - - - Ferry

0 150 miles
225 km

days 9–3, weekends 9–4; mid-Sept.–mid-Apr., weekdays noon–2:30, weekends 11:30–2.

Scandinavia's oldest secular building is the **Erkebispegården** (Archbishop's Palace). Dating from around 1160, it was the residence of the archbishop until the Reformation. After that, it was a Danish governor's palace and later a military headquarters.

Within the Erkebispegården is the **Forsvarsmuseet** (Army Museum; ☎ 73/99–59–97; 🎫 NKr 5; ⊙ June–Aug., weekdays 9–3, weekends 11–4; Feb.–May and Sept.–Nov., weekends 11–4), with displays of uniforms, swords, and daggers. The **Hjemmefrontmuseet** (Resistance Museum; ☎ 73/99–59–97; 🎫 NKr 12; ⊙ 9–3, weekends 11–4; Feb.–May and Sept.–Nov., weekends 11–4), also here, documents the occupation of Norway during World War II. ☎ *73/50–12–12.* 🎫 *NKr 20. Ticket also permits entry to Nidaros Cathedral.* ⊙ *Late June–late Aug., Mon.–Sat. 10–5, Sun. noon–5; late Aug.–late June, Mon.–Sat. 10–3, Sun. noon–5.*

Behind the **Biblioteket** (Library, ⊠ Peter Egges Pl. 1) you can see the remains of St. Olavskirke (St. Olav's Church).

Scandinavia's largest wooden building, **Stiftsgården,** was built in 1774–1778 as a private home, the result of a competition between two sisters who were trying to outdo each other with the size of their houses. Today it is the king's official residence in Trondheim. The interior is sparsely furnished. ⊠ *Munkegt. 23,* ☎ *73/52–13–11.* 🎫 *NKr 30.* ⊙ *June–mid-June, Tues.–Sat. 10–3, Sun. noon–5; mid-June–mid-Aug., Tues.–Sat. 10–5, Sun. noon–5; mid-Aug.–May, open 1 day per month.*

Off Munkegate near the water, you can see an immense variety of seafood at **Ravnkloa Fiskehall** (fish market). The **Sjøfartsmuseet** (Maritime Museum), housed in a former prison, displays galleon figureheads, ship models, and a large collection of seafaring pictures. ⊠ *Fjordgt. 6A,* ☎ *73/89–01–00.* 🎫 *NKr 25.* ⊙ *June–Aug., daily 10–4.*

Trøndelag Folkemuseum has a collection of rustic buildings from the turn of the century. The museum restaurant is from 1739 and serves traditional Norwegian food. ⊠ *Sverresborg,* ☎ *73/53–14–90.* 🎫 *NKr 40.* ⊙ *Late May–Aug., daily 11–6, Sept.–Dec., Sun. noon–4.*

OFF THE BEATEN PATH
RINGVE MUSIC MUSEUM – For an unusual museum visit, you can take a half-hour ride to Fagerheim and Ringve Gård, the childhood home of the naval hero Admiral Tordenskiold. Guides (music students) demonstrate the instruments on display and tell about their role in the history of music. Concerts are held regularly. ⊠ *Lade Allé 60,* ☎ *73/92–24–11.* 🎫 *NKr 60.* ⊙ *Guided tours in English late May–Aug., daily at 11:30, 1:30, and 3:30; schedule varies rest of year so phone ahead. Open April–mid-Sept., daily 11–6; mid-Sept.–Mar., Sun. noon–3. Tour lasts about 75 mins.*

Dining and Lodging

Trondheim is known for several dishes, including *surlaks* (marinated salmon served with sour cream). A sweet specialty is *tekake* (tea cake), which looks like a thick-crust pizza topped with a lattice pattern of cinnamon and sugar.

$$$–$$$$ ✕ **Bryggen.** The furnishings are in bleached wood, with dark-blue and
★   red accessories. The menu features reindeer fillet salad with cranberry vinaigrette and herb cream soup. ⊠ *Øvre Bakklandet 66,* ☎ *73/87–42–42. Reservations essential. AE, DC, MC, V. Closed Sun. No lunch.*

$$$ ✕ **Dickens.** This popular, international-style restaurant at Bryggen is housed in a 300-year-old building with a traditional, elegant interior. The wide-ranging menu includes a delicious sauté beef bearnaise as well as fish and some vegetarian dishes. ✉ *Kjøpmannsgt. 63,* ☎ *73/51–57–50. AE, DC, MC, V.*

$$–$$$ ✕ **Havfruen.** "The Mermaid" has an open kitchen at street level. Fish soup is the most popular starter; summer main dishes include poached halibut. ✉ *Kjøpmannsgt. 7,* ☎ *73/87–40–70. AE, DC, MC, V. Closed Sun. No lunch.*

$$ ✕ **Lian.** In the heights above the city, the views here are spectacular. The oldest part of the restaurant dates from 1700, but the round section, from the 1930s, commands the best view. The food is solid, honest, and hearty, with roast beef, reindeer, smoked pork loin, and the old standby, *kjøttkaker* (Norwegian meat cakes). ✉ *Lianvn.,* ☎ *72/55–90–77. MC, V.*

$$ ✕ **Tavern på Sverresborg.** This big, yellow, wooden former ferryman's house at the Trøndelag Folkemuseum has been an inn since 1739. The food is authentic Norwegian, including meat and fish prepared with old methods—pickled, salted, and dried. Choices include a plate with four different kinds of herring, fish cakes, cured salmon, meatballs, and rømmegrøt. Homemade oatmeal bread and rolls accompany all dishes. ✉ *Sverresborg Allé,* ☎ *73/52–09–32. MC, V.*

$ ✕ **De 3 Stuer.** Everything this small bistro chain serves is homemade, and the daily specials may be fish soufflé, fried fish with sour-cream sauce, asparagus soup, and roast beef, all served with dessert and coffee. For lunch there's smørbrød, crescent rolls, salads, and cakes. ✉ *Trondheim Torg,* ☎ *73/52–92–20;* ✉ *Gågaten Leuthenhaven,* ☎ *73/52–43–42;* ✉ *Dronningens Gt. 11,* ☎ *73/52–63–20. Reservations not accepted. MC, V. Dronningens Gt. closed Sun.*

$$–$$$$ 🏨 **Quality Prinsen Hotel.** Rooms in this hotel in the center of the city are light—monochromatic to the point of being dull. The restaurant, Pinocchio, serves a good early dinner. ✉ *Kongensgt. 30, 7417,* ☎ *73/53–06–50,* FAX *73/53–06–44. 81 rooms. Restaurant, coffee shop, pub, bar, meeting room. AE, DC, MC, V.*

$$–$$$$ 🏨 **Radisson SAS Hotel Trondheim.** The city's showcase hostelry, right on the river, was built in the same style as the old warehouse buildings that line the waterfront, but in glass and concrete instead of wood. ✉ *Kjøpmannsgata 73, 7001,* ☎ *73/80–30–00,* FAX *73/80–30–50. 297 rooms, 9 suites. Restaurant, grill, café, bar, indoor pool, exercise room, sauna. AE, DC, MC, V.*

$$ 🏨 **Ambassadeur.** From the roof terrace of this first-rate modern hotel, you'll see the deep-blue waters of the Trondheimsfjord reflect the dramatic and irregular coastline. The Ambassadeur is about 300 ft from the market square. Most rooms have fireplaces, and some have balconies. ✉ *Elvegt. 18, 7013,* ☎ *73/52–70–50,* FAX *73/52–70–52. 34 rooms. Bar. AE, DC, MC, V.*

$$ 🏨 **Comfort Home Hotel Bakeriet.** The hotel opened in March 1991 in
★ a building built as a bakery in 1863. Few of the rooms look alike, but all are large and stylish. There's no restaurant, but a hot evening meal is included in the room rate. ✉ *Brattørgt. 2, 7010, Trondheim,* ☎ *73/52–52–00,* FAX *73/50–23–30. 109 rooms. In-room VCRs, sauna, Turkish bath. AE, DC, MC, V.*

$$ 🏨 **Quality Panorama Hotel.** Ideally situated near the city center, this modern and well-appointed hotel has reasonable rates—you can use some of your savings to browse next door at City Syd, Norway's largest shopping mall. ✉ *Østrerosten 38, 7492,* ☎ *72/88–65–22,* FAX *72/88–86–26. 112 rooms. Restaurant, bar lounge, sauna, no-smoking rooms, children's programs. AE, DC, MC, V.*

\$–\$\$ ☒ **Rainbow Trondheim Hotel.** The building is old on the outside, with a curved corner and wrought-iron balconies, but inside it's new. The rooms are big and light. ☒ *Kongensgt. 15, 7013,* ☎ *73/50–50–50,* FAX *73/51–60–58. 131 rooms. Bar, meeting room. AE, DC, MC, V.*

Nightlife

Olavskvartalet is the center of much of the city's nightlife, with a disco, a jazz and blues club, and a bar and beer hall in the cellar. **Monte Cristo** (☒ Prinsensgt. 38–40, ☎ 73/52–18–80) has a restaurant, bar, and disco and is popular with the mid-20s and up set. Students and younger people in search of cheap drinks, music, and dancing gravitate toward **Strossa** (☒ Elgeseter Gt. 1, ☎ 73/89–95–10). **Cafe Remis** (☒ Kjoepmannsgt. 12, ☎ 73/52–05–52) is the center for gay nightlife in Trondheim.

Outdoor Activities and Sports

FISHING

The **Nidelven** (Nid River) in Trondheim is one of Norway's best salmon and trout rivers. You can fish right in the city, but, as usual, you'll need a license. Contact the tourist office.

SKIING

Bymarka and **Estenstadmarka,** the wooded areas on the periphery of Trondheim, are popular among cross-country skiers. At **Skistua** (ski lodge) in Bymarka, and at **Vassfjellet** south of the city, there are downhill runs.

En Route   Nord Trøndelag, as the land above Trondheim is called, is largely agricultural. Taken on its own, it's beautiful, with farms, mountains, rock formations, and clear blue water, but compared with the rest of Norway, it is subtle, with only an undulating landscape—so many tourists just sleep through it on the night train or fly over it on their way to the North. The first town of any size is Steinkjer, a military base.

Mo i Rana

   ⑫   *350 km (218 mi) north of Steinkjer.*

Mo i Rana (the poetic name means Mo on the Ranafjord) is a center for iron and steel production using ore from nearby mines.

Setergrotta is one of almost 200 caves 26 km (16 mi) northwest of Mo i Rana. With 7,920 ft of charted underground paths, many narrow passages, natural chimneys, and an underground river, this is for serious spelunkers. The caves are usually open from mid-June to mid-August; however, times vary with conditions. Check with the tourist office (☎ 75/15–06–22, or 75/15–28–87). ☒ *NKr 160 for a two-hour guided tour.*

Grønligrotta is Scandinavia's best-known show cave—it even has electric lights. A 20-minute tour goes deep into the limestone cave to the underground river. ☎ 75/16–23–44. ☒ *NKr 50.* ⊙ *Mid-June–mid-Aug. Tours daily on the hr 10–7.*

OFF THE BEATEN PATH   **SVARTISEN** – Glacier fans can hike on the Svartisen—literally, Black Ice—the second-largest glacier in Norway, covering 375 square km (144 square mi). The glacier is 30 km (19 mi) north of Mo i Rana, about 2½ hours by car, just south of Bodø. OVDS (☎ 76/96–76–00) offers seven-hour boat tours from Bodø to the ice cap on alternate Saturdays in summer. The easiest way to get to the glacier is from Mo, 32 km (20 mi) by car to Svartisvatn lake. A boat crosses the lake every hour to within 2½ km (1½ mi) of the Østerdal arm of the glacier. If you plan to get to the glacier on your own, you should inquire at the Svartisen Tourist Center (☎ 75/75–00–11) about connecting with a guide.

Glacier walking is extremely hazardous and should never be attempted without a professional guide.

Polarsirkelsenteret

73 *80 km (50 mi) north of Mo i Rana.*

A bleak stretch of treeless countryside marks the boundary line of the Arctic Circle. The **Polarsirkelsenteret** (Arctic Circle Center), on E6, presents a multiscreen show about Norway. The post office has a special postmark, and you can get your Arctic Circle Certificate stamped. There's also a cafeteria and gift shop. ⊠ *8635 Polarsirkelen,* ☎ *75/12–96–96.* 🎟 *NKr 45.* ☉ *May, daily 10–6; June, daily 10–8; July, daily 8 AM–10 PM; Aug., daily 10–8.*

Bodø

74 *174 km (108 mi) north of the Polarsirkelsenteret.*

Bodø, a modern city of about 40,000 just above the Arctic Circle, is best known as the terminus of the Nordlandsbanen railroad and the gateway to the Lofoten Islands and the North. The midnight sun is visible from June 2 to July 10. Like many other coastal towns, it began as a small fishing community, but today it is a commercial and administrative center. Like much of northern Norway, the Second World War inevitably touched Bodø. In 1940, the town fell victim to German bombs meant to destroy a British air base.

Bodø is the best base for boat excursions to the coastal bird colonies on the Væren Islands. It's also site of the **Nordland County Museum,** which depicts the life of the Sami and the regional history of the area, particularly fishing. ⊠ *Prinsengt. 116,* ☎ *75/52–16–40.* 🎟 *NKr 15.* ☉ *Weekdays 9–3, weekends noon–3.*

Down the road from Bodø's airport and a good 15 minutes from the ☺ town's center, the jumbo **Norsk Luftsfartssenter** (Norwegian Aviation Center) tells the story of Norwegian aviation with flight simulators and life-size displays of commercial and military planes dating back to 1912. ☎ *75/50–85–50.* 🎟 *NKr 65.* ☉ *Early June–mid-Aug., weekdays and Sun. 10–8, Sat. 10–5; mid-Aug.–early June, Tues.–Wed. and Fri. 10–4, Thurs. 10–7, Sat. 11–5, Sun. 10–6.*

Lodging

$$$ 🏨 **Radisson SAS Hotel Bodø.** This grandiose hotel pulses with life and has enough services to keep you entertained nearly around the clock. ⊠ *Storgt. 2,* ☎ *75/52–41–00,* 📠 *75/52–74–93. 190 rooms. 2 restaurants, bar, nightclub. AE, DC, MC, V.*

$–$$ 🏨 **Norrøna Hotell.** This no-frills establishment is plain yet comfortable and has a prime downtown location. ⊠ *Storgt. 4B,* ☎ *75/52–55–50,* 📠 *75/52–33–88. 99 rooms. Restaurant. AE, DC, MC, V.*

$ 🏨 **Comfort Home Hotel Grand.** This comfortable hotel is a stone's throw from the ocean and convenient for shopping, fishing, and sightseeing trips. ⊠ *Stogt. 3, 8006 Bodø,* ☎ *75/54–61–00,* 📠 *75/54–61–50. 97 rooms. Bar lounge, sauna, steam bath. AE, DC, MC, V.*

Saltstraumen

75 *33 km (20 mi) southeast of Bodø on Route 80/17.*

Saltstraumen is a 3-km-long (2-mi-long) and 500-ft-wide section of water between the outer fjord, which joins with the sea, and the inner fjord basin. During high tide, the volume of water rushing through the strait and into the basin is so great that whirlpools form. This is the legendary *malstrøm*—and the strongest one in the world. All that rush of water brings enormous quantities of fish, making the malstrøm a popular fishing spot. The nearby **Saltstraumen Opplevelsesenter** (Adventure Center) houses regional artifacts and presents a multimedia show that recount the scientific and human tales behind the malstrøm. ☎ 75/56–06–55. ⌧ NKr 50. ☉ Mid-May–late Aug., daily 10–6.

Dining and Lodging

$$–$$$ ✕⌹ **Saltstraumen Hotel.** This thoroughly ordinary hotel is practically on top of the malstrøm. The restaurant serves delicious steamed halibut in butter sauce. ⌧ 1056 ☎ 75/58–76–85. 28 rooms, 7 bungalows. Restaurant, meeting rooms. AE, DC, MC, V.

OFF THE   **BLODVEIMUSEET** – Ninety minutes southeast of Bodø in Rognan, the
BEATEN PATH   Bloodstained Road Museum re-creates the sinister atmosphere of an icy
              North Norway Nazi prison camp where Russian, Serb, and Polish prisoners of war were incarcerated. **Saltdal Bygdetun,** a collection of historic houses, is a few yards away. Call for a guided tour. ☎ 75/69–06–60. ☉ June–Aug., weekdays 9–4, Sat. 1–4, Sun. 1–6.

Narvik

➐ 336 km (210 mi) north of Saltstraumen.

Narvik is more easily reached by rail from Stockholm than from most places in Norway, as it is the end station on the *Ofotbanen,* the Norwegian railroad that connects with the Swedish railroad's northernmost line. Narvik was originally established as the ice-free port for exporting Swedish iron ore mined around Kiruna. From mid-June to mid-August, you can take a cable car 2,132 ft above town for a view of the city and Ofotenfjord.

Narvik was rebuilt after being flattened during World War II. The **Krigsminnemuseet** (War Memorial Museum) documents wartime events with artifacts, models, and pictures. ⌧ Torget, ☎ 76/94–44–26. ⌧ NKr 30. ☉ March–mid June and mid-Aug.–late Sept., daily 11–3; mid-June–mid-Aug., Mon.–Sat. 10–10, Sun. 11–5.

Lodging

$$ ⌹ **Inter Nor Grand Royal.** It looks like an office building from the outside, but inside it is a top-class hotel, with big, rather formal rooms. ⌧ Kongensgt. 64, 8500 Narvik, ☎ 76/97–70–00, ⎙ 76/94–55–31. 107 rooms. 2 restaurants, 2 bars, sauna, nightclub, convention center. AE, DC, MC, V.

Lofoten and the Islands of the North

Extending out into the ocean north of Bodø are the Lofoten Islands, a 190-km (118-mi) chain of jagged peaks. In summer the idyll of farms, fjords, and fishing villages draws caravans of tourists, whereas in winter the coast facing the Arctic Ocean is one of Europe's stormiest. The midnight sun is visible here from May 25 to July 17. If you are lucky enough to be visiting on a clear midnight, drive over to the western side, where the spear-shaped mountains give way to flat, sandy beaches that look oddly fluorescent in the hush of night. The sight is spectacular.

Until about 50 years ago fishing was the only source of income for the area (today tourism helps bolster the still thriving fisheries). As many as 6,000 boats with 30,000 fishermen would mobilize between January and March for the Lofotfisket, the world's largest cod-fishing event. During the season they fished in open boats and took shelter during stormy nights in *rorbuer*, simple cabins built right on the water. Today many rorbuer have been converted into tourist lodgings, but Lofotfisket is still an annual tradition.

The best way to visit Lofoten is by car. **Svolvær,** the main town and administrative center for the villages on the islands, is connected with the other islands by express boat and ferry, and by coastal steamer and air to Bodø. It has a thriving summer art colony.

A drive on E10, from Svolvær to the outer tip of Lofoten (130 km [80 mi])—the town with the enigmatic name of **Å**—presents an opportunity to see how the islanders really live.

The **Norwegian Fishing Village Museum** (☎ 76/09–14–88) at Å is a spread-out living fishing village with houses, a 19th-century cod-liver-oil factory, and a bread bakery. ⊠ *NKr 40.* ☉ *late June–mid-Aug., daily 10–6; Sept.–May, weekdays 10–4.*

Just south of Svolvær, the hamlet of **Kabelvåg** provides the perfect introduction to the string of islands, their history, and their inhabitants. A cluster of museums less than a mile from the quiet village center sits on the site of an old fishing settlement. Restored fishing cabins displayed at the **Lofotmuseet** (Lofoten Island Museum, ☎ 76/07–82–23) depict the rigorous life of a fishing community on the grassy edge of a fjord inlet. Next door, the **Galleri Espolin** (☎ 76/07–84–05) exhibits the dark, haunting paintings and lithographs of fishermen in stormy weather. Kaare Espolin Johnsen, who died in 1994, was a nationally renowned artist. The **Lofot-Akvariet** (Aquarium, ☎ 76/07–86–65) includes a salmon farm exhibit, a seal pond, and a slide show of sea creatures. ⊠ *Storvågan.* ☎ *NKr 60.* ☉ *Mid-June–mid-Aug., daily 10–9; mid–late Aug., daily 10–6; Sept.–Apr., weekdays and Sun. 11–3; May–early June, daily 11–3.*

Southwest of Kabelvåg is Henningsvær. This village is home to **Karl Erik Harr Gallery** (☎ 76/07–15–73), which exhibits Lofoten-inspired paintings by acclaimed Norwegian artists.

Viking enthusiasts might want to veer northwest to Borg, where archeologists unearthed a long, low chieftain's house—the largest Viking building ever discovered. Now rebuilt exactly as it was, the **Viking Museum Lofotr** houses the 1,000-year-old artifacts discovered there. Tour guides in Viking garb sit around crackling fires and demonstrate the crafts, customs, and cookery of their ancestors. ⊠ *Prestergårdsveien 59.* ☎ *76/08–49–00.* ⊠ *NKr 70.* ☉ *Late May–mid-Sept., daily 10–7. Groups in winter by appointment.*

Other scenic stops include tucked-away **Nusfjord,** a 19th-century fishing village on an official European Conservation list; **Sund,** with its smithy and small fisheries museum; and festive **Reine.**

NEED A BREAK?	The rustic **Gammelbua,** in Reine, serves excellent salmon mousse and chilled Norwegian beer. Locals and tourists flock here to eat, drink, and gossip.

Off the tip of Moskenesøy, the last island with a bridge, is **Moskenesstraumen,** another malstrøm that's not quite as dramatic as Saltstraumen (☞ *above*).

North of the Lofotens are the **Vesterålen Islands,** with more fishing villages and rorbuer, and diverse vegetation. There are fewer tourists in Vesterålen, but more whale sightings. Puffins populate area cliffs, as in the Lofotens. The coastal express boat (☞ Arriving and Departing by Boat *in* Trondheim to the North Cape A to Z, *below*) slithers in and around fjords along the coastline of these more subtle islands.

⑦ East of Vesterålen on Hinnøya, Norway's largest island, is **Harstad,** where the year-round population of 23,000 swells to 42,000 during the annual June cultural festival (the line-up includes concerts, theater, and dance) and its July deep-sea fishing festival.

Dining and Lodging

A word on the fishermen's cabins: although hotels have popped up in some of the bigger fishing villages, rorbu lodging is essential to the Lofoten experience. Rorbuer vary in size and comfort, some date back to the last century and others are new imitations. If you do stay in a rorbu, it is worth your while to bring a few days' worth of food to stick in the refrigerator. Some villages have few cafés, and you may find that the closest thing to a grocery store is a gas station. Unless you have your own linens, remember you'll have to pay extra—usually about NKr 100.

$$$ ✕ **Fiskekrogen.** This quayside restaurant in the fishing village of Henningsvær is a real gem. Chef-owner Otto Asheim's specialties include traditional Lofoten fish soup, seaweed soup, and panfried cod tongues. ✉ *8312 Henningsvær,* ☎ *76/07–46–52. AE, DC, MC, V.*

$$$ ✕ **Røkenes Gård.** The large white wooden building opened in 1750 as a commercial trading house and inn. It is today a cozy restaurant serving regional specialties, such as marinated reindeer and cloudberry parfait. ✉ *9402 Harstad,* ☎ *77/05–84–44. Reservations essential. AE, DC, MC, V.*

$$$–$$$$ 🛏 **Nyvågar Rorbu og Aktivitetssenter.** This lodging and recreation complex is a 15-minute drive from the Svolvær airport and a two-minute walk from the Storvågan museum complex. Activities are well organized, with fishing-boat tours, eagle safaris, and deep-sea rafting, as well as evening entertainment. The cabins are spotless. ✉ *8310 Kabelvåg, Storvågan,* ☎ *76/07–89–00,* 📠 *76/06–97–01. 60 rooms. Restaurant, meeting rooms. AE, DC, MC, V.*

$$$ 🛏 **Rainbow Vestfjord Hotel.** This simple hotel has spacious rooms and a lovely view of the harbor beyond. It used to be a cod-liver-oil factory. ✉ *8301 Svolvær,* ☎ *76/07–08–70,* 📠 *76/07–08–54. 63 rooms, 3 suites. Restaurant, bar, conference room. AE, DC, MC, V.*

$$$ 🛏 **Rica Hotel Svolvær.** Don't be fooled by the Rica's rustic rorbu look. It's an elegant hotel on the inside. Accommodations are in separate all-wood rorbu cabins, which are comfortably appointed, each with its own waterfront veranda (from which you can fish). The main lobby and restaurant are housed in an unusual boat-shaped building with panoramic harbor views. ✉ *Lamholmen, 8301 Svolvær,* ☎ *76/07–22–22,* 📠 *76/07–20–01. 147 rooms. Restaurant, bar, convention center. AE, DC, MC, V.*

$–$$$$ 🛏 **Reine Rorbuer.** In the heart of the village of Reine, these authentic fishing cabins are down the hill from Gammelbua (☞ *above*), a local eatery. The cabins all have typical Norwegian names, like Gro and Liv. Make reservations early as the cabins tend to get booked early in summer. ✉ *8390 Reine,* ☎ *76/09–22–22,* 📠 *76/09–22–25. 21 1-, 2-, or 3-bedroom rorbuer, most with shower. DC, MC, V.*

$–$$$ 🛏 **Henningsvær Rorbuer.** This small group of turn-of-the-century rorbuer is just outside the center of Lofoten's most important fishing village. Breakfasts can be ordered from the cafeteria. Reservations are essential for July. ✉ *8312 Henningsvær,* ☎ *76/07–46–00,* 📠 *76/07–49–10. 19 1- or 2-bedroom rorbuer. Cafeteria, grill, sauna, laundry service. V.*

$–$$$ 🛏 **Nusfjord Rorbuer.** Families stay at these secluded cabins for weeks at a time. There's plenty to do—hiking, fishing, boating—in the surrounding area. For a glimpse at the midnight sun, drive to the other side of the island at Flakstad. Rowboats are included in the price of a rorbu, and you can rent fishing gear and motor boats. The completely preserved village of Nusfjord is quaint at every turn. ⊠ *8380 Ramberg,* ☎ *76/09–30–20,* FAX *76/09–33–78. 34 1- or 2-bedroom rorbuer. Restaurant, pub, coin laundry. AE, DC, MC, V.*

$–$$ ⊞ **Grand Nordic Hotel.** This hotel is housed in a redbrick Bauhaus-style building; the public rooms are decorated with Norwegian leather furniture from the 1970s. ⊠ *Strandgt. 9, 9400 Harstad,* ☎ *77/06–21–70,* FAX *77/06–77–30. 82 rooms, 3 suites. Restaurant, bar, nightclub, convention center. AE, DC, MC, V.*

$ ⊞ **Wulff-Nilsens Rorbuer.** A five-minute drive from Reine, this tidy cluster of 19th-century rorbuer is an excellent starting point for fishing excursions and mountain walks. The rorbuer are rustic but comfortably equipped. Breakfast and light meals are served in the restaurant by request. ⊠ *Hamnøy, 8390 Reine,* ☎ *76/09–23–20,* FAX *76/09–21–54. 14 1-, 2-, or 3-bedroom rorbuer, all with shower. Restaurant, kitchenettes. AE, DC, MC, V.*

Outdoor Activities and Sports

BIRD-WATCHING

A constant shrieking hum emanates from some of North Norway's arctic island cliffs, which pulsate with thousands of birds. From Moskenes, just north of Å (or from Bodø), you can take a ferry to the bird sanctuaries of **Værøy** and **Røst.** Many different types of seabirds inhabit the cliffs, eider ducks in particular.

WHALE-WATCHING

The stretch of sea that lies north of Lofoten and Vesterålen is perhaps the best place to sight whales, porpoises, and white-beaked dolphins. Whale safari boat tours leave from the tip of Andøy, an island northwest of Hinnøya. Contact **Whale Safari** (☎ 76/11–56–00) for more information. Brush up on your knowledge of the seafaring mammal at the island's **Whale Center** (Destination Lofoten, ☎ 76/07–30–00) before the trip. Farther south from the Vesterålen coastal town of Stø, **Whale Tours A/S** (☎ 76/13–44–99) also scours the sea for sperm, minke, and killer whales. Reservations are necessary for both excursions.

Shopping

Lofoten is a mecca for artists and craftspeople, who come for the spectacular scenery and the ever-changing light; a list of galleries and crafts centers is available from tourist offices.

Probably the best-known craftsperson in the region is Tor Vegard Mørkved, better known as **Smeden i Sund** (the blacksmith at Sund, ☎ 76/09–36–29). Watch him make wrought-iron gift items. Another fun stop is Åse and Åsvar Tangrand's **Glasshytta and Ceramics Workshop** (☎ 76/09–44–42), near Nusfjord. **Sakrisøy Antiques & Second Hand Store** (☎ 76/09–21–43), which is just outside of Reine (above Dagmar's Museum of Dolls and Toys), sells sundry Lofoten keepsakes.

Tromsø

78 *318 km (197 mi) northeast of Harstad.*

The most important city north of the Arctic Circle, Tromsø looks the way a polar town should—with ice-capped mountain ridges and jagged architecture. The midnight sun shines from May 21 to July 21, and the city's total area—2,558 square km (987 square mi)—is the most expansive in Norway. Still, Tromsø is just about the same size as the country of Luxembourg, but home to only 58,000 people. The city's picturesque center itself sits on a small, hilly island connected to the mainland by a slender bridge. The 13,000 students at the world's northernmost university are one reason the nightlife here is more lively than in many other northern cities.

The **Ishavskatedralen** (Arctic Cathedral) is the city's best-known structure. It is meant to evoke the shape of a Sami tent and the iciness of a glacier. Inside, an immense stained-glass window depicts the Second Coming. ☎ 77/63–76–11. ☒ NKr 10. ☉ June–Aug., Mon.–Sat. 10–8, Sun. 1:30–6. *Times may vary according to church services.*

☾ The **Tromsø Museum,** part of Tromsø University, offers an extensive survey and wildlife. It's great fun for children. ☒ *Universitetet, Lars Thøringsvei 10,* ☎ 77/64–50–00. ☒ *NKr 20.* ☉ *June–Aug., daily 9–8; Sept.–May, Mon.–Tues. and Thurs.–Fri. 8:30–3:30, Wed. 7 PM–8 PM, Sat. noon–3, Sun. 11–4.*

The **Polarmuseet** (Polar Museum), in an 1830s customs warehouse, documents the history of the polar region, with skis and equipment from Roald Amundsen's expedition to the South Pole and a reconstructed Svalbard hunting station from 1910. ☒ *Søndre Tollbugt. 11b,* ☎ 77/68–43–73. ☒ *NKr 30.* ☉ *Mid-May–mid-June, daily 11–6; mid-June–Aug., daily 11–8; Sept.–mid-May, daily 11–3.*

☾ To get a real sense of Tromsø's northerly immensity and peace, take the **Fjellheisen** (cable car) from behind the cathedral up to the mountains, just a few minutes out of the city center. You'll get a great view of the city from **Storsteinen** (Big Rock), 1,386 ft above sea level. In the late afternoon and on weekends, summer and winter, this is where locals go to ski, picnic, walk their lucky dogs, and admire the view. ☎ 77/63–87–37. ☒ *NKr 50.* ☉ *Late Apr.–mid-May, daily 10–5; late May–Sept., daily 10 AM–1 AM if it's sunny. At other times, call for hours.*

OFF THE
BEATEN PATH

NORDLYSPLANETARIET – At the Northern Lights Planetarium, 112 projectors guarantee a 360° view of programs, which include a tour through the universe. It's just outside town in Breivika. ☎ *77/67–60–00.* ☒ *NKr 50.* ☉ *June–Aug., shows in English weekdays at 1:30 and 4:30, Sat. 4:30; Sept.–May call for show times.*

Dining and Lodging

$$–$$$ ✕ **Brankos.** Branko and Anne Brit Bartolj serve authentic Slovenian dishes, accompanied by their own imported wines. ☒ *Storgt. 57,* ☎ 77/68–26–73. *Reservations essential. AE, DC, MC, V.*

$$–$$$ ✕ **Compagniet.** An old wooden trading house from 1837 is now a stylish restaurant serving modern Norwegian food. Chef Anders Blomkvist prepares cream of lobster soup with a dash of brandy and escargot in garlic sauce for starters; main dishes include grilled crayfish and reindeer fillet in a sauce seasoned with blueberries. ☒ *Sjøgt. 12,* ☎ 77/65–57–21. *Reservations essential. AE, DC, MC, V. No lunch in winter.*

$$$–$$$$ ▦ **Comfort Home Hotel With.** This hotel on the waterfront has spacious rooms. The sauna-relaxation room on the top floor has the best view in town. ☒ *Sjøgt. 35–37, 9000,* ☎ 77/68–70–00, ℻ 77/68–96–16. *76 rooms. Sauna, Turkish bath, meeting rooms. AE, DC, MC, V.*

$$$–$$$$ ▦ **Rica Ishavshotel.** Tromsø's snazziest hotel sits atop a deck that stretches over the sound toward the Arctic Cathedral. Inside, shiny wood furnishings with brass trimmings evoke the maritime life that is inescapable in this North Sea region. The soft-carpeted rooms are decorated in bold golds, reds, and navy blues, and the bathrooms are shiny and white. Guests represent a mixture of business executives, tourists, and scientific conference attendees. ☒ *Fr. Langes Gt. 2, Box 196, 9252,* ☎ 77/66–64–00, ℻ 77/66–64–44. *180 rooms. 2 restaurants, 2 bars, meeting rooms. AE, DC, MC, V.*

$$$ 🖫 **Radisson SAS Hotel.** You'll get splendid views over the Tromsø shoreline at this modern hotel, but the standard rooms are tiny. ⊠ *Sjøgt. 7, 9008,* ☎ *77/60–00–00,* FAX *77/68–54–74. 195 rooms with bath, 2 suites. Restaurant, 2 bars, pizzeria, sauna, nightclub. AE, DC, MC, V.*

$$ 🖫 **Comfort Hotel Saga.** Central location on a pretty town square and a helpful staff make the Saga a good place to stay. Its restaurant has affordable, hearty meals, and the rooms—though somewhat basic—are quiet. ⊠ *Richard Withs Pl. 2,* ☎ *77/68–11–80,* FAX *77/68–23–80. 66 rooms. Restaurant, cafeteria. AE, DC, MC, V.*

$–$$ 🖫 **Polar Hotell.** This is a no-frills hotel with small rooms, but it's a pleasant, unassuming place. ⊠ *Grønnegt. 45, 9008,* ☎ *77/75–17–00,* FAX *77/ 75–17–10. 68 rooms. Restaurant, bar, meeting rooms. AE, DC, MC, V.*

Nightlife

Tromsø brags about the quantity of night spots, quite something for a city of only 50,000 at the top of the world. **Compagniet** (☞ Dining, *above*) has the classiest nightclub; **Charly's** (⊠ Sjøgy. 7) at the SAS Royal Hotel is also popular. **Victoria Fun Pub/Sub Circus/Amtmannen's Dattar** (⊠ Amtmann Gt., ☎ 77/68–49–06), a lively evening entertainment complex, with something for everyone. Sub Circus has live bands and attracts a younger crowd while the English-style pub heaves with a mixed age group. The train motif at **Tromsø Jernbanestasjon** (⊠ Strandgt. 33-35, ☎ 77/61–23–48) suggests that some locals are still crossing their fingers to get a railway. The lively bar attracts a young crowd who sit in booths akin to train compartments.

Outdoor Activities and Sports

HIKING

In Tromsø there's good hiking in the mountains above the city, reachable by funicular. Other regional possibilities begin anywhere outside town.

SKIING

In Tromsø, the mountains, only eight minutes away by funicular, are a great place to ski. Elsewhere, you'll have to ask specifics from the tourist board. Listen to the weather reports and heed warnings.

En Route   The drive from Tromsø to Alta is mostly on a coastal road. At one point you'll drive along the **Kvænangsfjellet ridge,** where Kautokeino Sami spend the summer in turf huts—you might see a few of their reindeer along the way. Thirteen kilometers (8 mi) west of Alteidet you'll pass by **Øksfjordjøkelen,** the only glacier in Norway that calves into the sea.

Alta

⑦⑨   *409 km (253 mi) north of Tromsø, 217 km (134 mi) from the North Cape.*

Alta is a major transportation center into Finnmark, the far north of Norway. Most people come just to spend the night before making the final ascent to the North Cape.

OFF THE   **ALTA MUSEUM** – It's worth a trek to Hjemmeluft, southwest of the city, to
BEATEN PATH   see four groupings of 2,500- to 6,000-year-old prehistoric rock carvings, the largest in northern Europe. The pictographs, featuring ships, reindeer, and even a man with a bow and arrow, were discovered in 1973 and are included on the UNESCO World Heritage List. The rock carvings form part of the Alta Museum. The museum has displays delineating the history of the area. ☎ *78/43–53–77.* 🎫 *Summer NKr 40; winter NKr 35.* 🕐 *May and Sept., daily 9–6; early-June–mid-June and mid-Aug.–late Aug., daily 8–8; mid-June–mid-Aug., daily 8 AM–11 PM; Oct.–Apr., weekdays 9–3, weekends 11–4.*

Lodging

$$$ 🏨 **Rica Hotel Alta.** Everything is light and bright in this hotel, from the reflectors on the ceiling of public rooms to the white furniture in the bedrooms. ✉ *Lokkevn. 1, 9501,* ☎ *78/48–27–77,* 𝔽𝔸𝕏 *78/43–58–25. 154 rooms. 2 restaurants, 2 bars, lobby lounge, sauna, nightclub, meeting rooms. AE, DC, MC, V.*

Outdoor Activities and Sports

DOGSLEDDING

Roger Dahl's **Canyon Huskies** (☎ 78/43–33–06), in Alta, arranges all kinds of custom tours along Finnmark's ancient travel routes, whether you want to stay in a tent or hotel, and whether you want to drive your team or stay in the sled. Like most Norwegian sled dogs, these are very friendly.

Shopping

Manndalen Husflidslag (☎ 77/71–62–73) at Løkvoll in Manndalen, on E6 about 15 km (9 mi) west of Alta, is a center for Coastal Sami weaving on vertical looms. Local weavers sell their rugs and wall hangings along with other regional crafts.

Hammerfest

⑧⓪   *145 km (90 mi) north of Alta.*

The world's northernmost town is Hammerfest, an important fishing center. At these latitudes the "most northerlies" become numerous, but certainly the lifestyles here are a testament to determination, especially in winter, when night lasts for months. In 1891 Hammerfest decided to brighten the situation and purchased a generator from Thomas Edison. It was the first city in Europe to have electric street lamps.

Hammerfest is home to the **Isbjørn Klubben** (Royal and Ancient Polar Bear Society). All the exhibits depict some aspect of Arctic hunts. ✉ *Town Hall Basement,* ☎ *78/41–31–10.* 🎫 *Free.* ☉ *Mid-June–mid-Aug., weekdays 7–7, weekends 10–3; Sept.–May, 11:30–1:30, or by appointment.*

Dining and Lodging

$$–$$$ ✕🏨 **Rica Hotel Hammerfest.** The rooms are functional and small, but the furniture is comfortable. There is also an informal pizza pub and a spacious bar. ✉ *Sørøygt. 15,* ☎ *78/41–13–33,* 𝔽𝔸𝕏 *78/41–13–11. 48 rooms. Restaurant, bar, pizzeria, sauna, convention center. AE, DC, MC, V.*

$$$ 🏨 **Quality Hammerfest Hotel.** Right on the pleasant Rådhusplassen, this guest house has handsome, harborview rooms for tolerable prices in a town where hotels are expensive. The hotel is very accessible for travelers with disabilities. ✉ *Strandgt. 2–4,* ☎ *78/42–96–00,* 𝔽𝔸𝕏 *78/42–96–60. 53 rooms. Restaurant, 2 pubs, bar, sauna. AE, DC, MC, V.*

Honningsvåg

⑧①   *130 km (80 mi) from Hammerfest.*

The last village before the Cape, Honningsvåg was completely destroyed at the end of World War II, when the Germans retreated and burned everything they left behind. Only a single wood church, which still survives, was not left in embers. The **Nordkappmuseet** (North Cape Museum), on the third floor of Nordkapphuset (North Cape House), documents the history of the fishing industry in the region as well as the history of tourism at the North Cape. ✉ *9751 Honningsvåg,* ☎ *78/47–28–33.* 🎫 *NKr 20.* ☉ *Mid-June–mid-Aug., Mon.–Sat. 11–8, Sun. 1–8; mid-Aug.–mid-June, weekdays 1:30–4.*

Lodging

$$ 🏨 **Arctic Hotel Nordkapp.** This simple hotel is cozy and centrally located, with small, spic-and-span rooms. No evening meal is served. ✉ *Storgt. 12, 9751 Honningsvåg,* ☎ *78/47–29–66,* FAX *78/47–30–10. 45 rooms. Cafeteria, meeting rooms. AE, DC, MC, V.*

Outdoor Activities and Sports

BIRD-WATCHING

There are tons of birds in Gjesvær on the east coast of the Honningsvåg. Contact **Ola Thomassen** (☎ 98/80–40–30) for organized outings.

Nordkapp

82 *34 km (21 mi) from Honningsvåg.*

On your journey to the Nordkapp (North Cape), you'll see an incredible treeless tundra, with crumbling mountains and sparse dwarf plants. Although this area is notoriously crowded in the summer, with endless lines of tour buses, it's completely different from fall through spring, when the snow is yards deep and the sea is frosty gray. Because the roads are closed in winter, the only access is from the tiny fishing village of Skarsvåg via Sno-Cat, a thump-and-bump ride that's as unforgettable as the beautifully bleak view. For winter information, contact North Cape Travel (☎ 78/47–25–99). Knivsjellodden, slightly west and less dramatic than the North Cape, is actually a hair farther north.

The contrast between this near-barren territory and the **North Cape Hall** is striking. Blasted into the interior of the plateau, the building is housed in a cave and includes the restaurant Louis Philippe, with incredible views. Exhibits trace the history of the Cape, from Richard Chancellor, an Englishman who drifted around it and named it in 1533, to Oscar II, king of Norway and Sweden, who climbed to the top of the plateau in 1873. Out on the plateau itself, a hollow sculptured globe is illuminated by the midnight sun, which shines from May 11 to August 31. ✉ *9764 Nordkapp,* ☎ *78/47–25–99. Entrance to the hall:* 🎫 *NKr 175.* ☾ *Mid-Apr.–mid-May and late Sept.–early Oct., daily 2–5; mid-May–mid-June, daily noon–1 AM; mid-June–mid-Aug., daily 10 AM–2 AM; mid-Aug.–early Sept., daily 10 AM–midnight; early Sept.–mid-Sept., daily noon–5.*

Outdoor Activities and Sports

RAFTING

Deep-sea rafting is as exhilarating as it is beautiful. Among the several tours is a three-hour trip to the North Cape. Call **Nordkapp Safari** (☎ 78/47–27–94).

Trondheim to the North Cape A to Z

Arriving and Departing

BY BOAT

Hurtigruten (the coastal express boat, which calls at 35 ports from Bergen to Kirkenes) stops at Trondheim, southbound at St. Olav's Pier, Quay 16, northbound at Pier 1, Quay 7. Other stops between Trondheim and the North Cape include Bodø, Stamsund (Lofotens), Svolvær, Sortland (Vesterålen), Harstad, Tromsø, Hammerfest, and Honningsvåg. Call ☎ 73/52–55–40 for information on Hurtigruten and local ferries.

BY BUS

Bus 135 (**Østerdalsekspress**) runs overnight from Oslo to Trondheim via Røros. Buses also connect Bergen, Molde, and Ålesund with Trondheim.

Nor-Way Bussekspress (☎ 23/00–24–40 or 814/44–444) can help you to put together a bus journey to destinations in the North. The **Ekspress 2000** (☎ 78/44–40–90) travels regularly among Oslo, Kautokeino, Alta, Nordkapp, and Hammerfest. Phone for information on destinations in the north leaving Alta.

BY CAR

Trondheim is about 500 km (310 mi) from Oslo: seven to eight hours of driving. Speed limits are 80 kph (50 mph) much of the way. There are two alternatives, E6 through Gudbrandsdalen or Route 3 through Østerdalen. It's 727 km (450 mi) from Trondheim to Bodø on Route E6, which goes all the way to Kirkenes. There's an NKr 30 toll on E6 just east of Trondheim. The motorway toll also covers the NKr 11 toll (6 AM–10 PM) for cars entering the downtown area. Anyone who makes it to the **North Cape** *sans* tour bus will be congratulated with an NKr 150 toll.

BY PLANE

Trondheim's **Værnes Airport** is 32 km (21 mi) northeast of the city. **SAS** (☎ 74/80–41–00 or 810/03–300), **Braathens SAFE** (☎ 73/89–57–00), and **Widerøe** (☎ 73/89–67–00 or 810/01–200) are the main domestic carriers. SAS also has two direct flights between Trondheim and Copenhagen daily.

With the exception of Harstad, all cities in northern Norway are served by airports less than 5 km (3 mi) from the center of town. Tromsø is a crossroads for air traffic between northern and southern Norway and is served by Braathens SAFE, SAS, and Widerøe. SAS flies to eight destinations in northern Norway, including Bodø, Tromsø, Alta, and Kirkenes. Braathens SAFE flies to five destinations, including Bodø and Tromsø. Widerøe specializes in northern Norway and flies to 19 destinations in the region, including Honningsvåg, the airport closest to the North Cape. **Arctic Air** (Kautokeino, ☎ 98/48–78–00) offers helicopter and small-plane charters throughout Finnmark.

BY TRAIN

The *Dovrebanen* has frequent departures daily and nightly on the Oslo–Trondheim route. Trains leave from Oslo S Station for the seven-to eight-hour journey. Trondheim is the gateway to the North, and two trains run daily in both directions on the 11-hour Trondheim–Bodø route. For information about trains out of Trondheim, call 72/57–20–20. The *Nordlandsbanen* has three departures daily in each direction on the Bodø–Trondheim route, an 11-hour journey. The *Ofotbanen* has two departures daily in each direction on the Stockholm–Narvik route, a 21-hour journey. Call 76/92–31–21 for local information for summer trains from Narvik to the Swedish border.

Getting Around

BY BOAT

Boat is the ideal transportation in Nordland. The *Hurtigruten* stops twice daily (north and southbound) at 20 ports in northern Norway. It is possible to buy tickets between any harbors right on the boats. **OVDS, Ofotens og Vesterlens Dampskibsselskap** (Narvik, ☎ 76/96–76–96), in partnership with **TFDS (Troms Fylkes Dampskibsselskap)** (Tromsø, ☎ 77/64–81–00; Trondheim, ☎ 73/51–51–20), operates the **Coastal Express** ferries and express boats that serve many towns in the region.

BY BUS

All local buses in **Trondheim** stop at the Munkegata/Dronningens Gate intersection. Some routes end at the bus terminal at Trondheim Sentralstasjon (✉ ☎ 72/57–20–20). Tickets cost NKr 12 and allow free transfer between buses (☎ 73/54–71–00) and streetcars (Gråkallbanen, ☎ 72/55–23–55).

North of **Bodø** and **Narvik** (a five-hour bus ride from Bodø), beyond the reach of the railroad, buses go virtually everywhere, but they don't go often. Get a comprehensive bus schedule from a tourist office or travel agent before making plans. Local bus companies include **Saltens Bilruter** (Bodø, ☎ 75/50–90–00), **Ofotens Bilruter** (Narvik, ☎ 76/92–35–00), **Tromsbuss** (Tromsø, ☎ 77/67–75–00), **Midttuns Busser** (Tromsø, ☎ 77/67–27–87), **Finnmark Fylkesrederi og Ruteselskap** (FFR; ✉ Alta, ☎ 78/43–52–11; Hammerfest, ☎ 78/41–10–00), and **Ekspress 2000** (Alta, ☎ 78/44–40–90).

BY CAR
The roads aren't a problem in northern Norway—most are quite good, although there are always narrow and winding stretches, especially along fjords. Distances are formidable. Route 17—the *Kystriksvegen* (Coastal Highway) from Namsos to Bodø—is an excellent alternative to E6. Getting to Tromsø and the North Cape involves additional driving on narrower roads off E6. In the northern winter, near-blizzard conditions and icy roads sometimes make it necessary to drive in a convoy.

You can also fly the extensive distances and then rent a car for sightseeing within the area, but book a rental car as far in advance as possible. There's no better way to see the Lofoten and Vesterålen islands than by car. Nordkapp (take the plane to Honningsvåg) is another excursion best made by car.

The best way to see the Lofoten Islands is by car since bus service is often limited and there is just so much to see. The main tourist office in Svolvær can point you to local rental agencies, whose rates tend to be quite high. Short distances between neighboring villages are doable by bicycle if you plan to stay in one village for several days.

BY PLANE
Northern Norway has excellent air connections through SAS, Braathens SAFE, and Widerøe (☞ Arriving and Departing by Plane, *above*).

BY TAXI
Taxi stands are located in strategic places in downtown **Trondheim.** All taxis are connected to the **central dispatching office** (☎ 73/50–50–73). Taxi numbers in other towns include the following: **Harstad** (☎ 77/06–20–50), **Narvik** (☎ 76/94–65–00), and **Tromsø** (☎ 77/60–30–00).

Contacts and Resources

GUIDED TOURS
Tromsø: The **tourist information office** (✉ Storgt. 61/63, 9001, ☎ 77/61–00–00) sells tickets for City Sightseeing (Dampskipskaia) and M/F *Polstjerna,* an Arctic vessel that runs a fishing tour in the waters around Tromsø Island.

Trondheim: The **Trondheim Tourist Association** offers a number of tours. Tickets are sold at the tourist information office or at the start of the tour.

LATE-NIGHT PHARMACIES
Trondheim: **St. Olav Vaktapotek** (✉ Kjøpmannsgt. 65, ☎ 73/52–66–66) is open Monday through Saturday 8:30 AM–midnight and Sunday 10 AM–midnight.

Tromsø: **Svaneapoteket** (✉ Kongensgt. 14, ☎ 73–52–23–01) is open daily 8:30–4:30 and 6–9.

VISITOR INFORMATION

Alta (⊠ Top Of Norway, 9500, ☎ 78/43–54–44). **Bodø** (⊠ Sjøgt. 21, 8006, ☎ 75/52–60–00). **Hammerfest** (⊠ 9600, ☎ 78/41–21–85). **Harstad** (⊠ Torvet 8, 9400, ☎ 77/06–32–35). **Lofoten** (⊠ 8301 Svolvær, ☎ 76/07–30–00). **Mo i Rana** (⊠ Polarsirkelen Reiselivslag, 8600 Mo, ☎ 75/13–92–00). **Narvik** (⊠ Kongensgt. 66, 8500, ☎ 76/94–60–33). **Tromsø** (⊠ Storgt. 61/63, 9001, ☎ 77/61–00–00). **Trondheim** (⊠ Torvet 7001, ☎ 73/92–93–94). **Vesterålen Reiselivslag** (⊠ 8400 Sortland, ☎ 76/12–15–55). **Nordkapp** (⊠ Nordkapphuset, Honningsvåg, ☎ 78/47–25–99). **Rognan** (Salten Tourist Board, ☎ 75/64–33–03).

11 SAMILAND TO SVALBARD AND THE FINNISH-RUSSIAN CONNECTION

On the roof of Europe, atop the vast, windswept Finnmarksvidda, roam the Continent's only nomadic indigenous people, the reindeer-herding Sami. Most still live in traditional tents and dress in colorful costumes, although the most visible evidence of their lifestyle consists of roadside souvenir stands and tourist exhibits. The desolate expanses and treeless tundra of this area is an inspiring trekking destination—you're almost guaranteed an encounter with reindeer.

EVERYONE HAS HEARD OF LAPLAND, but few know its real name, Samiland. The Sami recognize no national boundaries, as their territory stretches from the Kola Peninsula in Russia through Finland, Sweden, and Norway. Although still considered nomadic, they no longer live in tents or huts, except for short periods during the summer, when their animals graze along the coast. Their traditions survive through their language, music (called *joik*), art, and handicrafts. Norwegian Samiland is synonymous with the communities of Kautokeino and colorful Karasjok, capital of the Sami, in Finnmark.

Numbers in the margin correspond to points of interest on the Trondheim and the North map in chapter 10.

Kautokeino

⑧③ *129 km (80 mi) southeast of Alta.*

Kautokeino is the site of the Sami Theater and the Nordic Sami Institute. It is a center for Sami handicrafts and education, complete with a school of reindeer herding.

Guovdageaidnu (Kautokeino in the Sami language) Gilisillju, the local museum, documents the way of life of both the nomadic and the resident Sami of the area before World War II. ⊠ *9520 Kautokeino,* ☎ *78/48–58–00.* ☜ *NKr 20.* ☺ *Mid-June–mid-Aug., weekdays 9–7, weekends noon–7; mid-Aug.–mid-June, weekdays 9–3.*

The Arts
During Easter, Kautokeino holds its annual **Easter Festival,** including theater, joik (a haunting, ancient form of solo a cappella song, often in praise of nature), concerts, reindeer driving, snow-scooter racing, and traditional craft exhibits. Contact **Top Of Norway** (⊠ 9500 Alta, ☎ 78/43–54–44).

Shopping
Locals say **Juhl's Silver Gallery** (☎ 78/48–61–89) was Finnmark's first silversmith. Also sold are handicrafts and art from around the world.

Karasjok

⑧④ *178 km (110 mi) from Kautokeino.*

Karasjok, on the other side of the Finnmark Plateau, is the seat of the 39-member Sami Parliament and capital of Samiland. It has a typical inland climate, with the accompanying temperature extremes. The best time to come is at Easter, when the communities are celebrating the weddings and baptisms of the year and taking part in reindeer races and other colorful festivities. In summer, when many of the Sami go to the coast with their reindeer, the area is not nearly as interesting.

The **Samiid Vuorka-Davvirat** (Sami Collections) is a comprehensive museum (indoor and open-air) of Sami culture, with emphasis on the arts, reindeer herding, and the status of women in the Sami community. ⊠ *Museumsgt. 17,* ☎ *78/46–99–50.* ☜ *NKr 25.* ☺ *Mid-June–late Aug., Mon.–Sat. 9–6, Sun. 10–6; late Aug.–Oct., weekdays 9–3, weekends 10–3; Nov.–Mar., weekdays 9–3, weekends noon–3; Apr.–mid-June, weekdays 9–3, weekends 10–3.*

From late fall to early spring you can go **reindeer sledding.** A Sami guide will take you out on a wooden sled tied to a couple of unwieldy reindeer, and you'll clop through the barren, snow-covered scenery of

Finnmark. Wide and relatively flat, the colorless winter landscape is veined by inky alder branches and little else. You'll reach a *lavvu*, a traditional Sami tent, and be invited in to share a meal of boiled reindeer, bread, jam, and strong coffee next to an open alder fire. Contact **Karasjok Opplevelser** (☎ 78/46–69–00).

Dining and Lodging

$$–$$$ ✗⊡ **Rica Hotel Karasjok.** This establishment feels more like a ski
★ chalet than a hotel, with bright rooms, done in warm blues and reds. The wonderful Sami restaurant, Storgammen, serves traditional fare, including reindeer cooked over open fires. ⊠ *Box 38, 9731 Karasjok,* ☎ *78/46–74–00,* FAX *78/46–68–02. 56 rooms. 2 restaurants, bar, saunas, meeting rooms. AE, DC, MC, V.*

Outdoor Activities and Sports

DOGSLEDDING

Sven Engholm, who has won the longest sledge race in Europe, leads tours with his pack dogs. In winter, you can lead your own dogsled, accompany one on skis, or just go along for the ride. In summer, you can hike with the huskies. Contact **Engholm's Huskies** (☎ 78/46–71–66) for information. For snow-scooter rentals, contact Gerus Ans (☎ 78/47–73–00).

HIKING AND FISHING

In between the Alta and Karasjok areas, the **Finnmarksvidda** has marked trails with overnight possibilities in lodges. Contact the Norske Turistforening (⊠ Boks 1963 Vika, 0125 Oslo, ☎ 22/83–28–00) and **Arctic Wildlife** (⊠ Boedtkergt 7, 9950 Vardø, ☎ 92/64–64–86) for details of fishing and hunting trips and other safaris. Finnmark boasts some of Norway's best salmon and trout rivers. For more information, call **Top Of Norway** (☎ 78/43–54–44.)

Shopping

The specialties of the region are Sami crafts, particularly handmade knives. In **Samelandssenteret** (☎ 78/46–71–55) is a large collection of shops featuring northern specialties, including **Knivsmed Strømeng** (☎ 78/46–71–05).

Kirkenes

85 At its very top, Norway hooks over Finland and touches Russia for 122 km (75 mi). The towns in east Finnmark have a more heterogeneous population than those in the rest of the country. A century ago, during hard times in Finland, many industrious Finns settled in this region, and their descendants keep the language alive there.

A good way to visit this part of Norway is to fly to Kirkenes and then explore the region by car. Only Malta was bombed more than Kirkenes during World War II—virtually everything you see in town has been built within the past 45 years.

In winter this entire region, blanketed by snow and cold, is off the beaten track. As the Norwegians say, there is no bad weather, only bad clothes—so bundle up and explore.

During the bombings of Kirkenes, its residents sought cover in subterranean tunnels. One of them, **Andersgrotta,** is open to the public. ☎ *78/99–25–01.* ⊡ *NKr 40.* ☉ *Opening hours vary.*

From mid-June to mid-August, the **FFR** (⊠ Hammerfest, ☎ 78/40–70–90) operates visa-free day-cruises to Murmansk, Russia, on a high-speed catamaran. Booking is required two weeks in advance.

OFF THE
BEATEN PATH **ST. GEORGS KAPELL –** Forty-five kilometers (28 miles) west of Kirkenes is the only Russian Orthodox chapel in Norway, where the Orthodox Skolt-Sami had their summer encampment. It's a tiny building, and services are held outside, weather permitting.

Lodging

$$–$$$ ⌧ **Rica Arctic Hotel.** Do not confuse this hotel with the Rica Hotel Kirkenes, an older establishment, which ends up costing the same during the summer. Rooms here are spacious and pretty, with white-painted furniture and light print textiles. ⌧ *Kongensgt. 1–3, 9915,* ☎ *78/99–29–29,* ⏷ *78/99–11–59. 80 rooms. Restaurant, bar, indoor pool, sauna, exercise room, convention center. AE, DC, MC, V.*

Storskog

86 *About 60 km (37 mi) from Kirkenes.*

Just east of Kirkenes is Storskog, for many years the only official land crossing of the border between Norway and Russia. The tiny village of **Grense Jakobselv** on the Russian border is where King Oscar II built a chapel right at the border in 1869 as a protest against constant Russian encroachment in the area.

OFF THE
BEATEN PATH **ØVRE PASVIK –** The southernmost part of Finnmark, about 118 km (73 mi) south of Kirkenes, is Øvre Pasvik national park, a narrow tongue of land tucked between Finland and Russia. This subarctic evergreen forest is the western end of Siberia's taiga and supports many varieties of flora found only here. The area is surprisingly lush, and in good years all the cloudberries make the swamps shine orange.

Svalbard

87 *640 km (400 mi) north of the North Cape.*

The islands of Svalbard, the largest of which is Spitsbergen, have officially been part of Norway since only 1920. They might have remained wilderness, with only the occasional visitor, if coal had not been discovered late in the 19th century. Today both a Norwegian and a Russian coal company have operations there, and there are two Russian coal miners' communities. The islands offer ample opportunities for ski, dogsled, boat, and snowmobile exploring.

Because Svalbard is so far north, it has four months of continual daylight, from April 21 to August 21. Summers can be lush, with hundreds of varieties of wildflowers. The season is so compressed that buds, full-blown flowers, and seed appear simultaneously on the same plant.

The capital, **Longyearbyen,** is 90 minutes by air from Tromsø. It is home to only about 1,200 Norwegians. Only three species of land mammal besides humans (polar bears, reindeer, and Arctic foxes) and one species of bird (ptarmigan) have adapted to Svalbard winters, but during the summer months, more than 30 species of bird nest on the steep cliffs of the islands, and white whales, seals, and walruses also come for the season. Do heed warnings about polar bears: they can be a real hazard.

Traditionally, only the richest tourists and the most serious scientists traveled to Svalbard. Now the islands have become more accessible. If Hammerfest felt like the edge of Europe, Svalbard feels like the edge of the world. Striations of snow have singed their way across the wild, jagged mountains, splintered down by millennia of arctic conditions. In early summer, antlerless reindeer lounge on the soot-colored tundra. Rumors of hungry polar bears looking to gobble up lonesome travelers tend to precede a trip to the icy island. Adventurous trekkers should not miss the chance to experience this strange, icy wilderness. Just go with caution, and only travel outside Longyearbyen with an experienced tour guide.

Lodging

$$$$ 🏨 **Svalbard Polar Hotel.** The world's most northerly full-service hotel. An enormous window in the dining and bar area provides a view of Mount Hjorthavnfjellet across the waters of the Icefjord. In summer, you can watch the sun cross from one side of the mountain at dusk to the other at dawn. The gourmet Nansen restaurant's exotic menu features seal, white grouse, and polar bear. ⊠ *Box 544, 9170,* ☎ *79/02–35–00,* FAX *79/02–35–00. 67 rooms, 4 suites. Restaurant, bar, sauna, conference room. AE, DC, MC, V.*

The Arts

To get a sense of the frosty place during other times of the year, see the **Kaare Tveter Collection** slide presentation. One of Norway's most admired artists, Tveter donated 40 illustrations of Svalbard to the new Galleri Svalbard. Centuries-old Arctic region maps fill an adjacent exhibition room. ⊠ *Galleri Svalbard.* ☎ *79/02–23–40.* ⊘ *Tues.–Sun. 3–6.*

Samiland to Svalbard A to Z

Arriving and Departing

BY BOAT

Hurtigruten now cruises from Tromsø to Svalbard, dipping down to the North Cape afterward. Contact Bergen Line (☞ Norway A to Z, *below*).

*Also see*Trondheim to the North Cape A to Z, *in* Chapter 10.

Getting Around

See Trondheim to the North Cape A to Z, *in* Chapter 10.

Contacts and Resources

GUIDED TOURS

Contact **Sami Travel A/S** (⊠ Kautokeino, ☎ 78/48–56–00) for adventure trips to Sami settlements. Because of extreme weather conditions and the dangers of polar bears, the best way to see Svalbard is through an organized tour. Longyearbyen's tour operators lead even very small groups on exploring trips lasting anywhere from a day to several weeks. **Svalbard Polar Travel** (⊠ 9170 Longyearbyen, ☎ 79/02–19–71) arranges combination air-sea visits, from five-day minicruises to 12-day trekking expeditions on the rim of the North Pole. **Spitsbergen Travel** (⊠ 9170 Longyearbyen, ☎ 79/02–24–00) offers specialized walks and hikes that focus on plant and animal life. The day-long boat trip to Barentsburg provides a snapshot of the surrounding area's icy beauty.

VISITOR INFORMATION

Karasjok (9730 Karasjok, ☎ 78/46–73–60). **Lofoten** (8300 Svolvær, ☎ 76/07–30–00). **Svalbard** (9170 Longyearbyen, ☎ 79/02–23–03).

12 PORTRAITS OF NORWAY

Norway at a Glance: A Chronology

In Norway at Christmas

NORWAY AT A GLANCE: A CHRONOLOGY

2,000 BC   Tribes from Southern Europe migrate toward Denmark. The majority of early settlers in Scandinavia were of Germanic origin.

c AD 770   The Viking Age begins. For the next 250 years, Scandinavians set sail on frequent expeditions stretching from the Baltic to the Irish seas and even to the Mediterranean as far as Sicily, employing superior ships and weapons and efficient military organization.

c 870   The first permanent settlers arrive in Iceland from western Norway.

c 900   Norwegians unite under Harald I Haarfager.

995   King Olaf I Tryggvasson introduces Christianity into Norway.

1000   Leif Eriksson visits America. Olaf I sends a mission to Christianize Iceland.

1016–1028   King Olaf II Haraldsson (St. Olaf) tries to complete conversion of Norway to Christianity. Killed at Stiklestad in battle with Danish king, he becomes patron saint of Norway.

1028–1035   Canute (Knud) the Great is king of England, Denmark (1018), and Norway (1028).

1045–1066   King Harald III (Hardraade) fights long war with Danes, then participates in and is killed during Norman invasion of England.

1217   Haakon IV becomes king of Norway, beginning its "Golden Age." His many reforms modernize the Norwegian administration; under him, the Norwegian empire reaches its greatest extent when Greenland and Iceland form unions with Norway in 1261. The Sagas are written during this time.

1319   Sweden and Norway form a union that lasts until 1335.

1349   The Black Death strikes Norway and kills two-thirds of the population.

1370   The Treaty of Stralsund gives the north German trading centers of the Hanseatic League free passage through Danish waters. German power increases throughout Scandinavia.

1397   The Kalmar Union is formed as a result of the dynastic ties between Sweden, Denmark, and Norway, the geographical position of the Scandinavian states, and the growing influence of Germans in the Baltic. Erik of Pomerania is crowned king of the Kalmar Union.

1520   Christian II, ruler of the Kalmar Union, executes 82 people who oppose the Scandinavian union, an event known as the "Stockholm blood bath." Sweden secedes from the Union three years later. Norway remains tied to Denmark and becomes a Danish province in 1536.

1536   The Reformation enters Scandinavia in the form of Lutheranism through the Hanseatic port of Bergen.

1559–1648   Norwegian trade flourishes.

1660   Peace of Copenhagen establishes modern boundaries of Denmark, Sweden, and Norway.

1814 Sweden, after Napoleon's defeat at the Battle of Leipzig, attacks Denmark and forces the Danish surrender of Norway. On 17 May, Norwegians adopt constitution at Eidsvoll. On 4 November, Norway is forced to accept Act of Union with Sweden.

1811 University of Oslo is established.

1884 A parliamentary system is established in Norway.

1903 Bjørnstjerne Bjørnson awarded Nobel prize for literature.

1905 Norway's union with Sweden is dissolved.

1914 At the outbreak of World War I, Norway declares neutrality but is effectively blockaded.

1918 Norwegian women gain the right to vote.

1920 Norway joins the League of Nations. Novelist Knut Hansun receives Nobel Prize.

1928 Sigrid Undset receives Nobel Prize for literature.

1929–1937 Norway is ruled by a labor government.

1939 Norway declares neutrality in World War II.

1940 Germany occupies Norway.

1945 Norway joins the United Nations

1946–1954 Norwegian statesman Trygve Lie presides as first Secretary-General of UN.

1949 Norway becomes a member of NATO.

1952 The Nordic Council, which promotes cooperation among the Nordic parliaments, is founded.

1968 Norway discovers oil in the North Sea.

1971 North Sea oil extraction begins, transforming the Norwegian economy.

1972 Norway declines membership in the EC.

1981 Gro Harlem Brundtland, a member of the Labor party, becomes Norway's first female prime minister.

1991 King Olav V dies. King Harald V ascends the throne. His wife, Queen Sonja, becomes first queen since the death of Maud in 1938.

1993 Norway's Minister of Foreign Affairs Thorvald Stoltenberg is appointed peace negotiator to Bosnia and Herzegovina.

1994 Norway hosts the XVII Olympic Winter Games at Lillehammer.

1995 In a national referendum, Norwegians again decline membership in the EC.

IN NORWAY AT CHRISTMAS

EVERY CULTURE REINVENTS the wheel. But every culture reinvents it slightly differently. In Norway, a traditional dining table may rest not on four legs, as tables usually do elsewhere, but on a cubic frame, like an imaginary cage that imprisons your feet while you eat.

I am a Chinese who has fallen in love with Norway. I was invited by my good friends Ole and Else to spend Christmas and New Year's with them in Oslo. It turned out to be the most marvelous Christmas of my fifty-two years.

It was one long feast, moving from household to household. On Christmas Eve we held hands and sang carols and danced ring-around-the-Christmas-tree. We skied at night on an illuminated track, whose lights switched off at ten, plunging us into obscurity on the downward slope. We played squash on the Norsk Hydro court and afterward relaxed in the sauna. We ushered in the New Year with fireworks on Oslo's frozen streets.

I am probably one of the few Chinese in two thousand years to have had such an intimate glimpse of Norwegian life. Of course, it is presumptuous of me to write about a people after an eight-day visit. Yet I have the feeling that Norwegians don't very much mind presumption (as long as it is straightforward and honest). Indeed, this exceptional tolerance of friendly rudeness bespeaks their generosity and is, to me, one of their most endearing qualities.

To begin with, to a Chinese who has seen something of the world, Norway is a most exotic country. Even ordinary, everyday things are done exotically here. For example, I saw my Norwegian friends: drink aquavit at breakfast; eat breakfast in the afternoon; turn on an electric switch to heat the sidewalk in front of their house; get a thrill out of driving their car like a bobsled; leave the house lights on day and night, when they went out and when they slept; wash their dishes with soap without rinsing them.

Norwegians also love to give gifts and make philosophical speeches at festive dinners. They decorate their Christmas trees not with angels but with strings of Norwegian flags. They don't find it necessary to have curtains around their showers, because it's simpler to build a drain on the bathroom floor. Cold dishes are de rigueur in the winter. There is a national horror of hot, spicy foods, and a national pact to ignore vegetables.

The Norwegians and the Chinese share certain cultural traits. The most striking is their common fondness for rituals. Confucius insisted on the importance of rituals as a collective code of behavior that gives order to life. The Master said, "To suppress the self and submit to ritual is to engage in Humanity." This precept might just as well apply to the Norwegians as to the Chinese.

At Christmas, all the traditional rituals are performed, some older than Christianity in Norway. A great deal of effort goes into making sure that they are done right. After each one—the baking of the gingerbread houses, the decorating of the tree—the excitement palpably mounts.

Christmas begins on the eve, with the hostess welcoming the guests to the dinner table. She assigns to each a specific seat according to a careful arrangement. The seating plan is the one touch of originality that marks the occasion. It is, in some ways, the hostess's signature for the evening. (You find seating charts of past banquets faithfully recorded in a family book.) It's quite touching to see a young hostess assign a seat to her own mother, who has undoubtedly done the same many times herself. It signals the passing of the torch from one generation of women to another.

Once the guests are seated and the candles lit, the feast begins. It begins with the dessert: rice pudding (reminiscent of the rice gruel that Chinese eat for breakfast and when ill, albeit without milk and butter). Toasts are offered, followed by a chorus of *skaals*.

Then comes raw fish of every kind—salmon, eel, herring, enough to send a sashimi-loving, Japanese into ecstasy. From the sea, the food parade marches onto land. A whole side of roast pork, skin done to a golden crisp, is served with meatballs and sausage, and buried under potatoes. Throughout there is much toasting with aquavit.

Finally, after two hours the meal is done. You get up from the table and stagger into the living room. There, in a role reminiscent of her mother's, the little daughter of the house hands out the gifts—to each recipient with charming solemnity.

Great care is taken by each household to do everything the same way, so that, as with the retelling of a familiar tale, all expectations are happily satisfied. Once in a while, one may introduce an oddity, such as a Chinese guest from afar, to liven up the routine. But in general surprises tend to raise eyebrows.

If, for the Chinese, rituals recall the teachings of Confucius, for the Norwegians they go back to the pagans. In spite of the electric sidewalks, the past is very much alive in the modern Norwegian psyche. The feasting, the speech-making, the gift-giving, and especially the generous hospitality and the importance of friendship are all part of the Viking tradition. Yuletide was a pagan celebration of the winter solstice. The birth of Christ was a later liturgical imposition. In some families these days, it is celebrated almost as an afterthought.

The other thing that the Norwegians share with the Chinese is their strong attachment to the family. Like the Chinese, the Norwegians belong to extended families, practically clans. But what defines a family in Norway is not at all clear. The relations are so complex and intertwined that, rather than family trees, the Norwegians seem to have family bushes. To begin with, there is one's spouse and one's brothers and sisters and their spouses. And then there is one's former spouse and his or her present spouse. And then there is the former spouse of the present spouse of one's former spouse, who in some cases also happens to be one's present spouse. The children of the former spouse of one's spouse are somewhat like nephews and nieces. Beyond that, there are the living-together arrangements and the progeny thereof, which take on quasi-family status.

It's not unusual for people who are divorced to remain good friends. Their old pictures sometimes hang in each other's bedrooms, Christmastime finds them reunited with their old partners and all of their children, old and new. At first, this kind of marital pluralism is slightly unsettling. What, no bad blood? No bitterness or jealousy?

I ASKED A YOUNG NORWEGIAN if it upset him to be shuttling between his father's and mother's separate households. He looked at me with astonishment. "But that's normal," he said. "Every kid in my class is in the same situation."

His guileless reaction gave me food for thought. "And indeed what's wrong with that?" I asked myself. Why try to stay with an unhappy relationship when one feels the need to change? And once changed, why not try to reconcile the past with the present?

The Chinese family is a vertical structure. Like the society itself, it is hierarchical, ruled from the top down. Confucius said, "Let the prince be prince, the minister be minister, the father be father, the son be son." Patriarchy and gerontocracy are the order of things: old men will rule, and the young will obey. Repression is inevitable under such a hierarchy. The collective always takes precedence over the individual; order always takes precedence over freedom. This denial of the self is responsible for much of the envy, backbiting, and hypocrisy common in Chinese communities.

The Norwegian family, on the other hand— or perhaps I should say the *new* Norwegian family—is horizontal. Like a strawberry plant, it spreads in all directions. Wherever it touches soil, it sprouts a new shoot. An obvious sign of this strawberry-patch kinship is the diminished importance of the family name. These days people are known mostly by first names. Children, too, often address their parents by their first names. As more and more households are headed by women, the old nuclear family is giving way to a fluid tribalism.

One way to understand the difference between the vertical and the horizontal cultures is to compare their concepts of space. To the Chinese, any space must have a center. The Chinese name for China, Zhongguo, means precisely Center Country. Every Chinese knows that the center of

China is Beijing. Why? Because the vast expanse of China is not divided into time zones, and from the Pacific to Tibet every watch is set to Beijing time. Every Chinese also knows that the center of Beijing is the Forbidden City, the symbol of governmental power, and that inside the Forbidden City sits an old man whose word is law.

NO ONE WOULD DREAM of ordering Norway's space this way. Unlike elsewhere in Europe, you seldom see a square in a Norwegian town. People don't seem to feel the need to meet and sit in the sun and feed the pigeons. In some rural communities, the church stands not in the center of town but on a hill somewhere on the outskirts. The houses, in all forms and dispositions, are widely dispersed, disdaining to line up along a straight road. One gets the impression that zoning laws are not very strict in Norway.

The big question is, if the Norwegians are such confirmed individualists, how come they are so conformist? It's voluntary, true, they choose it, but it's conformity all the same. This is the question posed—but never answered—by Ibsen's plays.

For me, the key to understanding the Norwegians is to recognize that they are a nation of irreconciled opposites. They have taken on the contradiction of their seasons: the long happy summer days alternating with the gloomy nights of winter. They have inherited two pasts with totally different characters. For more than two hundred years, from the ninth to the eleventh centuries, they were the scourge of Europe. They raided Britain and discovered America; they ruled Kiev and besieged Paris; they served at the court of Byzantium, and—who knows?—maybe some of them even made it to China. Lusty, adventurous, destructive, and curious about the world, they were sea nomads, the maritime counterpart of the horsemen of Genghis Khan, who conquered Russia and China. Then, as suddenly as they burst upon the world in their splendid ships, the retreated, went back to their home in the north. They were converted to Christianity and not heard from again.

Why the seafaring Vikings turned into God-fearing Christians is one of those mysteries that history doesn't explain very well. What made them turn their gaze inward? Why did they change from thinking big to thinking small? What, finally made them give up violence for peaceful ways? There is no satisfactory answer.

In any case, as the final image of Ingmar Bergman's *Fanny and Alexander* so powerfully shows, there are two ghosts walking beside the Scandinavian soul: the ghost of the hard-drinking father and the ghost of the psalm-singing stepfather. They walk beside the boy, each with a hand on his shoulder, never exchanging a word.

So the Norwegian labors under a double identity. In one ear, the Viking ghost tells him to leave Norway, this cold, homogeneous, incurious community, and discover the world. Go! The center is elsewhere! There are wonderful places to see and fabulous riches to be had!

In his other ear, the Christian ghost tells him Stay! Go back to your roots! Embrace the tradition and preserve the social order.

This ambivalence is at the heart of Norway itself. You see it reflected on canvas in the National Gallery in Oslo. Among the painters of the late nineteenth century, one finds two divergent sensibilities: the naturalists, who took as their subject the Norwegian folk, and the cosmopolitans, who, having spent time in Paris or Rome, insisted that art was not sociology or geography but, simply and purely, a composition of color and light.

For eight centuries, Christian ethics held sway in Norway as in the rest of Europe. But since 1945 something important has changed. There is a gap between the values of the prewar and the postwar generations. Between the threat of nuclear destruction and the temptation of America, the influence of the church waned. More and more, people have stopped practicing their faith. As they do so, they are reverting to their ancestral Viking instincts.

One clue to this reemergence of pagan consciousness is the marital pluralism that I observed. Another clue, probably closely related, is women's push for equality, a push that has been more forceful and more widely accepted in Scandinavia than anywhere else. A third indication of this new pagan way, I believe—and here I'm sticking my neck out—is the nation's collective decision, in the seventies, to turn Norway overnight into an oil economy.

There have been a lot of arguments about the reasoning behind this decision, but none of them address the Viking-versus-Christian dilemma. If Norway had listened to its Christian voice, it would have been content to remain a frugal, hard-working nation, tending the farm or the machine. Instead, after the oil crisis of 1973, Norway chose the Viking solution and went for broke. It decided to plunder the sea.

Agrarian people, like the Chinese, are naturally patient: it takes time to make things grow. The Vikings, on the other hand, never had patience. If they could survive by fishing and gathering berries, they would not care to cultivate. Whatever they could get by raiding, they would not care to make. It is still so today. Norwegians are willing to put all their ingenuity and technical skill into building gigantic derricks and drilling kilometers beneath the sea. They will do so in order to avoid making clothes and toys to compete with Hong Kong. This is the message I got from that magnificent Christmas feast: If it tastes good raw, *don't bother to cook it*. Take it raw. Don't transform. And nothing is rawer than oil.

In 1066, King Harald Hardraade left the shores of Norway to grab the big prize: the throne of England. At Stamford Bridge, he was offered by his enemy seven feet of English ground, "and more—if you are taller." Harald fought and lost. By nightfall, mortally wounded, he said, "I will accept that piece of kingdom that was offered me this morning."

I said to my friend Ole—who, as an oil engineer at Norsk Hydro, has staked his whole future on a challenge against the North Sea—"One day your oil will be depleted, and then where will you be?" He grinned and said, echoing King Harald's insouciance, "And then I will have nothing."

–By Chunglu Tsen

Born in Shanghai, Chunglu Tsen grew up in Paris and received his education in England and the United States. Since 1974 he has worked as a translator for the United Nations in Geneva. This article appeared originally in the December 1990 issue of *Wigwag*.

NORWEGIAN VOCABULARY

English	Norwegian	Pronunciation

Basics

English	Norwegian	Pronunciation
Yes/no	Ja/nei	yah/nay
Please	Vær så snill	**vehr** soh snihl
Thank you very much	Tusen takk	**tews**-sehn tahk
You're welcome	Vær så god	**vehr** soh goo
Excuse me	Unnskyld	**ewn**-shewl
Hello	God dag	goo **dahg**
Goodbye	Ha det	**ha** day
Today	I dag	ee **dahg**
Tomorrow	I morgen	ee **moh**-ern
Yesterday	I går	ee **gohr**
Morning	Morgen	**moh**-ern
Afternoon	Ettermiddag	**eh-terr**-mid-dahg
Night	Natt	naht

Numbers

1	en	ehn
2	to	too
3	tre	treh
4	fire	**feer**-eh
5	fem	fehm
6	seks	sehks
7	syv, sju	shew
8	åtte	**oh**-teh
9	ni	nee
10	ti	tee

Days of the Week

Monday	mandag	mahn-dahg
Tuesday	tirsdag	**teesh**-dahg
Wednesday	onsdag	**oonss**-dahg
Thursday	torsdag	**tohsh**-dahg
Friday	fredag	**fray**-dahg
Saturday	lørdag	**loor**-dahg
Sunday	søndag	**suhn**-dahg

Useful Phrases

Do you speak English?	Snakker De engelsk?	snahk-kerr dee ehng-ehlsk
I don't speak Norwegian.	Jeg snakker ikke norsk.	yay **snahk**-kerr **ik**-keh nohrshk
I don't understand.	Jeg forstår ikke.	yay fosh-**tawr** **ik**-keh
I don't know.	Jeg vet ikke.	yay veht **ik**-keh
I am American/British.	Jeg er amerikansk/engelsk.	yay ehr ah-mehr-ee-kahnsk/ehng-ehlsk
I am sick.	Jeg er dårlig.	yay ehr **dohr**-lee

Please call a doctor.	Vær så snill og ring etter en lege.	vehr soh snihla oh ring **eht**-ehr ehn **lay**-geh
Do you have a vacant room?	Har du et rom som er ledig?	yay vil **yehr**-neh hah eht room
How much does it cost?	Hva koster det?	vah **koss**-terr deh
It's too expensive.	Det er for dyrt.	deh ehr for **deert**
Beautiful	Vakker	**vah**-kehr
Help!	Hjelp!	yehlp
Stop!	Stopp!	stop
How do I get to . . .	Hvor er	voor ehr
the train station?	jernbanestasjonen	yehrn-bahn-eh sta-**shoon**-ern
the post office?	posthuset	**pohsst**-hewss
the tourist office?	turistkontoret	tew-**reest**-koon-toor-er
the hospital?	sykehuset	**see**-keh-hoo-seh
Does this go to . . . ?	Går denne bussen til . . . ?	gohr **den**-nahbus boos teel
Where is the W.C.?	Hvor er toalettene?	voor ehr too-ah-**leht**-te-ne
On the left	Til venstre	teel **vehn**-streh
On the right	Til høyre	teel **hooy**-reh
Straight ahead	Rett fram	reht **frahm**

Dining Out

menu	meny	meh-new
fork	gaffel	gahff-erl
knife	kniv	kneev
spoon	skje	shay
napkin	serviett	ssehr-vyeht
bread	brød	brur
butter	smør	smurr
milk	melk	mehlk
pepper	pepper	pehp-per
salt	salt	sahlt
sugar	sukker	sook-kerr
water/bottled water	vann	vahn
The check, please.	Jeg vil gjerne betale.	yay vil **yehr**-neh beh-**tah**-leh

INDEX

Index 155